Addiction and Mood Disorders

Addiction and Mood Disorders

A Guide for Clients and Families

Dennis C. Daley

with Antoine Douaihy

UNIVERSITY PRESS

2006

OXFORD
UNIVERSITY PRESS

Oxford University Press, Inc., publishes works that further
Oxford University's objective of excellence
in research, scholarship, and education.

Oxford   New York
Auckland   Cape Town   Dar es Salaam   Hong Kong   Karachi
Kuala Lumpur   Madrid   Melbourne   Mexico City   Nairobi
New Delhi   Shanghai   Taipei   Toronto

With offices in
Argentina   Austria   Brazil   Chile   Czech Republic   France   Greece
Guatemala   Hungary   Italy   Japan   Poland   Portugal   Singapore
South Korea   Switzerland   Thailand   Turkey   Ukraine   Vietnam

Published by Oxford University Press, Inc.
198 Madison Avenue, New York, New York 10016

www.oup.com

Oxford is a registered trademark of Oxford University Press

Library of Congress Cataloging-in-Publication Data
Daley, Dennis C.
Addictions and mood disorders : a guide for clients and families / Dennis C. Daley
with Antoine Douaihy.
    p.   cm.
Includes bibliographical references.
ISBN-13 978-0-19-531129-7; 0-19-531129-9 (cloth)
ISBN-13 978-0-19-530628-6; 0-19-530628-7 (pbk.)
1. Dual diagnosis. 2. Substance abuse. 3. Affective disorders.   I. Title.
RC564.68.D365 2006
362.29'86—dc22   2006010662

9 8 7 6 5 4 3 2 1
Printed in the United States of America
on acid-free paper

In memory of Natalie Daley

Preface

Addiction, depression, and bipolar disorders create suffering and havoc for affected individuals and their families. Unfortunately, many people experience *both* an addiction and a mood disorder, a condition referred to as "dual disorders." This book is devoted primarily to educating individuals with dual disorders and their families about mood and addictive or substance use disorders. It not only gives a message of hope but also provides practical suggestions on ways to manage these disorders. Professionals and students in the behavioral health field will also find this book helpful in their work with clients who have these combined disorders.

This book is based on my clinical, research and personal experiences. During the past 30 years, I have had the opportunity to work directly with thousands of patients and their families in a psychiatric hospital, hospital detoxification unit, addiction residential rehabilitation program, and both addiction and mental health partial hospital and outpatient programs. This has given me a very broad exposure to all types and combinations of disorders. My colleagues and I at Western Psychiatric Institute and Clinic (WPIC) of the University of Pittsburgh Medical Center were one of the first professional groups in the country to develop treatment programs for addiction and mood disorders combined. We have treated thousands of patients in our inpatient, partial hospital, and outpatient programs and have learned much from them since we began offering dual-diagnosis treatment back in the 1980s.

At WPIC, we have or currently are conducting research studies of addiction combined with major depression or bipolar disorders. This research aims to increase our knowledge of people with these conditions, as well as treatment of these dual disorders. We have studied the severity of mood symptoms among addicted individuals, lethal behaviors (suicidal and homicidal thoughts, feelings, and behaviors), compliance with treatment, and the impact of treatment (therapy, medications, or combined treatment of both medications and therapy). We have learned much from these studies, and we believe we will continue to learn more as our research continues.

In our ongoing attempts to improve the clinical care we provide to patients in our treatment programs, we have also conducted many surveys to learn how they experience their disorders, how their families are affected, what contributes to their relapses and difficulties in recovery, and what helps their recoveries. As part of my work on several federally funded research projects on the treatment of addiction, bipolar illness combined with addiction, and depression combined with addiction, I have listened to or watched hundreds of audiotapes of individual therapy sessions and videotapes of group therapy sessions. Hence, as an objective observer I have heard firsthand the experiences of hundreds of patients with various combinations of disorders. These experiences have given me additional insight into both the suffering of patients with addiction and mood disorders and the resilience many have shown in their ability to manage their disorders and make changes in their lives.

I also include information and insights learned from other researchers, clinicians, individuals with addiction or mood disorders, and family members who have written about these serious disorders. Many scientific studies have been published, and numerous informative and hopeful books have been written. However, the major limitation is that most books provide information on either addiction or mood disorders, not both. This book is unique in that it provides detailed information on strategies for recovery from both addiction and a major mood disorder, regardless of which one is primary. Information is provided on the experience of having dual disorders; types, symptoms, effects, and treatment of addiction, depression, and bipolar disorders; how these dual disorders affect each other; therapy or counseling, medications, and electroconvulsive therapy; the recovery process; and practical strategies for managing moods, building a support system, working with the family, making lifestyle changes, and reducing relapse risk. These strategies are adapted from various treatments that have been proven effective for addiction, mood disorders, or both.

One of the most significant experiences I've had was growing up in a family with parental alcoholism and depression. I experienced firsthand the nega-

your loved one who has these dual disorders. Also, be sure to get help
port for yourself if you think you need it. Professionals who work with
who have both an addiction and a mood disorder will find this book
educational guide in their clinical work. It can also be used to help pa-
arn how to change and to teach recovery skills that they can use to
their disorders. Appendices at the end of this book provide sugges-
r readings, as well as self-help programs and Internet resources.

tive impact of these disorders on my family an
was emotionally hurt. I also saw how this pain
behaviors and relationships. Anger, anxiety, wor
ions for many years. Academic underachievem
were just a few of the "side effects" of alcoholism
I feel fortunate that my hurts have been healed
forgiveness have replaced my anger and bitterness
ful at the time, my family experiences ultimately
standing of what it is like for a family to face alcoh
is no doubt in my mind that the combination of d
and problems associated with either disorder alor
this personal observation.

Although I provide guidelines and strategies
orders, I do not promise any quick fixes or easy ans
any exist. Rather, I believe that recovery involves a
within oneself, hard work at changing, discipline, c
tion, and the ability to accept help and support from
the work of recovery pays big dividends and gives
grow as a person. Although many examples in this bo
tive changes, I also include examples and experience
the problems, struggles, and tragedies associated with
disorders in order to give a "balanced" view. Although
people make tremendous changes for the better, others
that last only temporarily. They struggle, they relapse,

This book advocates a "recovery" model in which t
responsibility for getting the most out of professional
programs and continues recovery even if a course of pr
finished. Being an active participant is necessary to gair
ery. Regardless of the severity of the addiction or mo
many things that can be done to manage these disorde
positive changes in one's life.

If you are suffering from the dual disorders of addi
or bipolar illness, share and discuss this book with family
cant others who are part of your support system. This w
understand dual disorders and recovery. Discuss questio
have about anything in this book with your therapist, cou
you are a family member, use this information to help y

support
and sup
patients
a useful
tients l
manag
tions f

Acknowledgments

I wish to thank Cindy Hurney, administrative coordinator at the Center for Psychiatric and Chemical Dependency Services (CPCDS) at Western Psychiatric Institute and Clinic (WPIC), for help with all aspects of research, writing, and designing this book. All of the time and effort she put forth helping me made it possible for this book to be written.

Thanks to Ihsan Salloum and Antoine Douaihy, my long-time friends and colleagues, for their review of this book and their suggestions on ways to improve it. I also wish to thank my colleagues at WPIC who have conducted clinical research on addiction, mood disorders, or dual disorders—I have learned much from their work and teaching. Thanks also to my colleagues at CPCDS with whom I have collaborated on providing clinical treatment programs, conducting research, and teaching the next generation of health care providers.

I also wish to thank my late wife, Natalie Daley, for her critical review of this manuscript and her support and patience during the time it took me to write this book. Thanks to my children, Chris and Lauren, for their patience as well.

Several people in recovery from dual disorders read and critiqued an earlier version this book. I am most appreciative for their willingness to take their time to help me. I remember vividly a meeting with several of them during which they gave me useful and constructive feedback. Their input helped make this a more readable book.

Contents

Addiction and
Mood Disorders

Chapter 1

Dual Disorders: Addiction Combined With Depression or Bipolar Illness

Double Trouble: Dual Disorders From the Inside Out

Late one cold December night, Senator George McGovern heard a knock on his door. When he opened it and saw a policeman and a member of the clergy, he knew something was terribly wrong. They told him that his daughter Terry, a mother of two young daughters, had died. She got drunk, passed out in the cold out of doors, and froze to death. In his book, simply titled *Terry*, the senator gives a brutally honest and eloquent description of his depressed alcoholic daughter's life and how heartbroken he and Mrs. McGovern were over her tragic and untimely death. I found myself shedding tears when I read about how deeply he loved her and how sad and despondent he felt when she died.

I also had the privilege of hearing Senator McGovern tell his personal story, so I knew that Terry had had two serious disorders. I also knew that her alcoholism and depression were chronic disorders and all too common among people in our society. The senator says of his beloved daughter that:

> She was dealt a double cruel hand: the companion demons depression and alcoholism. They were demons that warred ceaselessly against the other aspects of her being—a warm and sunny disposition, a quick wit to make you smile or laugh, a frank and open candor that disarmed you and pierced your pomp and hypocrisy, a keen mind with a sensitivity to literature, art, and poetry, an amazing insight into and concern about the

3

problems of others, a hunger for spiritual meaning, a love of animals, birds and flowers, and a devotion to her family and friends.[1] (p. xiii)

Several weeks before her death, Terry sent a letter to her mother that captured the insanity of her disorders, how bad she felt, and the hurtful impact on the family.

> I truly cannot believe I've let myself stay sick for so long. It's been 4 years relapsing—pulling my life apart and damaging the spirits of those I love most. I wonder if I can ever really have a full life knowing my children and I have lost precious time and not knowing what time I will be allowed now. I'm so sad mom. Please pray for Marian, Colleen and me to be reunited. I want to be a daughter to you and dad—not a source of worry, anger and sorrow. I want to be a sister to my brother and sisters. I've played around with my recovery—somehow unable to grasp how serious it is, how much suffering it has caused me and others.[1] (p. 9)

Another story shows the complexity of addiction combined with a severe mood disorder. Jack, a successful and well-to-do businessman, was evaluated by a psychiatrist and diagnosed with bipolar illness, cocaine addiction, and alcoholism. The severity of his conditions made it clear to the physician to that Jack needed a structured dual-diagnosis treatment program to help him establish and maintain sobriety and stabilize his mood. However, Jack refused and insisted he could manage his disorders with medications and occasional visits to a therapist, even though he had a past history of failure at this level of care. Over the next 2 years, Jack was admitted twice to addiction rehabilitation programs and twice to psychiatric hospitals. He usually left the program or hospital against medical advice, then seldom followed through with after-care treatment for more than several weeks or a month or two. Jack was very inconsistent in taking his medications, talking with his sponsor, and attending self-help meetings and therapy sessions. He often challenged his therapist and doctor and disagreed with his diagnoses. Jack often lied when using drugs or alcohol and created one excuse after another for being late or missing his sessions. He exaggerated his recovery and tried to present himself as doing much better than he actually was. Jack usually blamed his wife and employees for his problems. Eventually, Jack lost his business, had his cars repossessed, and had to sell his house. His wife became so disgusted and despondent that she left him and took their children, not so much because he had these disorders but because he kept lying to her about his recovery and did not stay in treatment as he had agreed.

Living with depression or bipolar illness or living with an addiction to alcohol or other drugs is very difficult indeed. When you have both types of illnesses together it creates double trouble. Not only is your life affected in many ways by having these dual disorders, but your family is affected also. The experiences of the McGovern family illustrate how everyone in a family can be hurt by these disorders. Terry also had four sisters and two daughters, all of whom were affected by this tragic loss of life. The case of Jack illustrates the difficulty some people have in accepting their disorders, accepting the need for treatment or a particular type of treatment, actually staying in treatment, or following the recommendations of doctors or therapists. Sadly, Jack paid a high price for his inability to manage his disorders, losing both his family and his financial security. His family paid a high price as well.

Double Recovery: Successful Management of Dual Disorders

Although the McGovern case and the case of Jack show the tragic and negative sides of dual disorders, there are many cases in which the individual who engages in professional treatment and works at a program of personal recovery puts his or her life back on track. The road to recovery is seldom smooth and free of difficulties, but it can lead to many successful changes and a better life. I have had hundreds of wonderful experiences, and I want to share three that illustrate the positive side of recovery.

The first occurred after I unexpectedly received a phone call from the wife of Larry, a former patient recovering from bipolar disorder and alcoholism. I had worked with Larry and his family many years ago, and my last recollection was that he had settled into recovery very nicely but certainly had his work cut out for him. Now his family was celebrating the 10-year anniversary of his sobriety with a surprise party. I was invited as the only nonfamily member because they felt my work as Larry's therapist in the past had played a part in his recovery. It was absolutely a beautiful time, as his adult children and their spouses and children acknowledged a major milestone in his life. During the course of the evening, I learned that despite a recurrence of his mood disorder several years ago, overall Larry was doing well. Life for him and his family was much better as a result. The amount of love, support, and appreciation shared that evening by his family was impressive, and I left with a tremendous feeling of happiness to see Larry doing so well. I also knew that he did well in recovery because he worked hard at it by attending AA meetings, complying with his medications, involving his wife in recovery, and doing all the things necessary to manage his disorders over the long run.

The second experience occurred at a bus stop when I encountered Janice, a woman whom I first met many years ago when she was in our psychiatric unit. She was with two of her children. Janice told me that she had stayed off cocaine for more than 2 years, that her depression was in remission, and that she was feeling good overall. She had gotten her children back from Children and Youth Services and felt that her life was much better now. It was clear from a brief discussion with Janice that staying connected with her sponsor and other addicts in Narcotics Anonymous (NA) played a major role in her success.

The third experience involved a telephone call from Mike, a former patient who called me over the Christmas holidays a few years after discharge from our clinic. We chatted about several different things, and he brought me up to date with his life. Mike then said, "I called because I just wanted to wish you and the others at the clinic a happy holiday season, and let you know I got three and a half years clean. I'm doing good and want to thank everyone for their help." Because Mike's bipolar illness was a recurrent and chronic condition, he was still taking medication and working on his recovery program. It was such a pleasure to hear that he was doing well and to feel his attitude of gratitude. There was no doubt in my mind that Mike was grateful for what we had done to help him—in fact, he even laughed when he reminded me that he wasn't exactly the "ideal" patient when he was in our program.

I see many current and former hospital and clinic patients throughout our Medical Center. Many times, I've been stopped on the street or in an elevator and given a brief update on their recovery. In almost every single case, the people who share positive news about recovery also share appreciation for the help provided by our hospital and clinic. And they usually tell me to thank a specific therapist or doctor who helped them in the past. These are reminders that people can recover from these disorders, no matter how much they have struggled or how bad off they have been at one time or another.

Following are two brief stories about Diane and Rob that show both their struggles and their successes in managing their disorders. See if you can relate to their experiences.

I've Been Doing Well for a Couple of Years

I was an addict long before I ever had depression or mania. Even though I had been in and out of psychiatric hospitals for mania and suicide attempts, it was easier for me to see myself as an addict than a mental case. Although I worked on my recovery from heroin addiction by attending NA and counseling, I did nothing for my mood disorder. A couple times I was put on mood medications when in the hospital, but I always stopped them once I felt better and was discharged. I kept telling myself addiction was my main problem. I struggled with relapses to addiction, depression, and mania. Fortunately, I finally came to grips with the fact that I had a serious mood disorder. I finally accepted treatment, which made it easier to stay drug free and enjoy my sobriety. It seemed like I suffered needlessly for a long time because I had this attitude that I should never see a shrink and that all of my problems were caused by my addiction. I've been doing well for a couple of years now by working hard at my recovery. I take lithium and attend NA meetings regularly. My experiences have helped me with the people I sponsor in NA.—Diane, age 33

My Depression Got a Lot Better

Me, an alcoholic or addict? No way. I thought the people treating me for my depression and anxiety were out of their minds when they talked to me about my drinking and use of tranquilizers. After all, the pills made my anxiety better, and the drinking helped me sleep. Plus, it got me through some rough times, too. I always thought if the doctor would only put me on the "right" medication, my depression and anxiety would go away and I would get better. My therapist and doctor convinced me to get detoxified. Even though I was alcohol and drug free and taking antidepressant medications, I still felt miserable. How could they not understand how bad I felt and give me more medicine? For a couple of sessions with my therapist and with my doctor, all I did was complain about how bad I felt, begging for some medication. I don't know how, but throughout this I didn't drink any alcohol. Eventually, my depression and anxiety got a lot better. So did my life. I still have some symptoms, but I've been this way for many years, so why should I expect everything to go away? I've learned to live with some of these symptoms and I'm sober. My life really is much better now. Don't get me wrong, things aren't always easy, but no matter how bad my depression or anxiety gets, I don't want to drink. And I can get by without taking more drugs for every single symptom I experience. Therapy helped me learn to accept and deal with my symptoms and deal with family problems and other things going on in my life. It took me a while to realize that getting better meant an improvement in my situation, not necessarily that all of my symptoms would go away totally.—Rob, age 49

Diane's addiction started long before her bipolar disorder, making it hard for her to accept that she had a serious mood disorder and needed medication to control her symptoms. Until she accepted both of her illnesses and got the right treatment, she suffered. Rob, on the other hand, saw his primary problem as his depression and anxiety. It took a while for him to accept his alcohol and drug abuse as a problem. Cases such as those of Diane and Rob require both disorders to be addressed if recovery is to be successful.

Prevalence of Addiction and Mood Disorders

Having both a mood disorder, such as major depression or bipolar disorder, and a co-occurring drug or alcohol abuse or dependency is a condition referred to as "dual disorders." A large community study conducted in the United States by the National Institute of Mental Health found that 1 in 3 people with depression and 6 out of 10 people with bipolar disorder experience alcohol or drug abuse or dependency during their lifetimes.[2,3] Studies conducted in psychiatric or alcohol and drug treatment settings also show high rates of depression and bipolar disorders combined with substance use disorders.[4–8] Many people have more than one psychiatric diagnosis or problems with more than one substance. In one of my recent studies I found that patients with dual diagnoses had an average of 3.13 active diagnoses compared with 1.6 for patients without dual diagnoses.

Relationships Between Addiction and Mood Disorders

There are many possible relationships between addiction and mood disorders.[9–13] First, having either type of these disorders increases the odds or risk of having the other type. Mood disorders are higher among people with alcohol and drug dependence than among the general population. For example, the risk of having a substance use disorder is 4 times higher if you have depression and up to 14 times higher if you have a bipolar disorder.

Second, depression or bipolar disorder can modify the course of addiction or recovery. Untreated, a mood disorder can influence your response to substance abuse treatment and your ability to remain substance free over time. Diane's case, discussed earlier, showed how her failure to accept her bipolar illness contributed to multiple relapses to drug addiction. Diane did not give herself a chance to get well until she addressed both of her disorders. In his personal memoir titled *Darkness Visible: A Memoir of Madness,* author William Styron provides an excellent and detailed description of how his depression significantly worsened after he stopped drinking alcohol.[14] He felt that his alcoholism initially covered up his depression but then became intolerable after he quit drinking, causing him considerable anguish.

Third, mood symptoms can result from the effects of alcohol or other drugs on your central nervous system. Many cocaine abusers feel energetic and high at first but then feel depressed and suicidal when "crashing" from a cocaine binge. In some cases it is hard to distinguish between a true mood disorder and symptoms caused by the effects of drugs. This is why it may be necessary to be alcohol or drug free for several weeks or longer before an accurate diagnosis can be made.

Fourth, you may become depressed as a result of the losses or life problems caused by your addiction or mania. You may have lost a job, an important relationship, your self-esteem, your financial security, or other things. It is not unusual for depression to result from such losses. You may become depressed after getting sober and taking a look at your life, only to discover that a lot of damage has been caused by your addiction. Or you may feel depressed because you lost your "healthy self" as a result of having bipolar illness.

Fifth, the problems and symptoms related to your disorders can become so intertwined and linked that it is difficult to tell what causes what. You cannot easily tell whether your drug and alcohol dependence causes your mood symptoms or vice versa because they are so closely tied together.

And, finally, it is possible that your disorders developed at different points in time and are unrelated. Some people who are sober from alcohol or other drugs for months or years develop an episode of major depression or bipolar illness. Similarly, people in recovery from a mood disorder can get hooked on alcohol or drugs months or years after they recovered from an episode of illness or during the course of active treatment.

If you have these disorders, any area of your life can be affected in a negative way. Following are quotes from people regarding the effects of behaviors associated with one or both of their disorders:

Deeply in Debt

During a manic high, I spent our family's savings and charged thousands of dollars worth of stuff, getting us deeply in debt. Since my judgment was all messed up, I said rotten things to my teenage boys and my wife. I know they are very upset and hurt and worried about what's going to happen to our family.—Rich, age 44

I Was Immobilized

I got so depressed I couldn't take care of my kids. If it wasn't for my husband, I don't know how we would've made it. He picked up the slack. When I got real depressed, I couldn't function very well as a wife or mother. It was like I was immobilized. To make things worse, I felt guilty and worthless, too, because I was letting my family down. At the time I wished I would've never awakened. I just wanted to die.—Linda, age 39

I Traded Sex for Crack

My kids were taken away from me by Children and Youth Services. My mother was mad at me and my boyfriend ditched me. I traded sex for crack cocaine because I was desperate. I felt emotionally and spiritually bankrupt. I got very depressed and tried to kill myself by overdosing on pills.—Lavitta, age 25

The effects of dual disorders can vary from mild to extremely severe. Any area of your life can be affected—physical health, mental health, relationships, hobbies and leisure interests, work, school, legal status, finances, and spirituality. Dreams can be shattered, potential squelched, and families hurt. The actual effects of your disorders depend on:

- How long you have had your depression or bipolar disorder and how severe it is
- How long you have had your substance use disorder and how severe it is
- How much alcohol or drugs you use and how often you use
- How you ingest your drugs and the types of substances you use

- Your personality and ability to deal with problems or stress
- Your willingness to accept the need for treatment and comply with it
- Your support systems
- Your health and health care habits
- Your overall lifestyle

One person may lose everything as a result of alcohol or other drugs or problems caused by a manic episode. Another person may still be able to function and maintain a job. Although everyone is affected differently, effects associated with these disorders may include any of the following. [6,15–36]

Physical or Sexual Health

Numerous infectious diseases and medical problems are associated with addiction due to failure to take care of oneself or to seek treatment or preventive care.[9] Heavy intake of alcohol increases the risk of liver, heart, kidney, or lung diseases, cancers of the mouth or pharynx, gastritis (inflammation of the esophagus or stomach), high blood pressure, peripheral neuropathy (deterioration of nerve functioning in the hands and feet), and complications with the menstrual cycle, pregnancy, or childbirth. Early death may result from more serious types of medical conditions that are caused or worsened by addiction.

A poor diet and bad eating habits can hurt your health, too. Sandra, who suffers from depression and cocaine and alcohol dependence, lost over 40 pounds when using cocaine. An attractive woman who once worked as a model, she became thin and sickly. "I even lost my bust," she said, "and reached the point where my clothes didn't fit. I dreaded looking in the mirror because I was so skinny." People with depressive illness may overeat and gain weight or lose their appetites and lose weight. Alcohol and drug addiction often cause poor eating habits, such as skipping meals or eating an inadequate diet. Money needed for food is often spent on alcohol or drugs.

A large study of depressed patients seen in primary care settings showed that they had worse physical, social, and role functioning than those without depression. This poor functioning was similar to or worse than that caused by eight major chronic medical conditions. Patients with depression spent more days in bed than those with hypertension, diabetes, or arthritis. Another study found that individuals with depression had a fivefold greater risk of disability than those without depression. Results of these studies show that, for many, depression is a chronic and disabling condition.[31] In a recent book discussing mood disorders, Dr. Max Fink stated that "a depressive disorder increases the likelihood of early death, not necessarily because of suicide but because the patient's body undergoes numerous changes associated with systemic diseases like cancer and heart disease."[32]

Use of substances or depression can cause you to lose your sexual desire or ability to perform. Substance use or mania may cause you to engage in inappropriate or excessive sex. Some people prostitute themselves for money to support their addiction or trade sex for drugs. If you inject drugs with needles or participate in unprotected sex or sex with strangers, you increase your risk of getting a sexually transmitted disease or becoming infected with the HIV virus and eventually developing AIDS. Or, if you are infected, you can transmit it to others.

Drugs and alcohol or mania can impair your judgment and jeopardize your physical safety. Many people get hurt in accidents, fights, or suicide attempts. Jack, for example, did well for more than 3 years: "My depression lifted and I stayed sober. When I relapsed to alcohol use, I went to bars where I got into several fights after getting drunk. In my last fight, I got several teeth knocked out and got roughed up pretty bad. I'm lucky it wasn't worse." While under the influence, you can be a target of violence or crime, whether you start things or someone else does. Many victims of assault or homicide were under the influence at the time of the crime.[33,34]

Emotional Health

Your disorders can contribute to low self-esteem or low self-confidence. You can show impulsive behaviors, especially when under the influence, acting before you think about what you are doing. This can then lead to trouble in your relationships or with the law.

Suicidal thoughts and behaviors are higher among people with dual disorders than among the general population or among people with only one type of psychiatric illness.[4,6] Mood disorders have long been associated with suicidal risk.[19,35–38] Depression and alcoholism in particular are common among suicide victims. Earl, a man with a long history of depressive illness, personality disorder, and crack addiction, put it bluntly when he said, "I became an emotional wreck. Crack wore me out mentally, made me empty. I became a

nobody, a beaten down, despondent, suicidal man and lost my will to live."
Fortunately, Earl is now sober and in recovery, and his suicidal feelings are gone.

Family and Interpersonal Relationships

Many books and reports document serious negative effects of addiction and/ or a mood disorder on family and other relationships.[20,25,39-51] You can lose or damage important relationships due to unusual, bizarre, violent, aggressive, or inappropriate behaviors or to mistreating, ignoring, or taking advantage of others. This in turn can make you feel guilty and shameful and even make your depression worse. Jolene, a mother of two young children, suffered from depression and anxiety, became addicted to antianxiety pills, and began abusing alcohol as well. Before coming to treatment, she reported that "my kids, who used to be the main focus of my life, took a back seat to my addiction. I was so focused on me, my problems and getting pills or drinking booze, that I became inattentive to them. This really upset my husband, who could see that our kids were hurt by my behavior."

I conducted a written survey of more than 100 outpatients who were in my clinic for treatment of their dual disorders (most had addiction and a mood disorder). *On average, they rated the negative effects of their dual disorders on their family as "very serious."* Some of the specific negative effects on their families were identified as follows:

- Creating an emotional burden on family (worry, anger, fear, distrust; 91%)
- Neglecting their families (84%)
- Being irresponsible (74%)
- Verbal abuse (70%)
- Money problems (64%)
- Physical abuse (45%)
- Giving kids away to relative or having them taken away (37%)
- Being arrested for domestic violence (27%)

You can see from this brief list that many specific problems are caused with the family when a member has dual disorders. I have heard countless stories from men and women with addictions or dual disorders who described not only the things they did or failed to do with their families but also how they felt about their behaviors. Guilt and shame were recurrent themes.

Hobbies and Leisure Interests

You may have given up activities or interests that didn't involve alcohol or drugs as your addiction worsened. As a result you may feel bored when you first get sober because you have no hobbies or interests to keep you busy or to look forward to with enthusiasm. Depression can lead to cutting down or stopping enjoyable activities. Don, a depressed alcoholic who became sober at age 58, said, "I went nuts at first, because I didn't have any interests. Everything in my life centered around my drinking. When I got help and finally stopped, I didn't know what to do with myself. I had no hobbies. Now, I'm involved in collecting antiques, visiting my grandchildren, and volunteer work."

Work or School

Work problems include an inability to get or keep a job, lack of motivation to get training or look for a job, problems with being on time or performing job duties, and impulsively quitting due to feeling upset with a boss or because things aren't going well at work. Some people jump around from one job to the next and never really establish themselves in an occupation or with an employer. Dropping out of school, not being able to complete assignments, and poor attendance at school are common, too. Shannon had to interrupt her college studies as a result of a severe episode of depression. She became so depressed that she could not attend class, finish her assignments, or talk with her professors about her struggles completing her academic work. Shannon isolated herself from friends and often drank until she passed out. It wasn't until the semester was almost over that her parents discovered how serious her condition was and withdrew her from school so she could receive treatment for her disorders.

Lisa, an attorney with bipolar disorder and alcoholism, lost her job in a law firm after several alcoholism relapses. Her employer was very supportive and understanding of her problems and need for treatment, at least for a while. However, after several relapses during which she showed up at work intoxicated, missed work without calling in sick, and failed to live up her agreement to stay in treatment for her disorders, she was fired. She said, "I can't blame them for firing me. I wonder sometimes if I did this so I would get fired."

Legal Problems

Committing illegal acts to get money for alcohol or drugs or getting into trouble while under the influence of alcohol or other drugs or during a manic episode are common behaviors. Substance abuse is a primary cause and contributes to homicides, rapes, assaults, larcenies, burglaries, and thefts.[34] A report by the National Institute on Alcohol Abuse and Alcoholism states that alcohol is involved in many criminal behaviors.[48] A review that I conducted of studies from the United States and other countries on substance abuse and criminal behavior found that alcohol and drug use are associated with a variety of violent crimes such as rape and murder, as well as nonviolent crimes.[34] People under the influence of alcohol or drugs are often victims of crimes, including murder. Many people are in jails and prisons or on probation or parole as a result of behaviors associated with substance use or dual disorders. Drug-related crime costs American society billions of dollars, especially when drugs such as heroin or cocaine are involved.

Financial Problems

Financial problems result from money spent on alcohol or drugs, inability to follow a budget or keep a job, poor decisions made during a manic episode, or loss of benefits due to failure to comply with treatment. Self-employed people lose jobs or function less efficiently than they could due to either or both disorders. Costs associated with the legal system or with treatment can also contribute to financial problems.

People with expensive drug habits often report spending thousands, tens of thousands, or even hundreds of thousands of dollars on drugs over the course of their addiction. Many people spend their paychecks or disability or welfare checks on alcohol or drugs, only to fall behind in their rent, utilities, or other bills. Some even run out of money to buy food, sell food stamps or household items, or borrow money from loan sharks.[50]

Financial problems also can result from or be worsened by behaviors caused by the mood disorder. Depressed people sometimes go shopping and buy things they cannot afford in an attempt to raise their spirits. People with bipolar illness may go on spending sprees during manic episodes or spend money in other ways that are irresponsible. For example, Melissa spent over $900 (which she couldn't afford to spend) on shoes and purses during a shopping spree. Andy ran up over a thousand dollars in phone charges in 1 month by calling a company that provides psychic and tarot card readings. Joe withdrew over $50,000 from his retirement account and lost it in a very bad business venture. In all three of these cases, their judgment was clouded by mania.

Spirituality

You may feel "lost" or "empty," or your values may change. Many people say that drugs and alcohol bring out the worst in them and lead to behaviors that are out of character for them. This, in turn, can lead to feelings of guilt and shame. You may even stop or reduce involvement in church or religious practices. I've heard many people talk about feeling empty and not having meaning in their lives. Some lose hope and feel despondent or depressed as a result.

Some people feel bad as a result of losing opportunities in life or not being able to use their talents or abilities. An addiction or mood disorder can interfere with your ability to finish school, keep a job, or use your talents, which can cause a sense of loss because your potential isn't reached.

Evaluating the Effects of Addiction and Mood Disorders on Your Life

A helpful recovery activity is to make a list of the different areas of your life affected by your addiction and mood disorders. Although this exercise can cause anxiety at first, it can help you see more clearly the actual impact of your disorders, both on yourself and on others. This realization, in turn, can help motivate you to work hard at recovery. Discuss the results of this task with your therapist, sponsor, or someone you trust. They can help you figure out how to use this information in your ongoing recovery. For example, Joan said of her completed review of the impact of her disorders on her life, "I realized that I hurt my children and had to include them in treatment sessions because they were affected by my mood swings and strange behavior. I felt bad at first, but getting my kids involved in my treatment helped me feel less guilty because my kids got to talk about their experiences and worries. Hearing my kids really opened my eyes. I just didn't realize how hurt, angry and upset they were."

Chapter 2

Understanding Addiction: Alcohol and Drug Abuse or Dependence

The Insanity of Addiction: A View From the Inside Out

People who don't have an addiction find it very difficult to understand why someone would use alcohol or other drugs if this use causes them immense harm and trouble in their lives and upsets their families. They don't realize that all of the normal rules of human conduct are thrown out of the window when a person is addicted. Nor do they realize that the obsession and compulsion to use are intricately affected by the brain in ways that even scientists still don't fully understand.

In *Alcoholics Anonymous,* a book written by alcoholics for others suffering from alcoholism, there is a passage that illustrates the insanity of addiction and how the alcoholic is controlled by obsessions and compulsions to drink.[1]

Our behavior is as absurd and incomprehensible with respect to the first drink as that of an individual with a passion, say, for jay-walking. He gets a thrill out of skipping in front of fast-moving vehicles. He enjoys himself for a few years in spite of friendly warnings. Up to this point you would label him as a foolish chap having queer ideas of fun. Luck then deserts him and he is slightly injured several times in succession. You would expect him, if he were normal, to cut it out. Presently, he is hit again and this time has a fractured skull. Within a week after leaving the hospital, a fast-moving trolley car breaks his arm. He tells you he has decided to stop jay-walking for good, but in a few weeks he breaks both legs.

On through the years this conduct continues, accompanied by his continual promises to be careful or to keep off the streets altogether. Finally, he can no longer work, his wife gets a divorce and he is held up to ridicule. He tries every known means to get the jay-walking idea out of his head. He shuts himself up in an asylum, hoping to mend his ways. But the day he comes out he races in front of a fire engine, which breaks his back. Such a man would be crazy, wouldn't he?

You may think our illustration is too ridiculous. But is it? We, who have been through the wringer, have to admit if we substituted alcoholism for jay-walking, the illustration would fit us exactly. However intelligent we may have been in other respects, where alcohol has been involved, we have been strangely insane. It's strong language—but isn't it true? (pp. 37–38)

Prevalence, Types, and Problems of Addiction

Over 16% of adults in the United States will have a problem with alcohol or drug *abuse* or *dependence* at some point in their lives.[2] These disorders are referred to as "addictive" disorders, so when I use the term "addiction," I am referring to either a substance abuse or dependence disorder. Another term commonly used for addiction is "chemical dependency."

There are many different patterns of alcohol and drug use. Some people use occasionally but at no regular intervals. Others use more regularly, and yet others use daily. The amount of substances consumed can vary from a small to a very large amount. For example, some people smoke a five dollar rock of crack cocaine because that's all the money they have. Others smoke continuously throughout the day, consuming hundreds of dollars worth of crack cocaine. Similarly, one person may drink two or three beers on one day and then drink a lot more several days later. Another person may consume a pint or a fifth of liquor a day for months. You don't have to use every day or get intoxicated each time you use substances to have a serious problem.

Despite all the current emphasis on drugs such as cocaine, OxyContin, or "club" drugs such as Ecstasy, *alcohol remains the number one drug problem in our country.* For each drug abuser or dependent individual, there are more than two with alcohol problems. Other drugs of abuse include marijuana, tranquilizers and sedative-hypnotics, cocaine and other stimulants, heroin and other narcotics, and hallucinogens. Following is a brief discussion of different substances and some of their effects.[3–11]

Alcohol

Alcohol is the most widely abused drug in our country. Even in small quantities, it can impair your coordination or judgment and change your mood. Alcohol can affect your sleep, appetite, energy level, or sexual functioning. It is a factor in medical diseases and problems such as inflammation of the stomach (gastritis) or pancreas (pancreatitis); fatty liver or cirrhosis; cancers of the mouth, nose, esophagus, pharynx, larynx, and lungs; hypertension; coronary artery disease; stroke; heart attack; infections; damaged nerve tissues; and swelling of the joints. It can affect any organ system in your body. Withdrawal can produce seizures. A toxic overdose of alcohol can cause respiratory and circulatory failure, leading to death. Accidents at home, work, or while driving are common among people under the influence of alcohol. Alcohol abuse is a factor in traumatic injuries and in miscarriages among pregnant women.

Depressants or Tranquilizers

Drugs classified as sedative-hypnotics, antianxiety agents, or tranquilizers are used to treat anxiety, insomnia, muscle tension, convulsions, and alcohol withdrawal. Some people develop an addiction as a result of using these medications to reduce anxiety symptoms or induce sleep. These drugs can affect your sleep cycle and contribute to depression, especially when mixed with alcohol. Although few known medical disorders are associated with these drugs, they may impair memory over an extended period of time. If these drugs are taken into the veins with a needle, a person can develop hepatitis, tetanus, or abscesses or may develop HIV from using dirty needles, cotton, or rinsing water. The sedation caused by these drugs can impair one's judgment or ability to work or to operate machinery or a vehicle. Similar to alcohol, withdrawal from these drugs can produce delirium and convulsions. These are the most common drugs used in attempted suicides, and an overdose of these drugs can be fatal.

Narcotics or Opiates

Narcotic drugs include street drugs such as heroin and opium, prescription pain medications such as morphine, or cough suppressants such as codeine. Opiates such as heroin have no medical use. These drugs produce analgesia, drowsiness, changes in mood, and a clouding of mental capacities when taken in high doses. Depressive disorders are very common among opiate addicts. Medical problems associated with opiate addiction caused by using dirty needles include hepatitis and other liver problems, tetanus, abscesses and other infections, and AIDS. Gastric ulcers, heart arrhythmia, endocarditis, anemia, bone and joint infections, tuberculosis, pneumonia and lung abscesses, and abnormalities in the immune system are associated with opiate abuse. An overdose of any of these drugs can be fatal.

Cocaine and Stimulants

This category includes amphetamines, cocaine, crack, and caffeine. These drugs cause feelings of well-being, decrease fatigue, decrease the need for sleep, inhibit appetite, and increase energy or sexual desire. In recent years there has been a significant increase in the abuse of the drug called crack cocaine. This is a cheap form of smokable cocaine that affects the brain within seconds after it is smoked. Many addicts report that they became hooked on crack much more quickly than on other drugs. Stimulant drugs can cause seizures, blockages in blood circulation, abnormal heart rhythms, stroke, weight loss, impotence, disruptions in the menstrual cycle, and loss of the fetus during pregnancy. These drugs can cause babies to be born addicted. And, as mentioned before, using drugs with needles increases the risk of acquiring or transmitting HIV. In the United States, 28% of AIDS clients are intravenous (IV) drug abusers. A person who smokes or snorts cocaine or other stimulant drugs is at increased risk for respiratory problems or damage to the nasal septum in the nose.

Abuse of stimulant drugs is sometimes associated with bipolar illness. Some who abuse cocaine or other stimulants describe themselves as very "hyper" and say that they like "action." They are easily bored, enjoy "living on the edge," and use stimulant drugs to keep feeling hyperactive.

Cannabis (Marijuana)

Cannabis is a widely abused illicit drug that comes from the leaves of the cannabis plant and that is usually smoked in cigarette form, called a "joint." Another form of cannabis is called *hashish*, which comes from the resin of the plant and is usually much more potent than the leaves of the plant. Although the negative effects of cannabis are mild compared with other drugs, this drug can affect you in a number of ways, especially if you are a heavy user. It can alter your performance; decrease your motivation; impair your ability to drive; trigger panic reactions, anxiety, or paranoia; increase heart rate; impair sperm production; decrease levels of hormones; cause short-term memory deficits and accidents; and interfere with your ability to perform any complex mental task. Because it is usually inhaled, cannabis can also affect your respiratory system, causing inflammation of the sinus. Some of the effects are magnified when alcohol or cocaine is mixed with cannabis. This drug is especially dangerous to diabetics because it can alter the body's acid-base metabolism, causing ketoacidosis.

Hallucinogens or Psychedelics

This category of drugs includes LSD, or acid; mescaline; peyote; psilocybin; and other synthetic drugs made in laboratories. These drugs produce hallucinations or changes in your perceptions (that is, how you see, hear, smell, or feel things) of the world. They can cause severe psychotic experiences that necessitate psychiatric hospitalization. Perception distortions caused by hallucinogens can lead to accidents and even death as a result of behavior such as trying to fly off a roof or walk in traffic. The user may have trouble telling the difference between himself and his surroundings. These drugs can also cause depressive reactions, acting-out behaviors, paranoia, flashbacks, altered body image, or confused thinking. These drugs pose a danger to pregnant mothers and their offspring.

PCP or Angel Dust

Called phencyclidine, this unpredictable drug is an animal tranquilizer that can cause a person to become psychotic, paranoid, or violent or to act in a wild or uncontrolled way. Confusion and agitation associated with PCP can lead to accidents, self-harm, and suicide. It may also contribute to memory deficits, affect pregnancy, and cause poor attention span and slow reflexes in offspring of heavy users.

Designer or Club Drugs

Designer, or "club," drugs are created in laboratories to "mimic" other illegal drugs and are used at "raves" or all-night parties or clubs where there is a lot of music and experimenting with drugs. Ecstasy (called "XTC" or "E"), a hallucinogenic-type substance, is one of these drugs and is dangerous because the amount needed to get high is close to the amount that is toxic. Rohypnol ("roofies," "rope," "R2," and "ruffie" are some of the slang names of this drug) is known as the "date rape drug" because it can be secretly put into a female's drink so she will become sedated and pass out. Males have sexually taken advantage of females impaired by this drug.

Nicotine

Many people with addiction to alcohol or other drugs also are dependent on nicotine, mainly in the form of cigarettes. More deaths are associated with long-term use of nicotine than any other substance. Because many people in our society smoke, nicotine addiction is often ignored, which is very unfortunate given the many health risks associated with it.

Other Types of Drugs

Other drugs that people with an addiction may use include: (1) volatile or organic solvents such as gasoline, kerosene, or benzene, amyl or butyl nitrates; (2) deliriants such as nutmeg, mace, or nitrous oxide; and (3) over-the-counter drugs used for sleep, to reduce anxiety, to relieve pain, or to curtail appetite. Many people abuse or are addicted to more than one substance. Regardless of the specific substances you use or of how much or how often you use, you can experience negative effects on your behavior, mood, motivation, and ability to function in daily life.

What Is Addiction? Signs and Symptoms

An addiction is diagnosed if the symptoms and behaviors meet criteria for a substance dependence disorder as defined by the *Diagnostic and Statistical Manual of Mental Disorders* of the American Psychiatric Association (these criteria are discussed later in this chapter).[12] Another category is substance "abuse," which usually refers to excessive use of substances, leading to problems in life. Dependence is generally seen as more serious than abuse, although either can cause serious problems for the affected person and his or her family. This is especially true for those with a coexisting depression or bipolar disorder. Substance abuse and dependence are both referred to as "addictive" disorders by some experts.

You don't have to use large quantities, use every day, or get intoxicated each time that you use alcohol or other drugs to be dependent. If you have three or more of the following symptoms, you meet criteria for an alcohol or drug dependence disorder (addiction) as defined by the American Psychiatric Association:[12]

- *Compulsion:* You have difficulty cutting down or controlling how much you use or when you use. Even when you don't want to use on a given occasion, or want to limit your use, you may have trouble consistently doing so.
- *Obsession:* You are preoccupied with alcohol or drugs, and they become too important to you. You think too much about acquiring or using substances or the circumstances in which you use these.
- *Loss of control:* You use more than you intend or over a longer period of time than you planned.
- *Impairment:* You are often under the influence of substances or impaired by their use; you give up important activities in order to get or use substances or recover from the effects of them; or you continue to use even though alcohol or drugs cause problems in your life or with your health.
- *Tolerance:* You develop tolerance or a need for more of the substance to produce the desired effects; or you get high on lesser amounts of substances than before.
- *Withdrawal:* You get sick and develop withdrawal symptoms when you cut down or stop alcohol or drugs. These symptoms may vary from mild to life threatening.
- You use alcohol or drugs to avoid experiencing withdrawal symptoms. You use in the morning to get started and quell your symptoms, or you use throughout the day to make sure you don't get sick.

Although any one of these symptoms represents a problem, the more symptoms that you have, the more severe your addiction. *An addiction can exist even if you aren't physically dependent in the sense that you experience withdrawal symptoms when you cut down or stop your use or if your tolerance hasn't changed significantly.* Psychological, family, social, financial, and spiritual damage can be great even in the absence of physical withdrawal symptoms or tolerance changes.

How Addiction Is Diagnosed

Addiction is diagnosed through a combination of methods, including interviews with the individual and his or her family, review of his or her medical records, physical examination, laboratory tests, and completion of written questionnaires about alcohol or other drug use. Although any health care professional (e.g., doctor, nurse, psychologist, social worker, therapist, counselor) may conduct an evaluation, those who specialize or are specifically trained or certified in addiction medicine or addiction counseling are usually the most experienced. It is not uncommon that an addiction is not properly diagnosed because the professional lacks adequate training or knowledge of the nuances of the disorder. Addiction professionals know the types of questions to ask and when to probe for more details, because people can be evasive and secretive about their addictions.

When you are interviewed, you will be asked questions about your substance use, such as:

- Types and amounts of substances you currently use or have used in the past
- Whether or not you "mix" substances or use different ones together
- When you started to use each substance
- Your methods of use (for drug users, oral, snorting, or IV)
- When, where, and with whom you use (the social context of use)
- How substances affect you and which ones you prefer using (for users of multiple substances)
- Problems associated with your use (medical, psychological, family, financial, legal, occupational, spiritual)
- How you view your problem
- Your motivation to change
- Your view of whether or not you need professional help
- Current or past withdrawal symptoms
- Whether or not your tolerance for substances has changed

A physical examination and laboratory tests may be used to help assess medical problems that may be caused or worsened by addiction. Breathalyzer and/or urinalysis tests may be used to help confirm current or very recent substance use, because individuals with addiction sometimes lie about their use by minimizing or denying their recent use. The preceding information is important for professionals to have, because it helps them in making diagnoses and treatment recommendations. For example, I saw a patient who was clearly under the influence of alcohol and who said that he wanted nothing more than to come in for weekly outpatient counseling. When I gave him a Breathalyzer test, his blood alcohol level (BAL) registered .51, which is extremely high and potentially very dangerous. This high BAL told me several things: that he had consumed a very large amount of alcohol recently; that he had a very high tolerance; and that he needed a different type of treatment than he was currently receiving. I treated this as a serious medical emergency and arranged for medical detoxification in a hospital, because he was at high risk for seizures and complications associated with alcohol withdrawal.

You will be asked other questions about your background and different areas of your life, such as school, work, family, social relationships, and so forth. You will also be asked questions about current or past personal, emotional, or psychiatric problems. All of this information helps the evaluator get to know your background thoroughly, and it is necessary in order to make the most appropriate treatment recommendations.

People with an addiction, family members, and professionals don't always agree on whether a problem exists or how serious it is. The individual who doesn't use large quantities, doesn't use substances every day, or doesn't lose total control during each episode of substance use may minimize the seriousness of the problem. Family members may also deny or minimize his or her substance problem. This failure to accept the disorder is one of the major reasons that the majority of people with addiction never seek help on their own or seek help only when pressured by others.

Causes of Addiction

Addictions are complex disorders or diseases that are not easily explained despite the fact people often look for simple explanations. Biological, psychological, social, and cultural factors contribute to both acquiring and maintaining a substance addiction.[8,13–20] It is usually not one factor but a number of factors working together that cause a person to become and stay addicted. Although many scientists view addiction as a brain disease, they acknowledge that psychological and social factors are also involved. The term *biopsychosocial* is used to describe *bio*logical, *psycho*logical and *social*-cultural factors that contribute to this disease.

Biological Factors

Addictive disorders run within families. Perhaps you were born with a "predisposition," or increased vulnerability, to become addicted. This means that there is probably something different in the way that your body metabolizes alcohol or drugs that puts you at high risk for addiction. The actual effects of alcohol or drugs may be different for you than for others who do not become addicted. Remember, rates of addiction are much higher among first-degree relatives (i.e., siblings or children) of someone with an addiction than among relatives in whom addiction is not present. Separation or adoption studies show that children of biological parents with alcoholism who are raised in other families in which the parents are not addicted have rates of alcoholism that are 3–4 times higher than those found in the general population. On the other hand, children whose biological parents are not alcoholic but who are adopted and raised in a home with parental alcoholism do not show higher rates of alcoholism than the general population.

Addictive drugs work on the mesolimbic dopamine, or "reward," pathway of the brain, which is the same part of the brain that makes food, sex, and social interactions pleasurable. Repeated use of alcohol and other drugs stimulates this reward pathway, causing the addicted person to "want, need, or crave" these substances. An addictive pattern of use develops in which substances become of central importance in life. Scientists are continuing to study these factors in an attempt to unlock the mystery of how the brain of an addicted person is different from that of a person not addicted to substances. These differences in metabolizing drugs and brain chemistry may account for the fact that addicted individuals often develop a tolerance for alcohol or drugs and require increased quantities of substances in order to achieve the desired effect. As a result, many are able to consume large amounts of alcohol or other drugs because their tolerance is so high. On the other hand, tolerance may decrease over time, and the addicted person may get high much easier than in the past. This is called *reverse tolerance* and indicates that the addiction has gotten worse.

Alan Leshner, the former director of the National Institute on Drug Abuse (NIDA), a federally funded agency that supports research on drug problems, is working hard to educate the public that drug addiction is a brain disease.[9,21] NIDA-funded researchers are studying this brain disease and trying to find the most effective treatments for it. Experts believe that repeated use of drugs and alcohol produce enduring and possibly permanent changes in brain circuitry, in the normal levels of many neurochemicals in the brain, and in the body's stress response system.[22] Impairments in brain chemistry can be present months after a person stops using substances.

Thomas McLellan and colleagues (a group of distinguished researchers in addiction medicine in the United States) recently wrote that drug addiction is best viewed as a chronic medical disorder similar to hypertension, diabetes, and asthma.[22] All of these disorders have diagnostic criteria or symptoms, are highly influenced by heredity, and have many factors that contribute to them (physical, psychological, and social or environmental). People with any of these disorders are often poorly compliant with treatment, increasing their chances of relapse. Relapse and recurrence rates are similar among these different medical disorders, including addiction.

Psychological Factors

Psychological factors include using alcohol or drugs to relieve emotional pain or discomfort, to help you cope with problems, to relieve stress, and to help you feel better, even though the improved mood may only be temporary. If you are a risk taker, need a lot of excitement, or are prone to impulsive behaviors, your risk of addiction may increase. Another factor is the experience of positive reinforcement obtained from using alcohol or drugs. This reinforcement may come in the form of feeling good psychologically (feeling high, mellow, euphoric, relaxed) or of feeling accepted as part of a social group in which others also abuse substances. Defense mechanisms such as denial lead to an individual's failure to see the seriousness of his or her addiction and may account for the fact that the majority of people with addictions do not seek help.[23,24] Those who seek help often do so because of pressure or encouragement from family, friends, an employer, the court system, a doctor, or another health care professional.

Family and Social Factors

Family and social factors include heredity influences, as well as values and behaviors that people learn from their parents or caretakers. Some people are exposed to family chaos and disorganization and end up drinking or using drugs at a very early age in order to escape emotional pain. Or they see their parents abusing alcohol or drugs, which gives them the message that substance abuse is acceptable. Many kids are exposed to alcohol and drugs by their siblings or peers. Social pressures during the teenage years are fairly common and account for the fact that almost one in two high school seniors tries an illicit drug at some point in his or her life.

Although a number of different factors contribute to addiction, it is difficult to identify the specific causes in a given case. Also, once you develop an addiction, it takes on a life of its own. You may continue to use alcohol or drugs simply because you are physically and/or mentally addicted. A formula for understanding addiction is as follows:

Biology + Psychology + Family Influences + Social Influences
+ Alchohol/Drugs = ADDICTION

Effects of Substances on Mood Symptoms

Substance use can cover up depressive or bipolar symptoms, making it hard to identify your mood disorder until you stop using.[16] For example, Don had been dependent on alcohol for over 20 years and drank large quantities nearly every day. Although he also had symptoms of panic disorder and depression, which came before his alcoholism, his alcohol use covered up these symptoms. When he got detoxified and began working on a program of recovery, his panic symptoms and depression worsened. Treatment for his panic disorder and depression was needed to help Don stay sober from alcohol, because his symptoms caused strong cravings and thoughts of using alcohol. Interestingly, Don had sought help from several psychiatrists and general medical practitioners over the years for his "bad nerves." Treatment was only partially effective because he continued drinking heavily.

Addiction can bring about a delay in seeking treatment among those with a mood disorder. One study reported that clients with alcoholism and bipolar disorder experienced an average of 203 days of illness prior to beginning treatment, compared with only 37 days for clients who did not have coexisting alcoholism.[25]

Substance use can cause symptoms of depression, as well as self-destructive behaviors or suicidal feelings. Melissa suffered her first episode of depression while in high school, after years of getting high on alcohol and marijuana. Phillip had his first episode of mania following the use of cocaine for several months. He ended up in a psychiatric hospital due to the severity of his bipolar symptoms and concern about his suicidal feelings.

Ihsan Salloum and Michael Thase report that the course of bipolar illness or recovery from it is modified by an addiction in several ways: (1) an earlier age of onset of bipolar illness, delayed time to recovery, and shortened time to relapse; (2) higher number of symptoms and frequency of rapid cycling, mixed and dysphoric subtypes, and longer episodes; and (3) more chronicity, disability, and mortality.[26]

Manic symptoms can be triggered by acute or chronic use of alcohol or other drugs. For example, a biologically vulnerable individual may experience a first manic episode following the use of stimulant drugs. Hallucinogens have been associated with psychotic forms of bipolar disorder in several studies.

Effects of Substances on Recovery From a Mood Disorder

Drug and alcohol abuse can cause your mood symptoms to worsen and complicate your recovery. Or these symptoms may not respond as well to medications or therapy. You may even lose your motivation to recover or change your life.

Drug and alcohol use affects your judgment so that you may act in ways that interfere with your recovery by dropping out of treatment, not following your plan, and blaming lack of improvement on the wrong medications or on your doctor or counselor. Using alcohol and drugs may cause you to think about, plan, or make suicide attempts or to behave violently toward others.

Continued use of alcohol and drugs often plays a major role in relapse to an episode of depression or bipolar disorder. For example, in a survey I conducted on 50 patients readmitted to a psychiatric hospital for mood or psychotic disorders, 60% reported that drug or alcohol use had played a major role in their return to the hospital. In most cases, substance use led to poor compliance with medication and psychological treatment or to stopping treatment completely. Or it interfered with the effectiveness of medications, and the patients' depressive or bipolar symptoms returned or worsened.

Treatment and Recovery Resources for Addiction

The treatment program and recovery resources you use to help you manage your addiction depend on your current symptoms, your past history of treatment, and the availability of resources. The latter depends on your ability to pay or on whether or not you have insurance or receive government support to pay for care. It is becoming harder to get financial coverage for treatment, especially more costly inpatient hospital or rehabilitation programs. Managed care has led insurance companies to pay for fewer inpatient days or outpatient treatment sessions.

Most treatment programs are not "good" or "bad" in and of themselves, although some are better than others are. Key factors in the effectiveness of treatment include your attitudes and how hard you work at changing yourself. The best program in the world won't do you any good if you don't apply what you learn or fail to change your life. I know of many cases in which an addicted individual attended a rehabilitation program with an excellent reputation only to get drunk or high on the day of discharge from the program.

The goals of addiction treatment are to help you get and stay sober and to change yourself and your lifestyle. Your goal may differ from that of a professional who provides treatment. For example, many alcoholics have the secret goal of "controlled drinking," even though they never say anything directly about this to their counselors. Understandably, they would like to be able to drink alcohol at times and not have to abstain totally. However, the evidence is very clear from many studies that only about 1–5% of alcoholics are able to moderate their drinking consistently over time (many seem to limit their use over the short term, a few days or weeks, but often relapse over the long run because they cannot consistently control their alcohol intake). Although it is hard to predict which alcoholics could successfully moderate their drinking, many alcoholics believe they are the ones who fit in this category. So keep in mind that if you have alcoholism the odds are extremely low that you can learn to moderate and control your alcohol intake.

Some programs offer families the chance to participate in sessions as well. If you are involved with your family or have a live-in mate, ask about services available for them.

Following is a brief summary of programs and resources that are available to help you recover from addiction.

Detoxification

Detoxification refers to medically supervised or monitored withdrawal from alcohol or other addictive drugs, usually under the care of a nurse or physician. This usually involves taking medication to ease the process of withdrawal. Detoxification may be provided at rehabilitation programs or in a medical or psychiatric hospital. Inpatient detoxification is usually appropriate for more severe types of physical addiction, for cases that involve serious coexisting medical or psychiatric problems, or for individuals with a history of prior complications when withdrawing, such as seizures or delirium tremens.

Some outpatient programs provide detoxification as well, although this is usually done in connection with a partial hospital or intensive outpatient program. Detoxification usually lasts 2–5 days unless there are complications. The main goals of detoxification are to rid your system of alcohol and other drugs and to get you connected with ongoing treatment. It does little good to become detoxified if you don't follow up with treatment.

Detoxification typically involves taking medicine to prevent withdrawal, getting rest and good nutrition, and getting other evaluations or tests. Education groups and counseling sessions may also be provided, mainly to help you decide on what steps to take next to help yourself once you are finished detoxifying.

Rehabilitation

Rehabilitation refers to structured inpatient or outpatient programs that usually last 2 to 6 weeks. Rehabilitation programs offer education on addiction and recovery; individual, group, and family counseling; and participation in Alcoholics Anonymous (AA), Narcotics Anonymous (NA), and other self-help groups. These programs help you come to grips with your addiction, learn recovery skills, and put together a longer term plan to follow once you finish. A rehabilitation program helps you set the foundation and get started on your recovery. But keep in mind that this is only a start.

A typical day in a rehabilitation program is a busy one, with little free time. You will attend lots of meetings and group sessions with other patients. Educational groups, therapy groups, recovery and relapse prevention groups, family education groups, and AA/NA meetings are some of the treatments provided. You will also see a member of the treatment team for individual counseling and discharge planning. A rehabilitation program provides you with plenty of opportunities to learn about addiction and recovery and to talk about your problems. You will probably be given "assignments," as well. These include things such as (1) readings from the "Big Book" of AA, the "Basic Text" of NA, or a guide on addiction; (2) completing written activities, such as your history of substance use or filling in a section of a recovery workbook; or (3) practice changing a behavior, such as asking another person for help or support or talking about angry feelings instead of steaming on the inside. It may be hard the first few days, but once you adjust to the routine, you can gain a lot from a rehabilitation program. Many programs hire counselors and other staff members who are also in recovery from addiction and who thus have firsthand knowledge of what you are going through.

Halfway Houses or Therapeutic Communities

Longer term residential programs such as halfway houses or therapeutic communities often last several months to a year or more. These are designed primarily for those who have been unable to stay sober despite participation in other rehabilitation, counseling, or self-help programs. These programs help you slowly rebuild your life by establishing long-term sobriety and getting job training or attending school. Recovering alcoholics and drug addicts often work as counselors and role models in these programs, where group counseling and participation in AA, NA, or Cocaine Anonymous (CA) meetings are emphasized. Some programs are tough and confrontative, forcing participants to face their responsibilities in an adult manner. These programs will expel people who don't work hard at recovery. You can't "fake it" for long in these programs, so you need to be motivated and committed to changing.

Outpatient Counseling

Outpatient counseling occurs in individual, group, and/or family sessions and lasts from several weeks to months or longer. Counseling involves becoming educated about addiction and learning to function without alcohol or other drugs. If outpatient counseling is not successful in helping you stay sober, a rehabilitation program can help you. Most outpatient programs recommend the goal of abstinence from all substances. Research on drug abuse treatment supported by NIDA shows that those who complete more than 3 months show better results than those who drop out early.

In counseling sessions, you talk about things that bother you, as well as how you can deal with problems without drinking or using drugs. What you discuss in an individual session, for example, is a private decision between you and your counselor. If you are struggling with relapse or a problem, your counselor would rather hear the truth rather than have you say that everything is going well for you. A counselor can also give you "feedback" and input on how you are doing. And he or she can help you figure out problems to work on in your sessions. It is usually a good idea to come to your counseling session with an idea of a problem or issue you wish to talk about.

After-Care Counseling

Individual or group therapy follows the completion of a rehabilitation program. It may last from a few weeks to several months. After-care programs help to build on the gains made in a rehabilitation program and provide a place for you to discuss your current problems and concerns related to being drug or alcohol free.

Psychotherapy

Whereas counseling usually focuses on what is happening in your life at the present time, professional psychotherapy has a broader approach. It aims to help you understand yourself and your past better so that you know why you do the things that you do. Psychotherapy also aims to help you change your attitudes, beliefs, behaviors, and coping skills so that you can handle your problems and feelings without relying on alcohol or other drugs. Some alcoholics and drug addicts get involved in psychotherapy after they have established several months or a year or more of continuous recovery, because they feel more ready to explore their pasts. Others begin psychotherapy early and use it to help them get sober.

Special Programs

Some outpatient clinics offer time-limited programs such as relapse prevention or skills training. These programs aim to help participants learn specific coping skills to stay sober and to make positive changes in themselves or their lifestyles.

Dual-Diagnosis Programs

Dual-diagnosis programs are inpatient, partial hospital, and outpatient treatment services for psychiatric patients who also have an alcohol or other drug abuse problem. The main difference between these programs, usually offered as part of a psychiatric treatment system, and the ones discussed previously are that these focus on an individual's psychiatric problems in addition to his or her addiction.

Medications for Addiction

There is no "magic bullet" for treating an addiction. Specific medicines used for alcoholism, cocaine addiction, and heroin addiction are discussed in Chapter 6. Medications are used in conjunction with therapy and self-help program participation rather than as the sole treatment for addiction.

Self-Help Programs for Addiction

The mainstay of self-help programs is the 12-step programs of AA, NA, and CA. However, other self-help programs, such as Women for Sobriety, Rational Recovery, and SMART Recovery, offer an alternative for some people who feel they can't benefit from AA, NA, or CA. Self-help programs offer a chance to get involved with others in recovery who offer strength, support, hope, and encouragement. All programs have numerous "tools of recovery" that can help you stay sober and clean and become a better person.

Self-Help Programs for Dual Disorders

Self-help programs are sometimes part of AA or NA and sometimes a separate program. They go by many names, such as Double Trouble (DT), Dual Recovery Anonymous (DRA), MISA (Mentally Ill Substance Abuser), CAMI

(Chemical Abusing Mentally Ill) and SAMI (Substance Abusing Mentally Ill). They have a "dual" focus—staying sober *and* coping with psychiatric illness. Although many people with dual disorders find AA, NA, or CA suitable, others are more comfortable in a dual-recovery-oriented self-help program such as DT or DRA.

Effectiveness of Treatment for Addiction

A considerable body of research shows that people who receive treatment for addiction do much better than those who go untreated. Those who don't drop out of treatment programs early and keep their counseling appointments are much more likely to get better than are those who are poorly compliant. Many scientific studies show significant positive effects of treatment, such as:[21,22,27–49]

- Stopping or reducing alcohol or other drug use
- Improved physical health
- Decreased transmission or acquisition of sexually transmitted diseases or HIV
- Improved mental health (mood, self-esteem)
- Improved spiritual health
- Reduced family problems
- Improved health in babies of pregnant addicted mothers
- Increase in mothers' reuniting with their children
- Reduced rates of crime, rearrests, and return to prison
- Improved motivation to change and compliance with treatment
- Improvements in ability to get and keep a job
- Decreased medical costs (for families, insurance companies, government)
- Decreased costs to the public

The good news is that we have learned from these scientific studies that alcohol and drug dependence can be effectively addressed in professional treatment provided by qualified doctors, nurses, psychologists, social workers, and certified addiction therapists and counselors. Treatment works best when you keep your scheduled sessions, remain in treatment long enough to benefit from it, and take medications (e.g., Antabuse, ReVia, Trexan) as prescribed if they are an adjunct to counseling. Developing a trusting relationship with your counselor or therapist and opening up to discuss your personal problems and inner thoughts and feelings pave the way to get the most out of your treatment.

We also know, from other studies on substance abuse combined with psychiatric disorders, that treatment that addresses psychiatric issues and addiction yields the most benefits. Treatment for mood and substance use disorders generally works best if it is "integrated" and focuses both on alcohol and drug abuse and on mood-related problems.[16,50–53]

Successful Recovery

Following are a few brief stories that show how different people experienced a successful recovery. These people vary in terms of the severity of their addiction, their reasons for seeking help, and how they benefited from recovery. You will see positive changes in both their external lives (e.g., relationships, work, etc.) and their internal lives (e.g., how they feel about themselves and life). These are just a few stories; there are thousands of others that echo the hopefulness of recovery and show that no matter how badly off or down a person has been, recovery is always possible—but only if you go after it.

I've Been Sober Now for Over 5 Years

I'm a retired schoolteacher. When my husband died a few years ago, my drinking increased, but never to the point where I thought that I needed help. During a visit by my daughter and grandkids over the holidays, I drank too much and made a fool out of myself. My daughter was worried about and upset at how I acted. She suggested I get help but I didn't think anything was wrong. However, since I was seeing a therapist for depression, I told him about this episode, and we discussed my drinking habits. He recommended some counseling sessions with another therapist who specialized in treating people with alcohol problems. I went to six sessions over several months. It helped me realize that my drinking was a problem even though I didn't drink every day or always get drunk. I also decided to go to AA meetings. I've been sober now for over 5 years. I feel much better physically, my family isn't worried about me, and I'm much more active in my community. I still go to AA each week because I need a reminder about my alcoholism. Plus I find the people there to be supportive and helpful.—Alice, age 66

Recovery Gave Me Back My Self-Respect

My addiction to cocaine got out of control and I lost everything—my business, my freedom, my self-respect, and the respect of my family. While in prison I got involved in NA meetings. When I was released from prison I went to a therapeutic community—a long-term residential treatment program for female addicts whose lives had been ruined by addiction. I stayed there over 6 months. I went to a lot of group therapy and NA meetings while there. It wasn't easy, but it helped me. I slowly put my life back together. I now have my own business and I'm making good money. I'm taking good care of my family now—before, I was irresponsible and didn't care much about anyone but myself. I learned how to handle my depression and anger, too. I used to have a short fuse and go off on others real quick. Now I'm in control over my emotions and I don't get angry easy or use it as an excuse to get high. Recovery also gave me back my self-respect. Lots of people helped me in the process—counselors, my NA sponsor, my mother, and my husband. I've been off drugs over 3 years and I can tell you that my life is much better now. I still take my recovery one day at a time, and I do the things they taught me in treatment, like talk about my problems instead of letting them build up, fight off negative thoughts about sobriety, and stick with people who care about me. I'm not taking anything for granted.—LaVette, age 42

I Learned to Live Life on Life's Terms

I went to rehab mainly to get people off my back and save my job. I figured I'd go through the motions, let the pressure from others die down, then do my own thing again after I finished rehab. I really didn't think it was anybody's business if I drank or used drugs, but I wanted to save my job so I entered treatment. But something happened in rehab that made me realize I wasn't conning anyone but myself. When I left the rehab program I went to counseling for a couple of months. I also went to meetings a couple times each week. I learned how to fight off my urges to drink, deal with outside pressures to drink, and how to be upset and not use any chemicals. Probably most importantly, I learned how to live life on life's terms—I wasn't any special case, and all the reasons I gave for getting high were a copout. I still have problems, but I learned I can solve them much better if I'm sober.—Jerry, age 23

I Care About the World Now

Sobriety has been hard for me at times, and I feel I've worked real hard to earn it. Now, I just accept the rough times and do my best living with them because they never last for long. Before, I complained or wished the bad times away. Hey, life is like this, everything ain't gonna go good all the time. Despite the BS I had to put up with, life truly is much better now that I've been sober for a long time. Sure, I'm doing good at my job, pay my bills, get along better with my family and stay out of trouble. But in sobriety I've learned other things that are just as important. I learned to let myself love other people and to show it in how I treat them. I've also learned all of my feelings are important, even sadness or depression. My emotional life is richer even if harder at times so I ain't trying to escape my feelings. I'm better at setting goals and in balancing my life so I don't burn myself out. I feel like I'm a much more spiritual person now. Not just in the sense of going to church, but how I treat others and see the world. I want to make a difference and I care about the world now. I want my actions to matter so I live my life in a way that I think is decent and respectful. I'd have to say the internal rewards of sobriety are better than the external rewards.—Mary Ellen, age 36

Managed Care

Professional treatment has to be paid for, and most people are covered by some kind of private or public insurance. Managed care refers to private or public health maintenance organizations (MCO) that oversee insurance benefits that pay for mental health, drug and alcohol, or dual-diagnosis treatment. The MCO usually requires you to get approval or authorization for clinical services or they will not be paid for. With most MCOs, you have to call your managed care company to request treatment services. You will be asked information about yourself so that they can determine what kind of treatment you need and where you may receive this treatment. Most MCOs approve only a limited number of treatment programs or professionals—in fact, they require providers to submit documentation before approving them. Depending on your specific MCO, you may have a yearly or lifetime limit on the number of days of hospital care, partial hospital care, or number of outpatient sessions that will be covered for the treatment of addiction. Treatment authorizations are usually needed when you first start treatment, when you move from one level of care to another (e.g., from inpatient to partial hospital, from partial hospital to outpatient), or when you need to continue treatment once your initial authorization has expired. Any questions you have about managed care benefits can be discussed with your MCO care manager or your therapist.

Chapter 3   *Understanding Mood Disorders: Depression and Bipolar Illness*

Prevalence and Types of Mood Disorders

There are two major categories of mood disorders (also sometimes referred to as "affective" disorders): (1) depression, which includes major depression, dysthymia, depressive disorder not otherwise specified, bipolar depression, and depression caused by a medical condition or substance abuse; and (2) bipolar disorder, which includes mania (with or without depression), hypomania, cyclothymia, and bipolar disorder not otherwise specified. Some people have symptoms of both a bipolar and a depressive disorder at the same time, a condition referred to as a "mixed state." Clearly, mood disorders come in many different varieties, and each case is different in some ways.

Depressive disorders affect about 20% of women and 12% of men at some time in their lives, and bipolar disorders affect a little more than 1% of the population, with men and women being affected equally.[1,2] Some individuals experience their mood symptoms at specific times of the year, a condition referred to as "seasonal affective disorder." Depression, for example, often begins in the fall or winter. Mania may begin in the spring, followed by a depression later on.

You may experience an *acute episode* of illness in which your mood symptoms are present for a specific period of time. These symptoms may go away in time, with or without treatment. However, treatment helps to decrease the length of time that the mood episode is experienced, the severity of the episode, and the problems or suffering that result from such an episode of illness. *Recurrent illness* refers to experiencing two or more different episodes of your mood disorder over time. In between episodes you may do quite well and experience few or no symptoms. The length of time between episodes may vary from months to years. Bipolar disorders and major depression are recurrent conditions for significant numbers of people who experience multiple episodes of depression, mania, or both over time.

Persistent or chronic mood disorders, such as dysthymia or cyclothymia, are lifelong forms in which mood symptoms may more or less be experienced continuously over time.[3–5] There may be flare-ups of symptoms and times in which they worsen. For example, some people with dysthymia experience a low mood even when they are doing fairly well. Although the symptoms of these disorders are persistent, they are less severe and debilitating than major depression or mania.

Symptoms of depression or bipolar disorder show in your moods, thinking, perception, behaviors and activities, and physical functioning (sleep, appetite, energy, activity level, sexual energy). Having a mood disorder means that you experience a combination of these symptoms over a period of time. These symptoms affect your relationships, your ability to function and take care of yourself, your judgment, your ability to cope with stress and to solve problems, and your substance use. Mood disorders underlie the majority of suicides.

The Black Dog of Depression

Thoughts, behavior, and activity are often slowed in depression. Fatigue and an inability to exercise are common. The person may sleep too little or too much and find it hard to get restful sleep. In more serious depressive states, moods are bleak, pessimistic, despairing, and hopeless. Decisiveness is replaced by indecision and by running things over and over in the mind, concentration is difficult, and it becomes hard to act. Irrational fears, panic, and obsessions and delusions (false beliefs) are also present in some types of severe depressions. In her book *Touched by Fire: Manic-Depressive Illness and the Artistic Temperament,* Kay Jamison provides numerous descriptions of famous people with mood disorders that convey the personal anguish and suffering of depression.[6] For example, F. Scott Fitzgerald said of his depression: "I could lie around and was glad to, sleeping or dozing sometimes twenty hours a day and in the intervals trying resolutely not to think . . . every act of life from the morning toothbrush to the friend at dinner had become an effort" (23).

Kathy Cronkite described her awful depression in her book *On the Edge of Darkness*.[7] She talked about how she struggled with the "black dog of depression" and even contemplated swallowing a can of liquid Drano. She interviewed actor Rod Steiger, who said this about his depression: "You have moments when you're locked in an ever-increasing terror. You begin to doubt your sanity. When you're depressed, there's no calendar. There are no dates, there's no day, there's no night, there's no seconds, there's no minutes, there's nothing. You're just existing in this cold, murky, ever-heavy atmosphere, like they put you inside a vial of mercury" (46).

Nancy Rosenthal, who is recovering from a mood disorder, coauthored a recent new book *Hope for People with Bipolar Disorder*.[8] She describes the dark side of her depression as follows: "There is no minimizing its shattering, destabilizing effects. . . . Depression is dark days and endless nights. Trivial, mundane tasks become insurmountable. . . . Depression has a domino effect—one defeat leads to another and another and another" (15).

Although not all cases are as severe as these, depression brings with it much personal suffering. It can affect any area of life and rob the person of motivation or even the will to go on living.

Symptoms of Depressive Disorders

A problem with the term *depression* is that it is used too casually to refer to all types of mood states, from being mildly "bummed out" because your favorite sports team lost a game, because you gained a few unwanted pounds, or because you got criticized by your spouse or boss to being "clinically" depressed. Clinical depression refers to a disorder in which a variety of mood, cognitive (thinking), and bodily symptoms are experienced. In some instances, psychotic symptoms such as delusions (false beliefs) may be experienced. The symptoms of clinical depression not only cause you to feel awful but also affect your ability to function or enjoy life.

Almost 1 out of 3 people with depressive disorders will also have problems with alcohol or drug abuse or dependence. About 1 in 10 people with major depression will also experience a bipolar disorder. Others will have an anxiety, eating, or personality disorder. Hence, people with clinical depression often have other psychiatric or substance abuse disorders as well.

Major depressive disorder involves symptoms that are present nearly every day for 2 weeks or longer. Over one-half of those with this type of depression will have a recurrent course and will experience two or more episodes during their lifetimes. In another type of depressive disorder, called *dysthymia,* low-level depressive symptoms are experienced most of the time and fairly continuously for 2 years or longer. Some people experience both major depression and dysthymia at the same time, a condition referred to as "double depression."

Depressive disorders include a combination of the following objective and subjective symptoms and behaviors:[2,9,10]

Mood Symptoms

- Depressed or low mood
- Persistent sadness
- Loss of interest in life or inability to experience pleasure (in food, sex, work, or activities)
- Feeling hopeless about the future or helpless about changing
- Feeling worthless or guilty

Thinking Symptoms

- Difficulty focusing
- Poor concentration
- Poor memory
- Difficulty thinking clearly
- Slowed thinking
- Trouble making decisions (indecision)
- Thoughts of suicide

Bodily or Physical Symptoms

- Decrease in energy, low energy, or fatigue
- An increase or decrease in appetite
- Weight loss or gain that is not intentional
- Sleep difficulties (trouble falling or staying asleep, inability to sleep through the night, or sleeping too much)
- Decrease in or loss of sexual energy or interest in sex

Other Symptoms

▨ Suicidal behaviors

▨ Isolation

▨ Psychotic symptoms (hallucinations, delusions, or catatonic states)

A list of symptoms can never truly convey the differences in the personal experiences of depression among various people. Nor can such a list adequately describe the personal anguish often felt by the person with a depressive illness. Symptoms are descriptors and are helpful to professionals in reaching a diagnosis. In reality, the number, intensity, and effects of depressive symptoms will vary from one person to the next. For example, Eric was so depressed and despondent that he could hardly get out of bed, often sleeping for 10 hours or longer. Getting through the day was very hard, and he had trouble taking care of his family. Eric was pessimistic about his future and often thought he would be better off dead. Despite being a successful professional, he felt tormented by feelings of incompetence and believed that he was a "fraud." Beth, on the other hand, was also clinically depressed but went to work and took fairly good care of her family. Her concentration was off, and her energy was low. Beth's sleep was not restful, and she awakened in the middle of the night. Overall, however, she was less impaired by her depression than Eric was, and she did not harbor any thoughts of suicide. Hence, the severity of a clinical depression may vary from mild to moderate to severe.

Bipolar Illness: A Disorderly and Unpredictable Disorder

Disorderly, unpredictable, chaotic, erratic, hectic, disorganized—these are just some of the terms used to describe bipolar illness. Ellen Frank and colleagues have been studying bipolar illness for many years. They refer to this illness as a "disorderly disorder" that causes considerable "chaos" for the patient and family. They state that bipolar disorder:[11]

is typically hectic and variable. A "roller coaster" for both patients and clinicians, extreme highs and lows intermingle with mixed states and subsyndromal symptom flurries to create hybrid symptom states that defy easy labels . . . hypomania can surge into . . . mania and then plummet into a debilitating major depression. A fall from mania can lead to endless months of major depression. . . . Treatments for those intolerable depressions may send a patient's mood back into the manic range, only to plunge back down into depression. (p. 593)

The Experience of Mania

Mania is often seasonal and recurrent and is characterized by a mood that is high, euphoric, self-confident, or extremely irritable. Mania usually starts gradually, and it can take weeks for the full syndrome to show. In the early phases of the change in mood, the person may actually feel better than usual. Mental activity increases, and thinking is more rapid, which then leads to more and faster speech or jumping from one topic to the next in conversation. Activity levels increase and can be frantic, aimless, and sometimes even violent. Some people become suspicious and isolated, whereas others seek out social interaction. Impulsive, bizarre, driven, risky, and paranoid behaviors are common. Although affected individuals may have a tendency to seek out other people, they may also be suspicious toward others. Poor judgment is common and shows in impulsiveness (e.g., quick decisions to get engaged or married or to change jobs), bad financial decisions (e.g., spending sprees or bad investments), and engagement in high-risk behaviors (e.g., promiscuous sex, sex with strangers, or involvement in sexual behaviors not ordinarily pursued). Failure to acknowledge the illness even in the presence of severe symptoms is common and, unfortunately, is a major factor in many people refusing treatment. The senses are more finely tuned, and hallucinations (alterations of the senses) may be experienced. Symptoms are usually unrelated to events in a person's life, and they can persist for weeks or longer if untreated.[6,12]

In milder forms, referred to as "hypomania," the increased energy, risk taking, and fluency of thought can lead to creativity and productivity. These milder mood and energy swings often precede mania by years. In her memoir *An Unquiet Mind,* psychologist and researcher Kay Jamison described her early hypomania as "intoxicating states that gave rise to great personal pleasure, an incomparable flow of thought, and a ceaseless energy." Jamison also described more severe mania, then a switch to depression.[12]

There was a particular kind of pain, elation, loneliness, and terror involved in this kind of madness. When you're high it's tremendous. The ideas and feelings are fast and frequent like shooting stars. . . . Shyness goes, the right words and gestures are suddenly there, the power to captivate others a felt certainty. There are interests found in uninteresting people. Sensuality is pervasive and the desire to seduce and be seduced irresistible. Feelings of ease, intensity, power, well-being, financial omnipotence, and euphoria pervade one's marrow. But, somewhere, this changes. The fast ideas are far too fast, and there are far too many; overwhelming confusion replaces clarity. Memory goes. Humor and absorption on friends' faces are replaced by fear and concern. Everything previously moving with the grain is now against—you are irritable, angry, frightened, uncontrollable, and enmeshed totally in the blackest caves of the mind. You never knew those caves were there. It will never end, for madness carves its own reality. (67)

Jamison provides numerous rich and detailed descriptions of the symptoms and behaviors associated with both depressive and bipolar disorders in her memoir, as well as in her other books, one of which discusses mood disorders among many well-known and distinguished writers, composers, and artists.[6] She has done a superb job in helping the public understand these mental disorders and providing a sense of hope that effective treatments exist for mood disorders. In addition to poignant descriptions of symptoms and the problems associated with mood disorders, Jamison discusses the "positive aspects" of mood disorders. Many accomplished writers or composers, for example, have used their depressions or manic states as an impetus to create poetry, literature, or musical works. Regarding bipolar illness, Jamison states:

the positive aspects of the illness that can arise during the milder manic states: heightened energy and perceptual awareness, increased fluidity and originality of thinking, intense exhilaration of moods and experience, increased sexual desire, expansiveness of vision, and a lengthened grasp of aspiration. . . . [T]his was an illness that could confer advantage as well as disadvantage, and for many individuals these intoxicating experiences were highly addictive in nature and difficult to give up.[12](128).

Symptoms of Bipolar Disorder

Bipolar disorder, previously referred to as manic depression, is a disorder that involves multiple types of symptoms: mood, cognitive, bodily, or psychotic. In mania or hypomania, the mood is high, euphoric, or expansive. A manic episode can last days, weeks, or even several months and involves the following mood and related symptoms:[2]

Mood Symptoms
- A period of abnormally and persistently elevated or expansive mood
- Feelings of joy or excitement that seem out of place or too extreme
- Irritable mood

Cognitive (Thinking) Symptoms
- Inflated self-esteem or feeling of grandiosity (i.e., increased belief in one's own importance)
- Racing or disconnected thoughts; jumping from one idea to the next
- Being easily distracted
- Paranoia
- Hallucinations
- Delusions (false beliefs about wealth, power, or special abilities)

Physical and Behavioral Symptoms
- Decreased need for sleep
- Being more talkative than usual or feeling a pressure to keep on talking
- An increase in goal-directed activities at home, work, or school (for example, involvement in many projects or activities)
- Odd or improper social behavior

Similar to depressive disorder, a list of symptoms cannot clearly convey the personal experience of having a bipolar illness. Nor can such a list adequately communicate the variability between people affected by this disorder.

Episodes of depression are very common with bipolar disorder. Some people switch from a manic state to a depressed state. Those who switch multiple times are referred to as "rapid cyclers." Others experience symptoms of both mania and depression at the same time, a condition known as mixed bipolar disorder. Hence, there are many variations of this illness.

Up to 60% of people with bipolar illness also have a problem with alcohol and drug abuse or dependency.[13] Both manic and depressive symptoms that are part of bipolar disorder can be caused or worsened by the use of alcohol or other drugs. Some people who have a biological vulnerability to mania can actually experience the first episode following the use of stimulant or hallucinogenic drugs such as LSD or PCP. Alcohol or drugs may be used to medicate symptoms of bipolar illness and can mask some of the symptoms. Substance abuse can also precipitate a recurrence of a mood episode after a period of remission, most often because it contributes to the decision to stop taking medications or stop going to therapy. For example, Ed had been stable from his bipolar disorder and sober from alcohol for more than 5 years when he decided to have a few beers. Over the next few weeks he began drinking more alcohol, sometimes to the point of intoxication. Ed also quit taking his lithium. Within a few weeks, he became manic and refused all efforts of his family to help him get back in treatment. Finally, Ed was hospitalized briefly to stabilize his mania and help him reestablish his sobriety from alcohol.

How Mood Disorders Are Diagnosed

Mood disorders are diagnosed through a combination of methods, including interviews with the individual and his or her family, interviews with other professionals who have worked with the person, review of his or her medical records, a physical examination, laboratory tests, and completion of written mood inventories. Because many medical conditions can cause depression, a thorough physical examination and laboratory tests may be ordered in order to rule out medical causes of depression.

During an interview with a psychiatrist, psychologist, psychiatric social worker, or other licensed mental health professional, you will be asked questions about your life and about current and past symptoms. This information will help the evaluator determine whether you have a mood disorder or whether additional assessments are required to reach an accurate diagnosis. These questions relate to your current moods, feelings, thoughts, interest in your life, appetite, sleep patterns, changes in weight, energy, concentration, interest in sex, alcohol or drug use, and overall health. You will be asked about suicidal thoughts or feelings and, if you endorse these, you will be asked if you intend to hurt yourself or actually have a plan to take your own life. Your evaluator will also ask you questions about other current (and past) psychiatric symptoms, medical problems, medications you take, involvement in treatment, and your overall life (school or work, social life, family relationships, hobbies and interests, and spirituality). You may also be asked to fill out brief mood questionnaires, which can take anywhere from 2–10 minutes. If your evaluator is not a psychiatrist or licensed psychologist, the results of your assessment will probably be reviewed with a psychiatrist who will help determine the diagnosis. If your behavior is grossly disorganized or out of control due to the nature of your mood symptoms (e.g., mania, psychosis, violence or the threat of it), the evaluation will be finished after your symptoms are brought under control. If you are initially evaluated in an outpatient mental health clinic or by a private practitioner, your initial evaluation will last between 1 and 2 hours. If you are seen in a psychiatric emergency room, the evaluation can take several hours or longer. In some instances, it may take more than one session to reach an accurate diagnosis.

A mood disorder is diagnosed if the symptoms and behaviors meet criteria for one of the specific types of depression or bipolar disorder as defined by the *Diagnostic and Statistical Manual of Mental Disorders* of the American Psychiatric Association (these criteria are discussed later in this chapter).[2] Although many physicians are knowledgeable about mood disorders, a psychiatrist has the most training and expertise in assessment and treatment of these disorders. If you are concerned about yourself or a loved one having a depressive or bipolar disorder, seek a consultation with a psychiatrist or other licensed mental health professional, such as a psychologist, psychiatric social worker, nurse, or mental health counselor.

Active alcohol or drug use can complicate the evaluation process, because substances can cause, worsen, or cover up mood symptoms. Therefore, be sure to tell whoever evaluates you about the details of your alcohol or other drug use. Also, it isn't unusual for you to have a different opinion from that of your family or even professionals regarding your mood disorder. You may think you are fine, even though a professional assessment reveals the presence of a serious depression or bipolar disorder.

Risk Factors for Mood Disorders

Dan Blazer recently reviewed many studies to identify risk factors associated with major depression and bipolar disorder.[14] Risk factors are characteristics of the individual or life circumstances that increase the likelihood of having a mood disorder. This does not mean that a person with some of these factors will experience depression or bipolar illness. Rather, it means that having these factors increases the risk for developing a mood disorder.

Risk factors for major depression include: (1) being female; (2) being younger (the average age at onset is between 20 and 40); (3) being from a low socioeconomic class; (4) being separated or divorced; (5) having a family history of depression; (6) early death of a parent and disruptive childhood environment; (7) experiencing negative stressful events (e.g., loss of a loved one); (8) chronic stress (e.g., financial problems, conflict at work, living in a dangerous neighborhood); (9) not having a confidant with whom to talk; and (10) living in an urban area.

For bipolar disorder, risk factors included: (1) being younger (typically, 20–40 years old); (2) being from a high socioeconomic class; (3) being separated or divorced; (4) having a family history of bipolar disorder; (5) experiencing negative stressful events; (6) and living in the suburbs. In relation to stressful events, it is more the person's view of the event rather than the event itself that affects mood and behavior.

Causes of Mood Disorders

According to experts, a variety of biological and environmental factors may contribute to episodes of major depression or bipolar disorder.[8–10,15–24] Michael Thase and John Rush, two experts in the treatment of mood disorders, put it best when they said, "often it is a combination of heredity and biochemistry, along with a person's psychological makeup and stressful life events, that may cause depression"[25] (3). The same holds true for multiple causes of bipolar disorder. However, in a given case it is not always easy to tell what caused the mood disorder. William Styron, the writer, who suffered from alcoholism and major depression, conveys the difficulty in isolating the precise causes of depression when he says in his personal memoirs:[26]

> I shall never know what "caused" my depression, as no one will ever learn about their own. To be able to do so will likely forever prove to be an impossibility, so complex are the intermingled factors of abnormal chemistry, behavior and genetics. Plainly, multiple components are involved—perhaps three or four, most probably more, in fathomless permutations. (38–39)

Biological Factors

Mood disorders run in families, so heredity plays a significant role. When a family member has a bipolar disorder, the risk of developing a bipolar disorder among other relatives is three to eight times higher than what would be normally expected. Studies of identical twins show that when one twin has bipolar disorder, 75% of the time the other twin will also have it. When a family member has a major depressive disorder, the risk is two to three times higher for other family members compared with the general population. Twin studies show that if one twin has depression, 40% of the time the other twin will also suffer from depression. However, not everyone with a genetic vulnerability will experience a mood disorder.

Impairment or imbalances in the transmission of brain chemicals (excesses or deficits), altered hormonal regulation, thyroid dysfunction, other physical diseases or trauma, medications, and abused substances such as alcohol or illicit drugs contribute to the onset of depression or mania. Depression in mothers may occur following childbirth. Caused by a combination of physical, psychological, and social changes associated with childbirth, *postpartum depression* can be especially severe for some mothers. Serious and terminal medical diseases or disabilities, other significant physical ailments, chronic pain, changes or limitations in physical or athletic abilities, decline in appearance, or weight gain common among middle-aged and older adults also may contribute to depression. A woman entering menopause, for example, may have difficulty accepting changes in her body and may perceive herself to look far less attractive than she once did. Or an active, athletic man who can no longer participate in certain sports as he ages may have difficulty accepting and adjusting to this new reality. Any of these types of situations may contribute to depression. Significant physical changes or problems usually involve psychological and social adjustments, as well.

Psychological Factors

Some people appear to have a temperament or certain personality attributes that predispose them to problems with their moods. These are people who are more or less depressed or hyperactive most of the time; it seems to be part of their nature or personality. A tendency toward negative and pessimistic thinking, helplessness, self-criticism, exaggerating the significance of problems, or low self-esteem also affect mood disorders. Martin Seligman has written extensively about the role of "learned helplessness" and he believes that depression could be caused by defeat, failure, and loss and the consequent belief that any actions taken will be futile.[27] Seligman also believes that people can learn to think differently and learn "optimism," which can help counteract depression. Some experts believe that ways of thinking about problems and life are initially learned in the family, often from parents or primary caretakers.

Major changes in life, such as a change in status caused by retirement or the unexpected loss of a job or career, can affect self-esteem and a person's view of life and the future. So can changes associated with a transition to another stage in life, such as moving from young to middle adulthood or from middle to older adulthood. Some people are prone to depression following such changes.

Social and Interpersonal Factors

Significant losses; serious interpersonal problems; negative family atmosphere or serious family problems; exposure to trauma such as rape, assault, physical or sexual abuse; feeling stuck in a hopeless and very negative relationship; legal, job-related, financial, or housing problems; and stresses such as negative life events may also contribute to an episode of a mood disorder, especially depression. However, it isn't necessarily these problems or stresses in and of themselves that cause mood problems. Rather, it is your view of these stresses or problems, your ability to manage or cope with them, and the availability of support from other people that determine whether you experience problems with your mood. Also, it is possible that biological factors contribute to how stresses are subjectively experienced.

Substance Use

An episode of substance use can precipitate mania or depression.[28] Another significant factor is relapse to addiction following a substantial period of recovery. Dana's comments capture this experience: "I worked very hard at staying sober from alcoholism and had over 7 years when I relapsed. I really thought I'd never drink again. It was devastating when I relapsed. I felt I let everybody down—my husband, kids, friends and two women in AA who I sponsor. Following my relapse, I went into a deep depression and seriously thought about killing myself." Fortunately, Dana had an excellent support system and quickly got back on the sober track. However, like many people with long-term sobriety who relapse, she initially reacted very negatively, judging herself harshly and labeling herself as hopeless and a failure.

A formula for understanding the multiple causes of a mood disorder is as follows:

$$\text{Biology} + \text{Psychology} + \text{Family/Social Influences}$$
$$= \text{MOOD DISORDER}$$

Other Psychiatric Disorders

Many people with depression or bipolar disorder, an addiction, or both types of disorders will experience other types of psychiatric illnesses, such as anxiety, personality, psychotic, eating, or other nonsubstance addictive disorders. Following is a brief discussion of some of these other types of disorders.

Anxiety Disorders

Anxiety disorders involve feelings of anxiety and worry that are excessive and unrealistic. Situations that cause anxious feelings are often avoided as a result. These disorders can cause significant personal distress and interfere with one's life. Following are specific types of anxiety disorders, each with its own set of symptoms.[2]

Panic Disorder Panic disorder involves sudden panic or anxiety states in which intense fear is experienced.[29,30] This fear usually lasts several minutes or longer and, during the time in which the attacks are experienced, you may worry about losing your mind or dying. Things "don't seem real" during panic attacks. Physical symptoms include feeling dizzy or faint, having difficulty breathing or catching your breath, feeling shaky, trembling, sweating, feeling sick to the stomach, or having hot or cold flashes, chest pains, and rapid heartbeat.

Phobias These include social phobias, simple phobias, and agoraphobia.[31–35] A *social phobia* is an irrational fear of being in situations in which you might be looked at, criticized, or rejected by other people or of acting in ways that will be embarrassing or humiliating. Common examples of social phobias involve fears of eating, speaking, or writing in public, dating, or taking tests. In a survey of 125 outpatients in my clinic, almost one-third reported high levels of social anxiety and avoiding groups (treatment and self-help) as a result. Talking in front of others was extremely anxiety provoking and often interfered with recovery. *Simple phobias* are irrational fears of things or objects, such as spiders, blood, or needles. Phobias may also involve irrational fears of traveling by bus or airplane, being in closed spaces such as an elevator, or being in high places, such as on top of a building. *Agoraphobia* is an intense fear of being alone or being in a public place from which you think you can't escape or can't get help if you need it. People with agoraphobia limit how far they will travel from their homes. Some even become prisoners in their own homes and seldom leave them unless they are with another person. Physical symptoms associated with phobias include having heart palpitations, feeling shaky, sweating, blushing, feeling dizzy, and being short of breath.

Obsessive-Compulsive Disorder   In obsessive-compulsive disorder, an individual has persistent and recurrent ideas or thoughts that repeat over and over in his or her mind.[36,37] These recurrent ideas, called *obsessions,* usually make little or no sense at all. In fact, sometimes you will find them quite distasteful. Examples include obsessions about harming yourself or another person; fears of germs, dirt, contamination, body fluids, or body waste; obsessions with order and perfectionism or with forbidden or perverse sexual thoughts or images; fears of doing something impulsive, embarrassing, or out of the ordinary; religious obsessions; and body obsessions (related to weight, height, body parts, or illness). *Compulsions* refer to repeating behaviors over and over again. These behaviors are often repeated as a way of blocking your obsessions or, in some cases, an attempt to prevent some future event or situation from occurring. Compulsions also appear to be senseless. Compulsive behaviors include rearranging things or putting them in order; washing hands or brushing teeth over and over; taking numerous showers; repeatedly checking doors, locks, windows, the stove, or car brakes; repeating words over and over silently to oneself; counting objects; or repeating some other ritual over and over.

Posttraumatic Stress Disorder   Posttraumatic stress disorder involves reexperiencing a past trauma that is outside the range of normal human experience.[38–40] The trauma may be something you experienced directly, such as violence, assault, or rape, or something that you have witnessed, such as watching other people get hurt or even killed in combat, in a natural disaster or an accident, or by murder. This trauma is reexperienced months or years after the event in the form of recurrent thoughts or dreams that actually feel as though the trauma is happening again, as well as intense anxiety in situations that remind you of the traumatic event. Many people with posttraumatic stress disorder avoid people, places, or things that may trigger thoughts or feelings about the trauma. Depression, trouble sleeping, angry outbursts, anxiety, and feeling on edge are other symptoms associated with posttraumatic stress disorder. Many people also feel guilty when the trauma involves the deaths of other people.

Generalized Anxiety Disorder   Having excessive and unrealistic anxiety about two or more life circumstances characterizes generalized anxiety disorder.[41] These worries are present for 6 months or longer and are accompanied by symptoms such as feeling shaky, irritable, tense or on edge, jumpy, and jittery. You may also experience sweating, pounding heart, feelings of dizziness, hot or cold flashes, an upset stomach, need to frequently urinate, diarrhea, and trouble relaxing or concentrating.

Some people become dependent on alcohol or drugs after using them to reduce or control anxiety symptoms. Others seek medical treatment for anxiety and become addicted to prescription tranquilizers.[42,43]

You may feel anxious when you first stop using substances. This anxiety is caused by:

- The physical effects of withdrawing from substances
- Difficulty adjusting to being substance free
- Worries about whether or not you can abstain from substances
- Psychological pain associated with facing life problems caused or worsened by your addiction

Personality Disorders

If the way you act or relate to others causes serious difficulties in your relationships or causes you significant distress, you may have a personality disorder.[2,44-47] A personality disorder involves long-standing traits that are rigid and ingrained in your personality. People with personality disorders often blame others for their problems and have difficulty accepting responsibility and controlling feelings and behaviors. Studies show that over 50% of individuals with alcohol and drug problems also have personality disorders.[28] These disorders may also be present in people with mood disorders.

A trait refers to a pattern of behavior. According to Aaron Beck and his colleagues, people with personality disorders often have traits that are over-developed or underdeveloped.[47] This means that they rely on certain behaviors far too much or that other behaviors are lacking. For example, with obsessive-compulsive personality disorder, the person is overdeveloped in terms of the need for control, organization, order, and responsibility and underdeveloped in terms of spontaneity and playfulness. The person with obsessive-compulsive personality disorder is often uptight and serious and has trouble relaxing and having fun.

Other Addictive or Compulsive Disorders

Other excessive behaviors can cause people distress and problems in their lives. The more common ones include compulsive smoking, gambling, sex, work, overeating, dieting, and computer or Internet addiction. You should discuss any other addictions you have with a therapist, because they often can affect recovery from other disorders.

Treatment Resources for Mood and Dual Disorders

Inpatient, partial hospital, and outpatient treatment services are available for mood and dual disorders. To get the maximum benefit from treatment, you need to focus on both of your disorders and involve your family, as they can be a source of help and support. They can benefit from information and a chance to discuss their concerns, questions, feelings, and experiences. Ask your therapist to include your family in some sessions.

The goals of treatment for depression or bipolar disorder are to help you accept your disorder, to eliminate or reduce your mood symptoms, to find the right medication for you if needed, to help you learn to manage your disorder and problems caused by it, to prepare you to spot early signs of relapse, and to introduce you to "recovery." Recovery refers to your use of skills to manage your disorders and stay sober. It often involves participation in self-help programs and working with others who are recovering from mood disorders and addiction.

Following is a brief review of treatment services for mood disorders, including those combined with substance abuse. These may or not be available to you, depending on where you live and your insurance coverage. Under managed care, it is harder to get insurance coverage to pay for hospital stays. Some insurance companies also limit the number of partial hospital or outpatient sessions they will pay for.

Psychiatric Hospitalization

Acute-care hospitalization is needed when a person is at high risk for suicide, represents a serious threat to others, or has symptoms that greatly interfere with the ability to function. In most instances, acute care lasts less than 2 weeks. It aims to stabilize severe symptoms with medication and therapy. Longer care hospitalization is used for the more chronically ill who need additional structure and treatment that can be provided only in an inpatient setting. These programs last several months or longer.

A day in the psychiatric hospital is likely to include a combination of the following treatment and related activities:

1. "Rounds," which involves a discussion of your current symptoms, problems, and progress with your psychiatrist and treatment team. Your doctor often makes decisions regarding medications during daily rounds. You can also discuss any questions or concerns you have about your diagnoses or treatment, medication side effects, or future plans to manage your illness over time.

2. Individual therapy or a discharge planning meeting with a member of your treatment team. This session focuses on your current mood symptoms, problems, and goals for treatment. You can use this time to talk about anything important to your recovery from your mood disorder (e.g., how to control suicidal thoughts, family or social relationships, the impact of your illness on your ability to work, the impact of addiction issues related to past trauma).

3. Group therapy with a small group of 6–10 patients and one or two professional staff members. Group therapy sessions are used to talk about any thoughts, feelings, or problems that members believe will

be helpful to discuss with peers. The patients in the group usually determine the focus of the discussions.

4. Recovery or educational groups that provide information about a particular topic such as depression, bipolar illness, mood disorders combined with addiction, or medications. Many of these groups also focus on helping participants improve or learn new coping skills to manage their disorders (e.g., ways to refute negative, depressed thinking or develop a support system).

5. Special groups such as multiple-family groups or groups devoted to art therapy, cognitive therapy, or dual-recovery therapy may also be used.

6. Community meetings at the beginning of the day to discuss the daily program schedule and your goal for the day and at the end of the day to reflect on how the day went for you. In addition, you will have some free time to relax, watch TV, socialize with other patients, or engage in recreational activities.

If you on are a dual-diagnosis unit for an addiction and mood disorder, you will also attend groups that focus on recovery from addiction. Some nights, you will attend self-help meetings of AA or NA. Your treatment team may also give you reading materials on mood disorders or writing assignments, such as keeping a mood diary. Even though professionals take care of you, treatment is very "active," and your participation is very important.

Community Residential Programs

There are a variety of treatment and special living arrangements for individuals with chronic disorders. These programs offer support, counseling, and supervision, and many people who participate in them also attend partial hospital or outpatient treatment at local mental health facilities. Community residential programs may be short or long term, depending on the problems and needs of the residents. Residents share responsibility for keeping the place in good order and are often assigned tasks to do during the day.

Partial Hospital Programs

Partial hospital (PH) programs are offered several hours per day, up to 5 days per week. PH programs provide medications and individual, group, and family treatments, although group therapies are the main treatment offered. These are structured programs that aim to reduce the need for inpatient care or that serve as a "step down" to people discharged from the hospital. PH programs are useful for those who need more than weekly outpatient therapy. A PH program may last several weeks. It aims to help you manage your disorders, build a support system, and develop coping skills to deal with problems that contribute to or result from your disorders. Many of the treatment activities described in the section on psychiatric hospitalization also occur in a PH program. You should receive individual therapy or counseling, in addition to group therapy.

Psychiatric Rehabilitation Programs

These programs provide group therapies that focus on "skill development" and vocational services (assessment, counseling, and training). They are designed to help people live with and successfully manage their chronic psychiatric disorders. For example, a mood management group may focus on helping you to understand causes and effects of mood disorders and to develop different strategies that you can use in your daily recovery to improve your mood.

Outpatient Therapy

In outpatient therapy, you meet regularly with a therapist, counselor, or group to discuss how to manage your symptoms and problems. Your family may be invited to some sessions. You may also see a psychiatrist for medication evaluation and management and for reevaluation of symptoms and treatment needs. Outpatient sessions taper off as you progress over time. Once your symptoms and problems are stable, you may be seen only once a month or less often. You may be discharged if your mood disorder is not a recurrent type.

Family Programs

Individual or multigroup family sessions may be offered. These aim to educate families about treatment, provide support, and give them an opportunity to discuss their questions, concerns, and feelings. Family members can learn how to support your recovery, as well as learn to avoid such behaviors as excessive criticism that can interfere with your recovery.

Medications

Psychiatric medications are used to eliminate or reduce symptoms of depression, bipolar illness, or other psychiatric disorders. Medication is the first line of treatment for bipolar disorder and is often used with depressive disorders. However, not all people with a depressive disorder will need medicine. Medications are usually used in cases of severe, recurrent, chronic, or psychotic depressions or in cases that do not improve with therapy or counseling alone. Specific types of medications used to treat mood disorders are discussed in Chapter 6. So are attitudinal issues that could get in your way of agreeing to take medications or continuing to take them once they are prescribed for your mood disorder.

Self-Help Programs

Self-help programs for mental health disorders—such as Emotions Anonymous or Recovery, Incorporated—are designed for anyone with a serious mental health problem. Other support groups are more specific to disorders, such as depression or bipolar illness. Dual Recovery Anonymous (DRA) and Double Trouble (DT) focus on recovery from dual disorders. Some AA and NA groups have "double trouble" meetings for members who have psychiatric disorders.

Intensive Case Management

Mental health agencies offer individuals with chronic psychiatric illness intensive case management (ICM) services. ICM can help with a variety of practical problems, such as getting community services (housing, economic benefits, medical treatment, etc.). An intensive care manager can also serve as an important member of your treatment team, giving input to your therapist or doctor. He or she can help with crisis situations and the transition from inpatient to outpatient care and can help you get back in the hospital if necessary.

Other Services

Some hospitals, agencies, and clinics also offer vocational or social work services to help with other personal or family problems.

Electroconvulsive Therapy

There are many misconceptions about electroconvulsive therapy (ECT), even though it has been used for more than 65 years to treat severe mental disorders. People mistakenly believe that it alters the brain or changes one's personality. Originally used with schizophrenia, ECT is a highly effective treatment used for individuals who have a severe and persistent mental disorder, including major depression or bipolar disorder, that severely impairs functioning.[9,48–50] ECT is sometimes used if other treatments such as psychotherapy or medications fail, if the person cannot tolerate medications, or if the person cannot take medications. It actually has fewer risks than treatment with medications.

ECT is used with patients with depressive disorder, often with melancholia, who do not respond adequately to medications or therapy. It is effective in up to 90% of such cases. ECT is sometimes used in mania and psychosis. ECT is also used with pregnant women who cannot take medications. ECT often brings about rapid improvement in mood symptoms and is lifesaving for some individuals.

Stages of Treatment

David Kupfer, Ellen Frank, and colleagues have been conducting studies on the treatment of mood disorders for many years.[11,51–57] They report that that there are three stages of treatment for mood disorders. The first stage is *acute* treatment and involves stabilizing the active symptoms of depression, mania, or both. This stage can last several weeks or months. The second stage is *continuation* treatment, in which the mood symptoms are further stabilized and the affected person addresses problems in life that contribute to or result from the mood disorder. This stage usually lasts 4 to 9 months after acute treatment. The final stage is called *maintenance* and involves ongoing treatment in order to reduce the risk of a recurrent episode. This phase is relevant for bipolar disorders, as well as recurrent major depression. Medications (and sometimes occasional therapy sessions) are continued so that mood symptoms do not return or early signs of relapse are identified and managed. Even patients with years of a stable mood can relapse if they stop taking medications for bipolar illness or recurrent major depression.

Effectiveness of Treatment for Depression and Bipolar Disorder

There is considerable evidence that medication and psychotherapy or counseling, alone or in combination, are effective in eliminating or reducing depressive symptoms and problems that contribute to or result from an episode of depression.[4,55–60] Cognitive-behavioral therapy (CBT) and interpersonal psychotherapy (IPT) have been used successfully to treat depression.[21,61–63] In addition, many medications, as well as treatment that combines medications and therapy, have been proven to be effective in treating depression.[60]

Medications are the main treatment for mania. However, therapy is recommended as well due to the debilitating effects of the disorder. CBT, IPT, interpersonal and social rhythm therapy, and family-focused therapy are treatments used with bipolar disorders.[11,56–59,61,63–66] All of these approaches have support from studies to show their effectiveness for treating bipolar disorder.

Frederick Goodwin's review of 28 separate reports involving more than 16,000 patients concludes that the suicide rate among bipolar patients treated with lithium is six to eight times lower than it is among bipolar patients not on lithium. These results show that treatment can actually save lives.[8]

Compliance with medications and therapy leads to improved outcome, so stick with your treatment plan, change it if it doesn't work, and trust your treatment professionals and take their advice. Although some people benefit from short-term treatment, those with persistent or chronic forms of depressive illness, such as recurrent major depression or dysthymia, and those with bipolar disorders need ongoing treatment to control symptoms and catch early signs of relapse. If you take medications for your mood disorder, it is critical that you comply with your doctor's prescription and take your medicine only as prescribed for maximum benefits.

If you focus only on your mood disorder and fail to address your addiction, your recovery from a mood disorder will be seriously hampered. You will put yourself at greater risk for relapse to depression or mania if you continue abusing alcohol or other drugs.

Chapter 4 | *The Recovery Process for Addiction and Mood Disorders*

Recovery as a Process

Recovery is the process of managing your addiction and mood disorder and making changes in your life.[1] Recovery requires hard work, discipline, a commitment to change, and a willingness to address both of your disorders.

Getting sober from alcohol or other drugs is one of your first recovery tasks. If you can't quit on your own, or if you relapse after short periods of abstinence, you may need to be detoxified or attend a structured substance abuse or dual-diagnosis treatment program to break the cycle of addiction. Abstinence is recommended because continued substance use can have a negative effect on your mood disorder and your motivation and can give an "incorrect" reading of the level of some antidepressant medications in your bloodstream. You also have to stabilize the acute symptoms of your mood disorder, such as mania, depression, or suicidality. Otherwise, it will be harder to stop using substances.

Recovery involves making internal and lifestyle changes so that you think differently, feel better about yourself, set goals, and develop a plan to meet these goals. This process usually involves professional treatment and participation in self-help programs. You must take an active role in identifying problems to work on. If you face your disorders, commit yourself to a program of recovery, and stick with it even during the rough times, you will make positive changes in your life.

Developing a trusting relationship with your treatment team is crucial for you to get the most out of your treatment. This requires a willingness to be straight with them and to share what's on your mind. Tell them if you feel like drinking or using drugs, feel suicidal, or feel that things aren't going well. Don't sugarcoat the truth and tell them what you think they want to hear. No professional can help if he or she doesn't know what's on your mind. Be open to accepting input and feedback from your therapist or treatment team. If your therapist talks with you about your lack of investment in your recovery, he or she is doing this to help you. It's a good idea to occasionally ask for feedback from your therapist on how he or she thinks you are doing in recovery.

The same holds true for working with a sponsor in NA, AA, CA, or Dual Recovery Anonymous (DRA). Level with your sponsor, say what you really think and feel, share your problems, and ask for feedback on your progress. It also helps to focus on what is going well for you and on positive steps you are taking to improve yourself.

Some people deal with conflicts with their therapists or sponsors by "firing" them and finding new ones. Although there are some instances in which this is a good decision, more often than not, firing a therapist or sponsor results from a person's dislike of hearing them speak some truth. If you feel like doing this, discuss it with the person you wish to fire, as you may be able to work through your differences. Or get an opinion from someone else who knows you.

Key Elements of Dual Recovery

There are four elements of recovery from addiction and depression or bipolar disorder: (1) education, (2) self-understanding, (3) social support, and (4) living recovery—changing yourself and your lifestyle.[2,3]

Education

Knowledge helps you understand your problems, prepares you to weather the difficult times you may face, and helps reduce the stigma, guilt, and shame associated with your disorders. It also helps you feel more in control of your options and of what is best for you. However, learning is not enough—you have to apply what you learn in treatment to your recovery and your life. For example, if you know that building structure and regularity into your daily life will help your bipolar disorder and reduce boredom, you have to figure out specific ways to add structure and regularity to your life. Or, if you know that you need to end an unhealthy relationship to reduce your depression, you have to take action to end it. If you know that talking with another person in recovery or talking yourself through a craving to use alcohol or drugs works, then you need to use one of these strategies in your daily life to help your recovery.

Self-Understanding

Self-understanding means that you personalize the information you learn in recovery. The more you understand yourself and why you do the things that you do, the better it is for your long-term recovery. Self-understanding is not always easy, as you will learn truths about yourself that can be hard to accept, and this can cause you to feel uncomfortable and anxious.

Social Support

Recovery is a "we" program in which you lean on others for support and share your problems, feelings, successes, and interests. These other people may include your family, friends, professionals, sponsors, and other members of support groups. If your family or friends do not understand your illnesses or the recovery process, or if they are upset at you for things you did, it may be difficult for them to give you the support you need. For example, if you spent your family's budget on drugs or went on a spending spree during a manic episode and your spouse is extremely upset and angry, you need to be realistic about the support you can get from him or her. Or, if you humiliated a family member while you were drunk, you need to give him or her time to get over this incident before asking him or her for help and support.

Living Recovery

"Living recovery" simply means that you "walk the walk," or apply the information you learn and the insights you gain in recovery to your daily life. You actually change your attitudes and behaviors. Expect to make mistakes along the way, because change is not always easy. It requires you to try out new behaviors and take risks. Recovery gives you a chance to grow as a person, as well as to get sober and stabilize your mood.

$$\text{DUAL RECOVERY} = \text{Abstinence} + \text{Change}$$

Recovery involves gaining information, self-understanding, and support from others and applying what you learn to make specific lifestyle and personal changes.

Phases of Dual Recovery

There are several phases that you may go through as your recovery unfolds.[2] You may not go through all of these phases, or you may not go through them in order. Some issues you deal with in one phase may be addressed in another phase in greater depth. If you relapse into depression, bipolar disorder, or addiction, this doesn't mean that you must start all over again.

Phase 1: Engagement and Stabilization

Recovery begins with getting alcohol and drugs out of your system and stabilizing your acute mood symptoms. When your symptoms are severe, and you're not able to get control of them with outpatient treatment, then you may need to be in the hospital or to attend a structured partial hospital or day treatment program. Or, if you're unable to stop using on your own, you may need to be detoxified in a hospital or to attend an addiction treatment program. Unless you stabilize, it will be hard to engage in treatment and gain the maximum benefit. You will "spin your wheels" and not get far. Medications may be needed to help you detoxify from substances or stabilize acute symptoms of your mood disorder.

This phase requires you to accept your disorders *and* the need for treatment. It is common to experience two different sets of feelings at the same time: (1) you accept that you have a problem and you want to get help and change; and (2) you don't accept that you have a problem and you don't want to get help and want to continue using alcohol or drugs. This is called *ambivalence,* and it is common in the initial phases of recovery.

The engagement and stabilization phase can take a few weeks or longer. Problems that occur during this phase include: worsening of symptoms, having trouble staying sober, refusing professional help, signing yourself out of the hospital against medical advice, not following up with outpatient or partial hospital treatment or self-help programs once you get out of the hospital, missing outpatient appointments, dropping out of treatment, not taking psychiatric medications as prescribed, believing that an improvement in symptoms means that you're well and don't need to stay involved in recovery, and not accepting the need to focus on both of your disorders.

Stay in treatment even if you don't feel like it and even if things are not going well. If you talk about your struggles and difficulties with your therapist or treatment team, they can help you change your treatment plan, work through your difficulties, or tolerate rough times. If you drop out of treatment early, you are at higher risk to end up in a psychiatric hospital, a detoxification unit, or a rehabilitation program for addiction. Symptoms of either disorder can worsen and cause you and your family much suffering.

Phase 2: Early Recovery

The early-recovery phase roughly includes the first few months following stabilization of your addiction and acute mood symptoms. However, some people will spend more time in the early-recovery phase because it is hard to maintain abstinence from alcohol or drugs and settle into recovery. For example, Stan was in and out of detox centers, psychiatric hospitals, partial hospital programs, and outpatient programs for several years before he became engaged in recovery. Before, he had seldom stayed sober for more than a month at a time. Nor did he stay on medications for his depression or stick with treatment long enough to give it a chance to work. Stan finally has accepted the need for abstinence and has been in treatment for almost 4 months.

Early recovery involves learning how to cope with your desires and cravings for alcohol or other drugs, identifying triggers, and avoiding people, places, and things that put you at high risk to relapse. You learn to resist pressures from other people to get high on alcohol or drugs or to stop your psychiatric medications.

In this phase, you build structure into your daily life so that you are regularly involved in recovery and leisure activities that keep you focused and busy.

Involving your family in sessions and in your recovery, participating in self-help programs, and finding a sponsor and a home group are important so that you have support from others.

Develop a list of problems and goals with your treatment team and as part of your involvement in self-help programs. This list will provide a focus for your recovery. For example, Theresa identified the following to work on: (1) reducing her negative, depressing thoughts; (2) coping with desires to drink alcohol or steal her mother's tranquilizers when feeling anxious; (3) controlling her bad temper so she doesn't break objects, scare her son, or say things to her husband that she will regret; and (4) returning to work.

Phase 3: Middle Recovery

In the middle-recovery phase you continue working on issues from early recovery, such as avoiding high-risk people, places, and things. You also work on relationship issues, such as making amends to others hurt by your behaviors, further developing your social support systems, and improving how you communicate with others. You work on changing negative beliefs and thoughts, increasing positive thinking, and learning to cope with upsetting feelings without relying on alcohol and other drugs. For example, Randy is an extremely pessimistic and negative person who tends to see the worst in everything. He is working on changing his beliefs that it's his destiny to get screwed by society and his family and that nothing will ever go right for him. Randy is learning to focus on positive events and experiences in his life, as he tends to downplay and ignore these. He is also changing his belief that his family should accept him with open arms and help him out financially. Randy has finally realized that, at age 39, he can't expect his parents to bail him out of his financial problems and that he must take an active role in working out conflicts between him and his parents rather than avoiding them.

Exploring and developing your sense of spirituality may start during this phase. Many people with dual disorders, as well as professionals, believe that spirituality is an important component of long-term recovery. Spirituality is seen as much more than formal religion, although this is part of some peoples' spirituality. It also refers to important issues such as honesty, hope, faith, courage, integrity, willingness, humility, compassion, justice, perseverance, forgiveness, meaning in life, and being of service to others.[5]

You should become aware of relapse warning signs, so that if signs of addiction or mood disorder relapse show, you have strategies to manage these signs. Such preparation is likely to reduce your relapse risk or prepare you to handle relapse should it occur.[6–8]

Phase 4: Late Recovery

In the late-recovery phase, you continue to work on the specific areas previously identified. Usually during this phase you'll delve into some of these issues in greater depth. By this time, you have made positive lifestyle changes and have become involved in recovery support groups. This phase aims to get you to focus more on your "internal self." The internal changes that you may work on in order to enhance your growth and improve your sense of self-esteem include making changes in your personality, improving how you cope with thoughts and feelings, and improving how you respond to problems or crises in your life. One problem that you may face in any phase of recovery is a return of your depression or bipolar symptoms or a relapse to alcohol and drug use. It helps to have a plan to manage your setbacks and cope with any emergency situations that may arise. I discuss this issue in greater detail in Chapter 12.

Expect ups and downs in recovery. If you prepare for them, you won't be taken by surprise. You may take a couple of steps forward in recovery and then fall back a step or two. Remember that recovery is not the absence of problems, but facing them. Staying sober makes it possible to focus on late-recovery issues. For example, Shawna has been drug-free for well over 1 year. She is now addressing psychological trauma experienced during her early years. Although it is painful and difficult to face, she's been able to experience intense and upsetting feelings without using drugs. And, although she had a temporary bout of depression during this time, Shawna was able to get through it with the support of her therapist, her NA sponsor, and a close friend.

Phase 5: Maintenance

Maintenance is an ongoing phase in which you maintain gains from earlier phases and continue to grow as a person. Many people choose to stay involved in recovery long after their symptoms and problems have improved. Some people with recurrent disorders require maintenance medications to control mood symptoms and reduce the risk of relapse.[9–11] Even if some of these persistent symptoms never go away totally, you have a better chance of managing them if you have remained involved in recovery.

Janet has a long history of alcoholism, depression, agoraphobia, and anxiety. After years of doing well, she had a recurrence of her agoraphobia and started drinking heavily. Following a brief inpatient hospital stay to detoxify her and stabilize her on medications, she attended AA and outpatient sessions. Janet has been sober for more than 3 years and has had no recurrences of her depression or anxiety disorders. She no longer needs counseling, but Janet continues regular AA meetings. She also meets with her doctor every 3 months for a medication check.

What Helps People Recover From Addiction and a Mood Disorder

I conducted a written survey of 140 outpatients in my dual-diagnosis clinic and asked them to tell me what helped them recover from their disorders. In terms of their mood disorders, they reported the following, beginning with the most helpful actions:

- Taking medications
- Staying active in therapy
- Using a support system and developing new, supportive relationships
- Changing thinking
- Changing lifestyle
- Praying or meditating
- Attending self-help meetings

Related to recovery from addiction, they reported the following, beginning with the most helpful actions:

- Regularly attending AA or NA meetings and talking to a sponsor in AA or NA
- Using a support system and developing new, supportive relationships
- Staying active in treatment

- Changing lifestyle
- Praying or meditating
- Changing thinking
- Taking medication

Although there are differences in how they viewed recovery from psychiatric illness or from addiction, their answers show that compliance with treatment, using self-help groups, obtaining support from other people, and changing their lives (relationships, spirituality, thinking, behaviors) were all important. Because most of the patients surveyed had more severe types of mood disorders, medications were seen as the most important factor in their psychiatric recovery. By reducing or eliminating mood symptoms, medications make it easier to address the challenges of recovery.

If you look closely at the strategies that have helped others manage their disorders, you can see that they all involve action. Change just doesn't occur without work and direct action on your part.

Helpful Recovery Attitudes

Half the battle in recovery is developing positive attitudes, as these affect your behavior. Following is a summary of healthy attitudes that can aid your recovery.

There are no simple solutions or short cuts. Don't look for recovery to be quick or easy. To get well and change your life means that you must work hard and pay your dues. You have to face your problems and learn to tolerate and get through tough times.

Make a long-term commitment. Change takes time and a willingness to learn from your mistakes. Your addiction or mood disorder didn't happen overnight, so your recovery won't happen overnight. Short cuts to recovery just don't exist. People who stick with recovery do better than those who look for short-term solutions. Dropping out of treatment raises your risk of relapse to either of your disorders.

Recovery requires effort, discipline, and sacrifice. Like anything worthwhile, you have to be disciplined in recovery and regularly follow your program. This means going to therapy sessions or self-help meetings, or calling your sponsor or therapist when you don't feel like it, and following your recovery plan when you'd rather just blow it off.

Take responsibility for your own recovery. Whether you change is largely a matter that is up to you. Others can help you, but you are the one responsible for your progress or lack of it in the way you approach recovery. Don't blame others for your problems. Take responsibility for your recovery and your own well-being.

Look for solutions; don't just focus on your problems. It's easy to focus only on problems and complain or feel overwhelmed. Search hard for solutions by looking at things you can do differently to solve your problems or make things better in your life. To get additional ideas, ask others how they have solved similar problems.

Accept small steps toward your goals as progress. Success can be measured in small steps toward your goals. Regardless of whether or not you struggle to reach your goals, be sure to put "success" into perspective. Any positive change or movement in the right direction can be viewed as success. Try not to overlook "small steps" to success.

Don't expect perfection; allow room for mistakes. Set realistic goals for change and don't expect things to go perfectly, because they won't. Expect to make mistakes along the way, and don't judge yourself harshly if you do. Instead, learn from your mistakes and use them as opportunities to discover new ways of changing.

Change what doesn't work well. If you are not coping successfully with a problem, try a new coping strategy. Change things that aren't working well; otherwise, you are doomed to repeat the same mistakes. Sometimes this requires you to take the advice of others who have ideas on how you can help yourself.

Helpful Recovery Attitudes

1. There are no simple solutions or shortcuts in recovery.
2. Make a long-term commitment to getting well and changing.
3. Recovery requires effort, discipline, and sacrifice.
4. Take responsibility for your own recovery.
5. Look for solutions; don't just focus on your problems.
6. Accept small steps toward your goals as progress.
7. Don't expect perfection; allow room for mistakes
8. Change what doesn't work well.
9. Trust and confide in your treatment team.
10. Remember that you *can* make positive changes.

Trust and confide in your treatment team. Learn to "open up" and share your inner thoughts, feelings, and struggles with your therapist or other members of your treatment team. This requires a willingness to take risks. No one can help you if you don't confide in and trust him or her. Throw out old negative beliefs about authority figures or beliefs that others can't help you unless they've been through what you've been through.

Remember that you can make positive changes. Remind yourself that you are capable of positive change. Believe in yourself and give yourself encouragement.

Recovery Habits That Promote Success

Habits refer to your behaviors or the actions you take to help yourself. Following are behaviors that can aid in your recovery:

Keep all scheduled counseling sessions. You can't get the maximum benefit from treatment if you cancel or fail to attend your sessions. Most of the time, people miss sessions for questionable reasons. Even when you don't feel like going, keep your appointments. Otherwise, you are more likely to drop out of treatment. And you lose continuity with your therapist if you don't attend your sessions regularly.

Take medications only as prescribed, and never stop on your own. Medications work most effectively when taken as prescribed, so don't adjust medicine on your own. Your depression or bipolar symptoms can return or worsen if you stop medications prematurely. Even if you've been symptom free for several months or longer, you should never stop medications without first talking with your psychiatrist and therapist. You don't have to like taking medications, but if you want to get well, you are going to have to take them as prescribed.

Discuss your problems and feelings in treatment sessions. Tell your therapist what's bothering you. You can then work on developing strategies to solve your problems and manage your disorders. One way to get started is to make a list of problems to work on in therapy, prioritize them, and then tackle them one at a time. Go to each session prepared to discuss one or two problems. In therapy sessions, it is generally accepted that you can express things that may be hard to express elsewhere. It should be a "safe" place to open up.

Reach out to others for help and support. Ask for help and support from AA, NA, CA, or DRA sponsors and members, professionals, or other members of your social network. Be assertive in asking for help, and don't expect others to read your mind, because they may not know you want their help. Talk with other members before and after self-help meetings. Invite others out after the meeting for a cup of coffee to continue discussing what you learned from the meeting.

Attend and participate in self-help meetings. You can gain a lot of information, support, and guidance from self-help meetings for addiction, mood disorders, or dual disorders. It helps to learn that you are not alone. Let others in the program teach you the ropes about recovery. Participate actively in the meetings. Don't sit quietly or keep to yourself. Use the "tools" of the program (slogans, steps, readings, etc.).

Get a sponsor and talk with him or her every day. Find someone with similar problems who is stable and active in support groups, and ask him or her to be your sponsor. A sponsor can guide you in working the 12 steps, can share your successes and problems, and can help you use the tools of the program. Regular, daily discussions in person or on the telephone are helpful, especially in the early months of recovery. Attend some meetings together, too.

Use the telephone to stay connected with others. Talk often on the phone with people you meet in support groups or with good friends or family members with whom you are close. This reduces isolation, especially in the early phase of recovery.

Keep busy and build structure and routines in your daily life. The more active you are, the less bored and depressed you will feel. Structure gives you direction and a sense of purpose, and it can protect you against relapse. It is helpful to have daily routines such as getting up, taking care of your apartment or house, working, eating, exercising, attending self-help meetings, and going to bed at similar times. These stable "social rhythms" are especially important in recovery from bipolar disorder.

Participate in something pleasant every day. No matter how small, make sure you do something every each day that feels good and brings you pleasure. Pleasant activities can lift your mood or reduce boredom.

Discuss all setbacks or relapses. If you have a relapse to depression or bipolar disorder, or if you begin to use drugs and alcohol again, let your therapist and sponsor know. They can provide support and help you get back on track. They can also help you learn from your experiences. Perhaps there were some warning signs of relapse that you ignored.

Read recovery literature. Information empowers! The more you learn about your illnesses and recovery, the greater sense of control you will feel over your life. Much recovery literature is inspirational, especially writings by others who have suffered and overcome serious problems. You will find suggested readings on addiction, depression, bipolar disorder, other psychiatric disorders, and dual disorders in the reference section of this book (they are marked by the * symbol).

Write your thoughts, feelings, and experiences in a journal. This can help you release feelings, clarify thoughts and options, and monitor your symptoms, problems, thinking patterns, and progress over time. Many excellent workbooks exist that provide structured recovery exercises on coping with feelings, managing relapse warning signs, or monitoring mood symptoms.

Regularly make a list of benefits of recovery. It is easy to take recovery for granted or to minimize the benefits you are gaining. Take a few minutes each week to review and write down benefits you've experienced in your recovery.

Give credit to yourself for efforts in recovery and for changes you made. Pat yourself on the back for any positive results you achieve in recovery. But, just as important, give yourself credit for trying and making efforts to change, even if you aren't making the progress that you would like.

Change one thing at a time. Prioritize your problems and work on changing one at a time. Start with something small and achievable that you know you can change. Work on more difficult issues later, after you've experienced some success.

Recovery Habits That Promote Success

1. Keep all scheduled counseling sessions.
2. Take medications only as prescribed; never stop on your own.
3. Share your problems and feelings in treatment sessions.
4. Reach out to others for help and support.
5. Participate in self-help programs.
6. Get a sponsor and talk with him or her daily.
7. Use the phone to stay connected with others.
8. Keep busy and build structure and routines in your daily life.
9. Participate in something pleasant every day.
10. Discuss all setbacks or relapses.
11. Read recovery literature for information and inspiration.
12. Write your thoughts, feelings, and experiences in a journal.
13. Regularly make a list of benefits of recovery.
14. Give credit to yourself for efforts in recovery and for changes you made.
15. Change one thing at a time.

Effectiveness of Treatment for Dual Disorders

Studies show that people with dual disorders generally have a more complicated course of recovery than those with a single disorder. However, there is evidence that "integrated" treatment is helpful for individuals with mood disorders and addiction.[4,12–19] Integrated treatment refers to clinical services such as counseling or a rehabilitation program that addresses both the addiction and the mood disorder. Combining therapy (individual or group) with medications appears to be the most effective approach to treatment for many people with dual disorders, especially those with chronic or recurrent mood disorders.

The key to successful treatment is complying with your treatment plan by taking medications as prescribed, keeping your therapy or counseling sessions, and working toward your individual treatment goals. You can measure your success by improvement in your overall life, less frequent and severe mood symptoms, and abstinence from, or reduction of your use of, alcohol or other drugs. Although I strongly encourage abstinence, any reduction of use of the amount and frequency of substance use is a step in the right direction.

Chapter 5

Setting the Foundation for Dual Recovery

Attitude and Motivation Roadblocks

Deana is recovering from recurrent major depression and heroin addiction. She has been in a psychiatric hospital once and completed two addiction rehabilitation programs. Deana struggled with low motivation and negative attitudes about taking medications for depression, attitudes that had prevented her from benefiting from treatment. Until recently, she focused mainly on her addiction and struggled with acceptance of her mood disorder. Now she is finally getting the help she needs because of a change in her attitude.

> I never trusted professionals, I thought they couldn't help me because they had never been through what I had experienced in life. What did they know about being depressed or being a junkie? I tuned them all out, figuring I knew how to change my life. Well, the problem was I never could stay motivated to change. I always went back to heroin. And I refused antidepressants or didn't give them a chance to work. Finally, I stayed on medication, which helped my depression. My therapist made an agreement with me that I had to call her directly if I felt like missing my appointment because in the past, I'd leave messages with her secretary and never rescheduled my appointments. My motivation still wavers sometimes, but talking about it helps me get through the times when

I feel like blowing off my sessions. Also, I finally understand the serious nature of my depression and how staying on medications will increase the chances that I won't get depressed again.

Recovery roadblocks are barriers that get in your way of getting or staying sober, managing your mood disorder, or changing your lifestyle.[1-2] Attitudinal and motivational roadblocks are very common during the early months of recovery. The most common one is difficulty admitting that you have an addiction and/or mood disorder or that you need help. Motivation can change from one day to the next. Your best defense against this roadblock is to stay in treatment, to keep working your recovery program, and to talk about your thoughts, feelings, and struggles with your treatment team and other people whom you trust. A key to successful long-term recovery is staying involved in treatment and support groups even when you don't feel like it and want to say "the hell with it."

Another roadblock is believing that the people working with you don't understand you, can't help you, or don't deserve your trust. You have to trust other people and give them a chance to help you. It is easy to find reasons why your doctor, therapist, or other professional can't help you because "they don't know what it's like to have dual disorders."

Not using recovery support groups or sponsors because you think that you don't need them, that they can't help you, or that self-help programs aren't right for you is another roadblock. Although no recovery program can help everyone in the same way, people who stay involved have a better chance of getting well and making progress. A related roadblock is getting involved with support programs for a brief period of time and then dropping out. Don't drop out of treatment or stop going to self-help group meetings without first discussing this with someone who knows you well.

Other roadblocks are negative attitudes about taking medications or incorrect beliefs about what medicine can do for you. You may believe that you don't need medicine for your depression or bipolar disorder or that the side effects you experience aren't worth the trouble. If your mood disorder is serious enough to warrant medications, then you have to take them as prescribed in order to get well. It may take several weeks or longer to experience the maximum benefits of medication or for side effects to lessen. Another roadblock is the belief that medications will eliminate all of your symptoms or make your problems go away. You may think that any time your symptoms flare up or worsen your doctor should change your medicine. You have to be realistic about what medication can and cannot do for you.

Personality Roadblocks

Edwin has been in and out of many detoxification centers and psychiatric hospitals over the years. He often went against medical advice and wouldn't listen to doctors, nurses, or therapists trying to help him. Edwin often saw professionals as his adversaries, not his helpers. He said the following about finally accepting advice from professionals and not letting his stubborn tendency lead him to bad decisions:

> Y'all been telling me for years what I need to do to stay clean and give myself a chance to stay out of the psych hospital. People in NA had been telling me some of the same things, too. But you think I'd listen? Hell no, I wasn't gonna let nobody tell me a damn thing to do. It had to be on Edwin's terms. I'm very stubborn and don't like to be told what's best for me. But you know what? My way ain't never worked. I'm going to try to be more open this time and listen to what y'all have to say. I know I'll never stay clean if I don't go to no meetings or get me a sponsor. I need someone who can get in my face when I'm messin' up.

Your personality style has a major impact on how you participate in and benefit from recovery. It plays a major role in whether you make changes in yourself, your lifestyle, and your relationships. Personality roadblocks show in the following behaviors:[3]

- Not wanting to do what others recommend to help your recovery
- Being stubborn and assuming the stance that you will only do things your way
- Acting impulsively and doing things before you think them through
- Being perfectionistic and having standards that you or others can't meet
- Having a low frustration tolerance and giving up too easily when things don't go your way or you don't get what you want
- Becoming too dependent on other people to solve your problems, take care of you, or tell you what to do

- Not opening up to share your feelings, thoughts, or problems with other people in your recovery network
- Using anger or hostility to keep people from getting close to you
- Blaming other people for your lack of progress or your problems

These roadblocks can be changed by long-term involvement in a recovery program. There is no easy way to change personality problems, or what 12-step programs refer to as "character defects." A key to overcoming personality roadblocks is accepting that change occurs in small steps. You have to try new behaviors to see whether they are going to work for you. For example, if you believe that you'll never do what others advise you to do as part of your recovery, you may want to test this belief by actually taking their advice and applying it. You just may find that it works.

Relationship Roadblocks

Jason, recovering from crack addiction, alcoholism, bipolar disorder, and a personality disorder, talks about his relationships with "snow queens" and what he had to change. His disorders had caused him problems in many areas of his life, and he didn't get on the right track until he changed some of his relationships. Poor choices in relationships often led him to relapse back to drug use. Listen to what he did to change:

> It took me a long time, but I finally figured out something I was doing over and over that brought me down. I'd be clean, then get calls from women I used to get high and have sex with. Some were what we called crack whores or snow queens cause they'd give you sex in a minute for a $5 rock of crack. At first I'd have sex and get high with them. Later, I changed this pattern and would get them some rocks so I could have sex, but I wouldn't use myself. How long do you think this lasted? Every single time I'd go back to using crack. Sometimes, it happened fast, other times it took a while. Sex with the snow queens was a big-time trigger for me. The solution was simple—I couldn't be hanging with these women and giving them drugs for sex. I got 7 months clean, the longest in my life. It's still tempting sometimes, but I'm hanging in there with the help of my sponsor and Higher Power. I keep telling myself that losing my re-

covery for sex with someone who don't mean nothing to me just ain't worth it.

One common roadblock is involvement with a partner, spouse, roommate, or family member who still gets high on alcohol or other drugs. Involvement in social groups or relationships in which getting high is a major activity is a relapse risk. Avoiding people who get high and staying away from parties and social situations in which the primary purpose is to party are the best strategies for managing this roadblock. Cutting loose relationships that are based primarily on sharing drugs or getting high is another useful strategy. If your spouse or live-in mate abuses substances, ask your therapist or sponsor to help you figure out how to deal with this situation.

Another roadblock is difficulty relating to people who don't get high. Your best way to deal with this is to get involved in support groups and recovery clubs where you can be around other people who are sober. You'll be able to identify with these people and what they've been through. Also, you can get involved in social or recreational activities that don't threaten your recovery. In time, you can learn to relate to nonusers.

Lacking close, supportive relationships is another roadblock. If you don't have anyone you can lean on for support, have no friends, have difficulty asking others for help, or can't trust anyone, you are likely to feel alone. In chapters 8 and 9 I talk more in depth about families, social relationships, and support systems.

Staying involved with a spouse or partner who emotionally or physically abuses you can sabotage your recovery by leading you to alcohol or other drug use. It can cause you to feel fearful, anxious, depressed, suicidal, or victimized. It's hard enough to work on staying alcohol and drug free and to cope with a mood disorder. Putting up with an abusive relationship is just too much to expect. The solution is very difficult yet simple: Don't stay in a relationship with a partner who abuses you or is unwilling to get help to stop the abuse.

Lifestyle Roadblocks

C.J., a military veteran recovering from addiction, depression, and posttraumatic stress disorder, talks about how he changed his lifestyle. He discovered that socializing after work at a bar wasn't in his best interests and that he was only fooling himself if he expected to hang out with work buddies while they drank alcohol.

> One of the biggest changes I made was to quit hanging with most of my work buddies. They always stopped at a bar after work for a few drinks. At first, I tried to hang with them and not drink, but it was a drag. I didn't fit in, felt awkward, and felt like I was missing the action of getting high. When I stopped hanging, I got real bored and more depressed. I didn't have any idea how to spend my time. It's really amazing how much time partying with my buddies took up in the past. So I joined the Y and started working out a few nights each week and on weekends. I also hooked up with some other vets in recovery who liked sports, too. We'd play ball, go to games, and watch sports on TV. I also made it a point to visit my family at least once a week. All this stuff together, plus going to AA and my vets' therapy group kept me busy. After a while, I didn't miss my old drinking buddies. Not only have I been sober a long time, I don't feel the daily temptation to drink like I used to when I'd go to the bar after work and drink soda.

If your lifestyle centers around getting high, you have to change the people with whom you socialize, your activities, and how you spend your time. You have to find positive people and non-substance-centered activities to keep you busy and give you a sense of fulfillment. If your living situation is a threat to your recovery, you have to change it, develop a support system, and develop coping strategies so that it doesn't bring you down or cause you to use alcohol or other drugs.

If you have too much free time on your hands or little direction in your life, you have to structure your time. Otherwise, you place yourself at greater risk for boredom and are more likely to relapse. You are also likely to feel depressed and dissatisfied with your life if you have too much free time and nothing important on which to focus. Structuring your life takes discipline and commitment, as well as a concrete plan.

You can ask your therapist to help you structure your time. Build in recovery activities, such as support group meetings and regular contact with other recovering people, treatment sessions, and social-recreational activities. As you structure your life, you'll be less bored and less likely to use substances. And the longer you stay sober, the better position you put yourself in to set goals and figure out the direction you want to take in your life.

Denial is a psychological defense mechanism that protects you from anxiety that comes with facing truths about your life, such as having a mood disorder and addiction. Denial is a factor that prevents the majority of people with dual disorders from seeking or benefiting from treatment. Denial can show in a variety of ways, such as:[4–5]

- Not accepting that you have a mood disorder despite evidence to the contrary
- Blaming your mood disorder on your use of alcohol or other drugs
- Not accepting that you have an alcohol or drug problem despite evidence to the contrary
- Blaming your addiction on other people, bad breaks in life, bad luck, or your mood disorder
- Believing that you can give up your main drug of abuse but still use other substances (such as giving up cocaine but continuing to smoke marijuana or drink alcohol)
- Believing that you can't have an addiction because you don't use every day, don't suffer withdrawal symptoms, or don't always have a desire to drink alcohol or use other drugs
- Believing that all you have to do is stop using alcohol and drugs and everything will get better, including your mood disorder, and you won't need professional treatment or involvement in recovery

As a result of denial, many people never get help, or they stay involved in treatment or self-help programs for only a short time. Some people seek treatment only as a result of pressure by the court system, family, friends, or a social service agency. In some cases, people with severe mood disorders enter treatment as a result of being involuntarily committed due to suicidal behaviors or behaviors that put other people in danger.

Bipolar illness can involve a lack of insight or poor judgment, each of which influences denial. It isn't uncommon for people in a manic episode to think there is nothing wrong and that they don't need treatment, even when their behavior is out of control. If you have depression, you can blame it on some external problem, or you might see it as a case of the blues rather than a serious case of clinical depression. Some ways to work through your denial follow:

- Review the symptoms of your mood disorder with a professional to identify the specific symptoms, how long they've been present, and how they've affected all areas of your life, including your substance use.
- Review your alcohol and drug use history with a professional. Go over the specific details of what you've used, how long you've used different substances, your patterns and methods of use, and the effects on your life, including your relationships and your depression or bipolar illness.
- Review what you'll miss about using alcohol or other drugs. You have to be honest about the fact that there is a good chance that you are going to miss using substances and getting high.
- Discuss with your doctor and therapist the type of mood disorder that you have. If you have recurrent depression, bipolar illness, or chronic dysthymia, discuss what this means to you. Ask your doctor or therapist about the importance of ongoing professional care to help you cope with the symptoms of a recurrent or persistent mood disorder.
- Write a list of all the effects of your addiction and your depression or bipolar illness on your physical and emotional health, relationships, and life.

Physical Recovery

Having an addiction puts you at a higher risk for medical problems. It isn't uncommon for existing problems to worsen or new medical problems to develop as a result of: (1) the effects of substances on your body over time; (2) using street drugs that are mixed (or "cut") with other compounds; (3) poor health care habits or poor diet; (4) complications involved when you mix drugs, smoke drugs, use dirty needles, cotton, or rinsing water, or share needles with other people; (5) engaging in high-risk behaviors such as unprotected sex, prostitution, violence, or criminal acts; (6) falls or accidents resulting from driving or being under the influence of alcohol or other drugs. Among people who use substances, it is common to ignore medical problems or not to comply fully with treatment.

Many studies and books document the medical effects of alcohol and drugs on the central nervous system, liver, digestive, cardiovascular, respiratory, and musculoskeletal systems, as well as other parts of the body.[6–14] There has been an increase in the number of drug abusers who become HIV-positive as a result of unprotected sex, sharing dirty needles, sharing dirty cotton or rinsing water, or failure to properly clean needles after shooting drugs. Physical recovery includes the following:

- Getting substances out of your body and adjusting to being sober
- Getting a physical and dental exam and treatment for medical or dental problems
- Eating a balanced diet and getting proper nutrition
- Getting sufficient sleep and rest
- Exercising on a regular basis
- Managing cravings to use alcohol or drugs
- Taking medication as prescribed for your mood disorder and/or addiction

Managing Cravings to Use Alcohol or Other Drugs

Cravings may be experienced for weeks or longer after you stop using alcohol or other drugs. Usually, the longer you abstain from substances, the fewer and less intense your cravings will be over time. Nora Volkow, a researcher who has studied cravings, believes that dopamine (a brain neurotransmitter) stimulation that occurs with long-term drug use disrupts the brain circuitry involved in regulating drives. This in turn leads to a craving (or a "conditioned response") when the person is exposed to stimuli, which then leads to compulsive drug use.[15] Thus cravings are best understood as involving physical, psychological, and environmental components.

Cravings are triggered by *external factors,* such as people, places, experiences, or events, that are associated with using. Such factors include parties; family celebrations; payday; objects or things that you associate with using or preparing substances, such as smelling smoke or seeing drug paraphernalia; or such situations as getting a flu shot or visiting a doctor. When possible, avoid people, places, and things that you associate with using substances. Because you can't avoid all people, places, and things, you need other strategies for refusing offers to use or for getting quickly out of situations in which strong pressure to use substances may build and make you feel very vulnerable to using.

Strategies to Manage Cravings

1. Be aware of how a craving shows in your body, behaviors, and thoughts.
2. Talk about it with other people in recovery.
3. Go to a support meeting and share it during or after the meeting.
4. Talk yourself through it: "I'm going to put off using until tomorrow." Or remind yourself of the benefits of staying sober.
5. Remind yourself that you've handled cravings before and you can do it again.
6. Redirect your energy to an activity to take your mind off of your craving.
7. Write about your craving in a journal.
8. Get rid of alcohol, drugs, or paraphernalia in your home.
9. Be aware of high-risk people, places, and situations and avoid these if at all possible, especially during times of strong cravings.
10. Pray or ask your Higher Power for strength.
11. Keep a list of coping strategies that you or others have used to handle cravings and use this to remind yourself of what you can do to get through a craving.
12. Read the "Basic Text" of NA or the "Big Book" of AA.
13. Accept that cravings are normal and will pass in time.

Internal triggers include feelings of boredom, depression, anger, or anxiety and thoughts such as "I can't handle things without using; I'll die if I don't get some alcohol or drugs," or "I just can't have fun unless I'm using alcohol or drugs." Physical symptoms such as being sick or symptoms associated with a previous withdrawal syndrome can also trigger a craving.

Sometimes you will be aware of the craving, a condition called *overt craving*. Other times you won't be aware of it, and your craving will show in a *covert* way, such as feeling irritated, on edge, or anxious. The chart above summarizes strategies to manage cravings.[2]

Avoiding and Coping With People, Places, Events, and Things

When possible, avoid or minimize contact with people who pressure you to use alcohol or other drugs; who abuse you physically or mentally; who are highly critical of you or who bring you down with their negativity, constant whining, or complaining; or who cause you emotional distress. For example, Alice was unable to make much progress in her recovery from depression until she re-

Strategies for Coping With People, Places, and Things

1. Identify the social pressures you expect to face in your recovery.

2. Avoid high-risk people, places, and events when possible (dealers, addicts still using, parties, bars, clubs, etc.).

3. Be aware of thoughts and feelings you experience when you are pressured to use substances.

4. Take a support person to events that cannot be avoided and where some pressure may be felt to drink (weddings, work parties, family picnics).

5. Assertively say straight out that you are not using anymore.

6. Tell the person offering you substances that you are in recovery and don't want them to offer anything.

7. Avoid long discussions involving using or why you are sober.

8. Leave situations in which the pressure is hard to handle.

9. Break off relationships that are destructive and a risk to your physical safety or mental health (e.g., with an abusive partner).

10. Avoid or minimize contact with people who are extremely critical, nonsupportive, or negative.

11. Spend your time with family and friends who care about you and support your recovery and toward whom you feel positive or with whom you share mutual interests.

12. Get involved in mental health, addiction, or dual-disorders support groups and recovery clubs so you can develop a positive recovery network.

13. Build in enjoyable and fun activities in your day-to-day life.

duced contact with her mother. Alice's mother was extremely critical and negative, and visits with her often left Alice feeling guilty and depressed. Latisha had to end an abusive relationship with her boyfriend in order to recover from her depression. She had to learn to resist his hollow apologies and attempts to get back together, because his violence always resurfaced. Tyrone had to cut ties with some friends because they were always scheming to rip people off to get money for drugs. It wasn't until he cut loose this group of men that Tyrone could get his act together. Above is a summary of strategies for coping with high-risk people, places and things.[2]

Managing Persistent Symptoms of Depression or Bipolar Illness

If you have a recurrent or persistent form of a mood disorder, you may continuously experience some of your symptoms at times. These are referred to as "persistent symptoms" because they don't go away totally. For example, Patricia has had anxiety and depressive symptoms for more than 20 years. Although her symptoms have improved, she still sometimes feels depressed and anxious. However, Patricia has learned to live with and manage these symptoms. She knows that when her depression and anxiety lead to isolating herself and becoming afraid of leaving her house, it is time to get help. Patricia, who used to experience depression almost every single day, also knows that spending fewer days depressed and having less severe levels of depression mean that she is getting better.

You can track and rate your chronic symptoms on a daily basis. You do this by first establishing a baseline and figuring out what is "normal" for you. Use a 1–10 rating scale, with 1 meaning the symptom is not present at all, 5 meaning the symptom is moderate, and 10 meaning the symptom is at its worst ever. For example, your baseline may be a 4, which indicates a "fairly moderate" rating of depression. If your daily rating rises for several days or longer, then you need to take action because your depression is worsening.

Complying with your treatment plan (taking medications, keeping appointments, and working on your problems and goals) and regularly attending self-help groups can help you manage persistent symptoms. Find out how others with similar disorders live with their persistent mood symptoms. You can learn a lot from them.

If your mood symptoms worsen over time and interfere with your ability to function or cause you considerable distress, ask for help from your treatment team. Extra sessions or phone contacts may help you. Sometimes, medication adjustments may be needed.

Coping With Suicidal Thoughts and Feelings

Suicidal thoughts and feelings are common with mood, addiction, or dual disorders.[16–18] Often, the suicidal person doesn't want to die but wants to be rid of pain caused by problems that seem endless, unavoidable, and insolvable.

If you have suicidal thoughts and feelings, talk with your treatment team so that you can get help in controlling them and figuring out why you feel suicidal. For some people with chronic disorders, suicidal thoughts and feelings come and go from time to time. However, there is a big difference between having suicidal thoughts and feelings and actually having a plan or making an attempt to end your life. If you have a plan, call your treatment team or a crisis line or get to a psychiatric or medical emergency room right away. This will help protect you from giving in to any impulse to hurt yourself. If your plan involves using a gun or a weapon or overdosing on pills, get rid of these objects immediately to reduce your risk of suicide. Also, if you are under the influence of alcohol or other drugs and feel suicidal, the risk of hurting yourself increases. Remember, suicidal thoughts and feelings go away in time, so the more difficult you make it to follow through with suicide, the better your chances of not acting impulsively or irrationally.

Your family or other close people can help, too. If they are aware of your condition, they can provide extra help and support during rough times. They can also help make arrangements for hospitalization or emergency psychiatric treatment if needed. If you feel that you are at risk for making a suicide attempt, make a "no-suicide contract" with your treatment team. This contract should state that you agree to take certain steps to resist suicidal impulses and work with others (your therapist, hospital, agency, or crisis hotline, etc.) to help you during your time of crisis. Your contract may also state steps you will take if you feel you are unable to resist suicidal feelings and are at risk to do something to harm yourself.[18]

Use therapy to help you figure out the reasons you feel suicidal and address the problems that contribute to these feelings. For example, if you feel depressed and hopeless due to a recent loss of a job or relationship, therapy can help you adjust to this loss. If you feel hostile and want to get revenge on someone else by ending your own life, therapy can also help you work through this feeling. Once your immediate crisis stabilizes, therapy can help you find ways to make your relationships and life more satisfying, thus reducing feelings of hopelessness, bitterness, or depression that can fuel suicidal feelings. Even if you currently feel depressed and hopeless, you can feel better in time. And remember, suicide is a permanent solution to a problem that is probably only temporary. Problems that trigger suicidal feelings can often be dealt with and reversed, whereas suicide cannot be.

Changing negative thoughts about yourself and the future can help you cope with suicidal thoughts. If you have thoughts such as "I'll never get better," "I don't deserve to live," or "life is terrible and full of problems," look for proof that they are not true and then replace them with more positive thoughts. For example, you can examine the proof that you'll never get better again. Then you can coach yourself to make coping statements such as, "I know it seems like I'll never get better, but if I stick it out, things can improve"; "I feel like a nobody now but my family cares about me and I know I deserve the chance to get better"; or "life is full of problems at times, but I can stand up to my problems. Sure, they might not go away, but I can learn to deal with them." Searching for proof often leads to the realization that your negative thoughts are exaggerated and not based on logic. Fighting off negative statements and creating positive ones can reduce hopelessness and depression and help you feel more in control of your feelings.

Another strategy is to focus on reasons for living. Your religious beliefs, relationships with family or friends, a task you wish to accomplish, or other reasons can keep you going, especially in the short run. If you can't find any reasons for living, make an agreement to give yourself time to find reasons to live and get over your suicidal feelings.

Suicidality is often one of several symptoms of a mood disorder rather than an independent symptom. Therefore, by paying close attention to early warning signs of mood relapse, you can spot trouble early and get help, which may prevent a new episode of illness. Or catching early relapse signs may lead to getting help before symptoms become severe and incapacitating. Relapse prevention strategies are discussed in Chapter 12.

Abstinence from alcohol and other drugs reduces suicidal risk. Alcohol or drugs can impair your judgment or give you false courage to try suicide. Attempts at suicide are grounds for involuntary commitment to a psychiatric hospital. If your family, friends, or others initiate a commitment, keep in mind that they are doing it to ensure that you are in a protective environment until your suicidal feelings lessen or go away.

How to Measure Your Progress

The "ideal" in recovery is to achieve and maintain abstinence from alcohol and other drugs, to eliminate or reduce mood disorder symptoms, and to make positive changes in yourself and your lifestyle. However, in "reality," progress is sometimes measured in small steps in the right direction. Progress means that you are getting better in terms of your addiction or mood disorder or in other areas of your life. To some people, it may mean fewer days in the hospital and less impairment by substance use or mood symptoms. To others, progress may mean major changes in lifestyle and improvements in their ability to function.

There are many ways to measure your progress. Examples include a decrease in your obsession to use drugs or alcohol, better control over your cravings, improved mood or ability to care for yourself and solve your life problems, greater control over your emotions, improved relationships, increased structure in your life, or increased satisfaction with yourself.

For example, Randy's pattern for years was to keep his feelings and problems to himself and get drunk when upsetting things built up. Recently, Randy went through a bad time and came close to drinking. For the first time in his recovery, he called his AA sponsor *before* he drank. With the support of his sponsor, Randy got through his crisis and stayed sober. Using his sponsor was a significant sign of progress for him. Holly often felt depressed after a serious quarrel with her husband. She used to take the blame for these arguments and often felt guilty and shameful. Now she is more realistic and accepts her husband's role in their quarrels and doesn't blame herself. She's learned to express her feelings to him in an assertive, yet appropriate way. Holly believes her depression has improved as she's gotten more skillful in communicating with her husband.

Chapter 6 | *Medications in Dual Recovery*

Dennis C. Daley and Antoine Douaihy

Purpose of Medications in the Treatment of Mood Disorders

Medications are used to treat the acute symptoms and prevent relapse and recurrence of an episode of depression or bipolar illness.[1-10] In addition, treatment goals with medications include a full return of functioning. Antidepressants and mood stabilizers, the medications commonly used to treat depression or bipolar illness, do not produce dependence and have no potential for abuse. They are safe for individuals in recovery from alcoholism or drug dependence.

Depression is no longer attributed simply to too little neurochemicals such as serotonin or norepinephrine. Instead, depression is associated with a dysregulation of neurochemical firing patterns. Antidepressants treat specific symptoms of depression such as depressed mood, sadness, fatigue and suicidality, and they also regulate the altered brain chemistry that may contribute to these symptoms.

In the case of recurrent major depression, bipolar illness, or chronic mood disorders, medications decrease the chance of having a relapse to the mood disorder and reduce the potential severity of a future episode, should it occur. Medications are also used to treat dysthymia, a more chronic from of depressive illness.[11-13]

More recent studies have shown that antidepressant medications can improve outcomes for a mood disorder and sometimes for a substance use disorder as well.[14] Still, it is important to use them in conjunction with therapy or counseling.[8,15] However, some individuals in the maintenance phase of treatment whose mood symptoms are stable may stop their involvement in therapy or counseling and only see their physician periodically for medication monitoring.

Purpose of Medications for Treatment of Addiction

Medications are used in the treatment of addiction to manage intoxication states, overdose, and acute withdrawal syndromes, and as maintenance or "replacement" therapy.[16–34] In the treatment of addiction, there are two goals for medications: to help the addicted individual establish an initial period of abstinence and to reduce the risk of a future relapse. Medications can help prevent or stop withdrawal symptoms and help the addicted person safely detoxify from alcohol or other addictive drugs such as opiates or benzodiazepines.[24]

Benzodiazepines such as diazepam (Valium), chlordiazepoxide (Librium), lorazepam (Ativan), oxazepam (Serax), or other depressant drugs are usually used to manage alcohol withdrawal. Other medications used for treatment of alcohol withdrawal syndrome include anticonvulsants such as divalproex sodium (Depakote, Depakote ER) and carbamazepine (Tegretol, Carbatrol). These medications are sometimes used in combination with benzodiazepines. Medicines used to manage withdrawal from physical dependence on antianxiety drugs (referred to as tranquilizers), sedative-hypnotics, or barbiturates may even include the drug the person is dependent on such as alprazolam (Xanax) or clonazepam (Klonopin), or a medication from a similar class of drugs.

Medicines used to manage withdrawal from heroin or other opiate drugs include methadone, buprenorphine (Subutex, Suboxone) or clonidine (Catapres), a drug used for treating high blood pressure, which reduces the distress of opioid withdrawal. Other drugs used to help with symptoms of opioid withdrawal include the mild antianxiety medication hydroxyzine (Vistaril, Atarax), the antidepressant trazodone (Desyrel) to help with insomnia, and diphenoxylate (Lomotil) to help with diarrhea. In addition to short-term detoxification, treatment for opioid dependence includes long-term treatment addressing the cravings for the drug and other physical dependence factors in the body.

In another method of opioid detoxification that has been termed "rapid" or "ultrarapid" detoxification, withdrawal is precipitated by administering either naloxone (the opioid antagonist Narcan) or naltrexone (ReVia) in combination with a heavy sedative or anesthesia to ease withdrawal symptoms. This type of detoxification is very costly and not covered by health insurance. This procedure has been associated with serious life-threatening complications related to the anesthesia, but it has rarely resulted in death.[26]

Antidepressant medications and dopamine agonists such as bromocriptine and amantadine have been used to alleviate depression or cravings associated with withdrawal from cocaine addiction; however, studies show mixed results with these drugs, and they are not widely used.[27] A promising medication, modafinil (Provigil), which is FDA approved for the treatment of narcolepsy (excessive daytime sleepiness), is currently being evaluated for treating cocaine dependence. Other agents such as topiramate (Topamax), baclofen (Baclofen), tiagabine (Gabitril), and disulfiram (Antabuse) have also shown some benefits for clients with cocaine dependence. However, currently there is no medication that is FDA approved for treatment of cocaine dependence.

There are no specific drugs used for withdrawal from cannabis, hallucinogens, inhalants, or other stimulant drugs since these drugs do not usually cause physical withdrawal symptoms. However, antianxiety or antipsychotic drugs may be used to alleviate psychiatric symptoms that some people experience either when using or stopping these drugs. Vitamins, good nutrition, and supportive care are also helpful in alleviating withdrawal symptoms.

Acute withdrawal symptoms usually remit within a week, though some may remain longer, depending on the frequency, amount, and types of drugs used. Withdrawal may take longer as your body adjusts to being substance free. It is not unusual for some alcoholics and drug addicts to take weeks to months or longer to feel "normal" and overcome anxiety, sleep disturbances, irritability, mood instability, and cravings commonly associated with longer-term withdrawal. Persons experiencing such symptoms are more vulnerable to relapse.

The second use of medication in the treatment of addiction is for maintenance. There are currently four drugs approved for the maintenance treatment of opioid dependence: naltrexone, methadone, LAAM, and buprenorphine. Synthetic opiates such as methadone (Dolophine, Methadose) or Levomethadyl (LAAM) (Orlaam) are used to replace the addict's heroin or other narcotic drugs.[28] Methadone is an important tool in decreasing the spread of hepatitis C and HIV in and by injection drug users. LAAM is longer-acting but is no longer a first-line treatment choice opioid dependence because of serious cardiac problems associated with its use. Methadone maintenance programs help many opioid dependent individuals, particularly those who remain in the program for an extended period of time. Unfortunately, methadone is sometimes diverted away from the clinic and onto the streets for illicit use. Another observed phenomenon has been the increasing use of benzodiazepines among patients on methadone, which can result in severe and even dangerous neurological reactions. Methadone and LAAM are usually not recommended unless the drug dependent individual has failed several other forms of treatment for narcotic addiction such as rehabilitation or outpatient therapy.

An opiate antagonist medication called naltrexone (Trexan) can be used by those who do not want to be maintained on opioids. This medication blocks the euphoric effects of the high produced by heroin or other opiate drugs. The addict who ingests opiate drugs while on this medication won't feel the high and may be less inclined to continue using opiates.[29] Naltrexone has few side effects, the most common of which is nausea. Hepatic function should be monitored before and during administration. A form of long-acting, injectable depot formulation of naltrexone was recently approved for treatment of alcohol dependence.

A relatively new medication, buprenorphine, an opioid partial agonist, has more recently been used to help opiate addicts. This drug has several advantages over methadone—it is safer, produces less severe withdrawal symptoms, has less potential to induce an opiate "high," and has a reduced risk for drug overdose.[30,32]

The biggest advantage to buprenorphine is that it is the first opioid therapy for the treatment of opioid dependence that can be obtained by prescription from the client's primary care physician or psychiatrist. However, a physician must have special certification to be able to prescribe buprenorphine.

Some medications can help alleviate or reduce strong cravings for alcohol or reduce the chances of relapse.[16,18,19,25] Disulfiram (Antabuse) serves as "aversive therapy" for alcoholics. It interferes with the breakdown of alcohol in the liver and if you drink on it you'll get very sick. It remains in your system up to 7–14 days and buys you time to stay sober if you have a strong urge to drink. The craving to drink alcohol may be gone by the time this medication washes out of the alcoholic's system. Disulfiram is most appropriate for alcoholics who are motivated to get sober, not generally impulsive, and who are willing to participate in psychosocial treatment (a rehab program, therapy, or counseling).[31] Naltrexone (ReVia), a drug previously used mainly with heroin addicts, not only helps reduce cravings for alcohol but also lessens relapse rates and the severity of relapses among alcoholics.[25,33,34] This drug has also been used successfully with depressed alcoholics.[35] Acamprosate (Campral), a drug widely used in Europe, is currently available in the United States. This agent appears to reduce discomfort—including restlessness, anxiety, insomnia, and dysphoria—commonly experienced within the first six months of alcohol abstinence. [36] In recent studies, it prolonged early alcohol abstinence for clients who had completed initial detoxification. It works best in clients with good family support and for those who are monitored by health professionals. It does not make a client sick if he or she should drink alcohol. The drug is found to be well tolerated and acceptable to most clients.[18, 36]

Serotonin agents, including buspirone (BuSpar) and ondansterone (Zofran), have been studied as possible treatment options for alcohol dependence but results have been limited. Studies are underway to test whether the anticonvulsant topiramate (Topamax) can be helpful for treating alcohol dependence.

Addiction to nicotine is very common among individuals with addictions to alcohol or other drugs. Some people benefit from help withdrawing from nicotine or managing intense cravings for nicotine. Nicotine replacement therapy takes many forms: nicotine gum, transdermal patches, nasal spray, oral inhalers, sublingual nicotine tablets, and nicotine lozenges. They are all effective in aiding smoking cessation.[37,38] Combining two forms of nicotine replacement may be more effective than a single form.[39] More recently, the medication bupropion (Zyban SR) was approved by the FDA to help in stopping smoking.[37]

Medications can help jump-start recovery. However, they are best viewed as an adjunct to recovery, not as the main way to stay sober. Treatment and self-help programs are the main mechanisms to help you get and stay sober. Medications can be used as "crutch" but learning to deal with problems and stresses, changing your lifestyle, and developing recovery skills are the mainstay of recovery.

Medications for Depression and Bipolar Disorders

Most medications for psychiatric disorders are taken in tablet, capsule, or liquid form. Some are taken by injection into a muscle or directly into the bloodstream. Although they can be prescribed by many different kinds of doctors, psychiatrists have the most training and experience in prescribing and managing medicines for mood or other psychiatric disorders.

Some medical conditions can affect the type of medications that you can tolerate. Also, medications used for mood disorders may cause problems when mixed with other medications. Therefore, make sure that you tell your psychiatrist your current medical problems and all of the medications you are taking. Any questions you have about medications or their side effects should be discussed with your doctor or your pharmacist.

The medication prescribed will depend on the type and severity of symptoms of your mood disorder as well as the presence of other psychiatric symptoms. Although some people with mood disorders require the use of only one medication, others require several. Medications may be added or changed over time based on your response and changes in symptoms. The length of time you take medications depends on the nature and course of your mood disorder. Chronic and recurrent forms of illness often require ongoing medications as a "preventive" measure. While medications reduce the odds of a future episode, it is still possible for some mood symptoms to return.

Following is a brief discussion of medications used for depression, bipolar illness, and some of the other psychiatric or substance use disorders that people with mood disorders may also experience.[1–13,43–46]

Depressive Disorders

If your depression does not significantly improve with abstinence from alcohol or drugs, if it causes suffering in your life or an inability to enjoy life as you once could, if you do not respond to non-medication treatments such as therapy, or if you have a recurrent form of depression, then antidepressant medications are probably necessary. Antidepressants have no potential for abuse compared with other kinds of drugs such as some antianxiety drugs (i.e. benzodiazepines). The specific antidepressant your doctor prescribes will depend on your past history of response to medicine, your current symptoms, as well as his or her preferences and experience.

There are several major categories of antidepressants. The first group of antidepressants includes selective serotonin reuptake inhibitors (SSRIs). Fluoxetine (Prozac, Prozac Weekly), sertraline (Zoloft), citalopram (Celexa), escitalopram (Lexapro), and paroxetine (Paxil, Paxil CR) are common medications in this group. These drugs regulate the firing patterns of the neurotransmitter serotonin that communicates between nerve cells in the brain. These medications may take up to three to four weeks before they "kick in" and improve your depressive symptoms. To experience their full benefits, it may take few more weeks. Some people who take an SSRI may experience side effects such as agitation, sleep disturbance, and sexual dysfunction. Overall, SSRIs have fewer side effects than other antidepressants, and some may have a sedating effect. They are safer for people with heart problems and when taken in an overdose.

A second group of antidepressant drugs include mirtazapine (Remeron, Remeron Soltab), venlafaxine (Effexor, Effexor XR), bupropion (Wellbutrin, Wellbutrin SR, Wellbutrin XL), duloxetine (Cymbalta), and trazodone (Desyrel). These medicines work on regulating other neurotransmitters such as dopamine and norepinephrine in addition to serotonin. Side effects are somewhat similar to those of the SSRIs.

A third classification is that of "tricyclic and tetracyclic antidepressants" (TCA) and includes amitriptyline (Elavil), imipramine (Tofranil), desipramine (Norpramin), nortriptyline (Pamelor), doxepin (Sinequan), clomipramine (Anafranil), and trimipramine (Surmontil). TCAs take up to 10 days or longer to improve depressive mood symptoms. These drugs can produce unpleasant side effects such as dry mouth, blurred vision, dizziness upon standing, sexual dysfunction and difficulty urinating. These drugs are not used as first-line treatment for depression because of the side effects and the risks of death if taken in an overdose.

The fourth class of antidepressants is called "monamine oxidase inhibitors" (MAOIs) and includes phenelzine (Nardil) and tranylcypromine (Parnate). These drugs are used when other medications are not effective or in cases of "atypical" depressions. MAOIs require adherence to a special diet of foods that do not contain a compound called tyramine. Cheddar cheeses, sausage, some pickled and smoked meats and fish, banana peel fiber, and a few others, and even some and drinks need to be avoided because of their high levels of tyramine. Combining them with an MAOI can be highly dangerous due to the risk of high blood pressure and stroke. MAOIs should only be taken by those who can adhere to these dietary restrictions. These medications may cause also side effects such as headaches, trouble sleeping, weight gain, and some sexual problems.

If you are being treated for an acute episode of depressive illness you should stay on your medication at least 6 to 12 months or longer after your symptoms are under control.[4,5,10] Stopping too early raises your risk of symptoms returning. If you have a recurrent depression, you should remain indefinitely on medication as a way of reducing the risk of a future relapse. If you respond only partially to a specific antidepressant your doctor may add another one or add another type of medicine such as a mood stabilizer.

Alcohol or drug use can cause antidepressant medication to be less effective as these substances can raise or lower antidepressant blood levels. Cocaine and other stimulants can produce fatal interactions with MAOI medications. Recovery can be greatly enhanced by the proper medication for depression *and* abstinence from alcohol and drugs.

Some antidepressants are used in the treatment of other disorders, too. These include panic disorder, chronic pain, anorexia nervosa and bulimia nervosa, and obsessive-compulsive disorder.

Bipolar Disorder

A number of pharmacologic agents have been approved by the FDA for the treatment of bipolar disorder. Until recently the primary psychiatric drug for the treatment of either mania or bipolar disorder has been lithium carbonate (Lithobid, Eskalith CR). This medication treats the acute symptoms of mania and helps prevent future episodes (maintenance therapy). However it is effective in only 60% of bipolar patients, a percentage that sinks as low as 50% if all types of bipolar disorders are considered.[43] The presence of substance abuse predicts a poor response to lithium, which means it is not a good first-line option for clients with dual disorders.[44] If you are on lithium, you must undergo periodic blood testing to check lithium levels and avoid its potential toxic effects on your thyroid and kidneys. Side effects such as tremors, weight gain can be problematic. If your Lithium level is too high, you can experience convulsions, kidney failure or even death.

At present three anticonvulsant agents—divalproex (Depakote, Depakote ER), lamotrigine (Lamictal), and carbamazepine extended-release capsules (Equetro)—are approved by the FDA for the treatment of bipolar disorder. People with a form of bipolar illness called *rapid cycling* usually respond better to Depakote than to Lithium.[45] Since most bipolar clients with substance use disorders appear to have more mixed and/or rapid cycling bipolar disorder, divalproex seems to be the best option for them. In addition, a recent study in our research clinic has shown that divalproex is well tolerated and effective in bipolar alcoholics.[46] Among the anticonvulsants, divalproex is the one most strongly associated with weight gain. Lamotrigine is associated with serious rashes in less than 1%. Antimania medications may take up to a week or longer to stop or alleviate symptoms. In individuals who do not respond to one medication alone, they may be used in different combinations or with other medications such as antipsychotics, benzodiazepines, or thyroid supplements (Synthroid). If you have a bipolar disorder, you should not be taking an antidepressant by itself without a mood stabilizer; doing so will increase your risk of have a manic or hypomanic episode. Being on both mood stabilizer and antidepressant decreases that risk.

Prior to taking any of these medications, you should get a physical examination along with medical tests (urine tests, blood-work testing for liver enzymes and blood count, and EKG). Also, you need to have regular blood levels taken (except in the case of lamotrigine) to ensure that you have a therapeutic level of medications in your system but also that their levels in your blood aren't too high.

Atypical antipsychotics are a relatively recent addition to the agents used to treat bipolar disorder. They include aripiprazole (Abilify), risperidone (Risperdal), quetiapine (Seroquel), ziprasidone (Geodon), and olanzapine (Zyprexa, Symbyax: Zyprexa with Prozac). Compared to the conventional antipsychotics, they are better tolerated. However, they have their own safety and tolerability concerns. Side effects include weight gain, increase in blood sugar, changes in lipid profile (increased cholesterol and triglyceride), cardiovascular problems, sedation, and galactorrhea. Certain newer agents such as topiramate (Topamax), gabapentin (Neurontin), and oxcarbazepine (Trileptal), which are less proven to work, may nonetheless help some people. The biggest challenge for clients is to stay adherent to the medications and discuss any difficulties with their doctors.

Electroconvulsive therapy (ECT), disparagingly labeled as "shock therapy" is the treatment of choice for persistent and severe mood disorders that are resistant to medications.[47] ECT involves the passage of a brief electrical current through the brain in order to induce a seizure. The clients undergoing ECT are sedated so that they do not feel pain during the procedure. It is a safe procedure and one of the most powerful treatments for bipolar disorder. ECT works quickly. The most common side effect is memory loss that resolves gradually and disappears with time.

Many complementary and alternative treatments such as light therapy may help improve feelings of depression and enhance mind-body health in general.[48]

Medications for Other Psychiatric Disorders

Anxiety Disorders

Medications prescribed to treat anxiety disorders will depend on the specific type of anxiety disorder and the severity of symptoms. Medicines are recommended when anxiety symptoms are severe enough to interfere with daily functioning and when symptoms do not respond to non-medication treatments. Remember that it is impossible to get an accurate reading of anxiety symptoms if you continue to use alcohol or drugs, because substances can cause, worsen, or cover up your symptoms.

Panic Disorder

The most common medications used in the treatment of panic disorder include the SSRIs. Venlafaxine (Effexor XR) was recently FDA approved for treatment of panic disorder. Also TCAs (especially Tofranil), and MAOIs may be used. Benzodiazepines such as alprazolam and clonazepam are also used to treat panic attacks but are usually not recommended for long-term use with alcoholics or drug addicts because of their addiction potential.

Phobias

The same antidepressants used to treat panic disorder are used in the treatment of agoraphobia. Some severe social phobias (social anxiety disorder) are treated with SSRIs (the first-line treatment choice) and MAOI's. People with severe performance anxiety who are required to speak or perform in front of others benefit from beta-blockers such as propranolol (Inderal), medicines that have no potential for abuse or addiction.

Obsessive-Compulsive Disorder (OCD)

OCD typically is treated with antidepressants such as clomipramine, fluoxetine, paroxetine, sertraline, or fluvoxamine (Luvox), which is an SSRI. These medications help decrease obsessions and the compulsive behaviors that accompany obsessive thoughts.

Post-Traumatic Stress Disorder (PTSD)

SSRIs (particularly Zoloft) are the medicines most often used to treat PTSD. Addiction and/or depression are common among people with PTSD.

Generalized Anxiety Disorder (GAD)

Some antidepressants such as venlafaxine and SSRIs are effective in treating GAD. Antianxiety medications such as buspirone (BuSpar) may be used in "anxious alcoholics" with benefits. Benzodiazepines should be avoided in patients with GAD due to the risk of abuse and dependence.

Benzodiazepines such as diazepam, alprazolam, and clonazepam are frequently used for treating anxiety disorders. However, because these medications are addictive and habit-forming, and because many people with addictive disorders may have gotten hooked in the first place as a result of taking these drugs for long-term use, they usually are not recommended, especially not for extended periods.

The length of time that you take medications will depend on the severity of your anxiety disorder. Similar to antidepressants, it is recommended that you stay on these for several months or more after your symptoms improve or go away. If you are being treated for a chronic or recurrent anxiety condition you may need to stay on medication indefinitely.

Psychotic Disorders

Drug and alcohol induced psychosis, mania with psychotic symptoms, schizoaffective disorder, and psychotic depression are treated with medications called antipsychotics (previously called neuroleptics). Psychotic symptoms are treated with atypical antipsychotics such as olanzapine, risperidone, quetiapine, ziprasidone or conventional antipsychotics such as perphenazine, chlorpromazine, haloperidol or thioridazine. Antipsychotic medications help to decrease or eliminate psychotic symptoms, as well as agitation and anxiety. They also help to organize thinking processes.

Prior to starting antipsychotic drugs, you should undergo a physical examination and other tests such as a neurological exam, blood count, lipid profile, kidney and liver tests, EKG, and other tests. Although most antipsychotic drugs are taken orally, some are available in injectable form (Risperdal Consta, Haldol Decanoate, and Prolixin Decanoate). This method of use releases the medication into the body over a period of weeks and is especially helpful for individuals who are unwilling or unable to comply with regular daily doses of oral medication.

Side effects of antipsychotic drugs may include drowsiness or sedation, weight gain, dry mouth, blurred vision, constipation, difficulty urinating, increased heart rate or pulse, stiffening of muscles, and restlessness. One of the most serious side effects is a neurological condition called *Tardive Dyskinesia*, which is seen mostly with conventional antipsychotics. This condition involves involuntary movements of facial muscles or movements of arms and legs.

Personality Disorders

There is no specific medication treatment used for personality disorders. However, specific symptoms or behaviors of a personality disorder may be treated with medicine. For example, depressive symptoms are treated with antidepressants, psychotic symptoms are treated with antipsychotics, and severe mood swings or trouble controlling angry, violent, or self-destructive impulses are treated with mood stabilizers.

Attention-Deficit/Hyperactivity Disorder (ADHD)

Stimulants such as amphetamine (Adderall, Adderall XR), methylphenidate (Ritalin, Concerta), and dextroamphetamine (Dexedrine, and Dextrostat) are used to treat ADHD. These medications pose a risk of abuse and dependence for individuals recovering from other types of addiction, so these must be used under medical supervision. Non-stimulant medications such as bupropion, desipramine, and atomoxetine (Strattera) are possible alternative medication choices, because they do not have a potential for abuse and dependence.

Eating Disorders

There is substantial evidence that eating disorders and SUDs co-occur at higher than expected rates. A particular association has been noted between alcohol abuse and bulimia. Another association can be found between bipolar disorder and bulimia nervosa or anorexia nervosa. SSRIs such as fluoxetine offer potential benefits in women with alcohol abuse and eating disorders.

Off-Label Usage of Psychotropic Medications

More physicians have been using medications for purposes other than those specified by the FDA when they were first approved. The practice is referred to as off-label usage. This kind of "cross over" medication use is on the rise, so it is important that you ask your physician about exactly what condition the medication is prescribed for, whether there is evidence it may work for that condition, and how safe it is.

Medications for Medical Co-Morbidities

Clients with a history of serious mental illness carry a 20% risk of being infected with hepatitis C virus (HCV).[49] Hepatitis means inflammation of the liver. Persons may have gotten HCV if they *ever* injected drugs, even if they have experimented only a few times and many years ago. People who share works to inject drugs are at greatest risk. Most individuals who get hepatitis C carry the virus for the rest of their lives. Over time, some with liver damage may develop cirrhosis of the liver and liver failure, which is fatal if not treated. Others have no long-term effects. Many persons with HCV have no symptoms. Alpha-interferon and alpha-interferon injectable therapies are the gold standard for treating hepatitis C. They help the body to get rid of infected cells while preventing healthy cells from being infected. Ribavirin is a pill form of a medication that is sometimes used with alpha-interferon. Side effects of alpha-interferons include mood changes such as depression and suicidal tendencies. SSRIs are safe and effective for treating this depression. Your doctor is an important partner in your fight against hepatitis C.

Exchanging needles among users of injectable drugs like heroin and cocaine is one of the primary ways that HIV/AIDS is spread in the United States. HIV infection is a common comorbid condition with opioid dependence. An association between methamphetamine abuse and increased high-risk sexual behaviors has also raised some concerns. Unfortunately there is no cure for HIV infection. The currently available treatment called "antiretroviral cocktails" can reduce the amount of HIV (viral load) to the point that is "undetectable" which is the goal of treatment. These antiretrovirals can interact with psychotropic medications. Being sober makes it much easier to stick to HIV treatment program and medications, which in turn increases the chances of living a longer, healthier and more productive life.

Other medical comorbidities such as obesity, diabetes, and migraine headache occur more commonly in clients with bipolar disorder than in the general population).[50] Working with your primary care doctor on treating and coping with these problems is very important. Nutritional counseling or support groups such as Overeaters Anonymous may be helpful.

Medications for Non-Substance Addictions and Impulse Control Disorders

Sexual Addiction

Estimated to affect 3% to 6% of the U.S. population, addictive sexual disorders often co-occur with chemical dependency and are a frequently unrecognized cause of chemical dependency relapse. Treatment goal is more to "manage" than to "cure." Drug therapy has a small place in the treatment of sexual addiction and only as part of a treatment plan that includes therapy. SSRIs, imipramine (Tofranil), or lithium (Eskalith) may help with the intensity of sexual obsessions and compulsions.[51]

Pathological Gambling

Pathological gambling is considered a disorder of impulse control that is characterized by recurrent and maladaptive gambling behavior. Gambling problems tend to co-occur with drug problems. Many agents such as SSRIs, mood stabilizers, topiramate (Topamax), Fluvoxamine (Luvox), and naltrexone (ReVia) may improve this condition.[52]

Side Effects of Medication

Medications can produce side effects such as dry mouth, urinary retention, constipation, sedation, dizziness, balance problems, confusion and memory difficulties. Sometimes these go away or decrease to the point where you can tolerate them. In other cases, additional medications may be used to manage side effects. Because of the complexity of psychiatric disorders, some people actually have an episode of illness as a result of being on a medication. That is why when you first start taking a new medication you need to be in close contact with your doctor and therapist to report the effects of the medication on your symptoms and to let them know if new symptoms develop. All medications must be taken responsibly and as prescribed. Otherwise, you place yourself at risk for relapse or other problems. Be careful to tell your doctor about any medicines you are taking for medical conditions such as diabetes or high blood pressure since drug interactions may pose a problem such as worsening of side effects.

Attitudes About Taking Medication

There are several attitude problems you may face regarding medication. First, you have to accept that mood disorder medications are different than alcohol or drugs that are used to get high. You are taking medications to treat a mood disorder and get better. You shouldn't feel guilty for taking medication or believe that they are a "crutch" or you are "weak" for needing them. Some people resent the idea that they have to take a medicine for a mental disorder. They argue with doctors, therapists, and family members. Some even refuse medicine altogether or take it only for a few days then stop.

A second problem is the desire to stop taking medication once your mood symptoms are under control and you feel better. Never stop your medications unless you first talk this over with your therapist and doctor. Many people relapse to depression or mania after they stop or cut down on their medication following a period in which they feel better. Just as you shouldn't stop taking medications for high blood pressure, diabetes, or other medical conditions on your own, you should not stop taking psychiatric medications without first consulting the people taking care of you.

A third problem is side effects from medication. If you are having unpleasant side effects that don't go away, call your doctor to ask if your medicines need to be changed or you need to do something to offset these side effects. Some side effects go away in time. Others become more tolerable over time.

A fourth problem is feeling frustrated that your symptoms are not improving as much as you would like. Some individuals do not respond to certain medications as well as others. They may be tried on several different types of medication over a period of time and feel very frustrated that they don't quickly find the medication that works for them. You have to be patient if this happens. Although doctors know what kinds of medications work for what types of symptoms and disorders, there are exceptions to every rule. Therefore, all medications aren't equally effective with everyone who has the same mood symptoms.

A fifth problem is expecting medications to make all of your symptoms or problems go away. Although medication can control or reduce symptoms, some chronic or persistent symptoms may remain with you. You have to learn to live with these as best you can. Also, medications cannot take away problems in your life. That is why medications should be used with therapy and/or participation in self-help programs.

Effects of Drug and Alcohol Use on Psychiatric Medications

Using alcohol, street drugs or other non-prescribed medications can have a negative effect on your antidepressant medications by causing the level of medication in your blood to increase or decrease. You can get a false reading of the level of medication in your blood in some cases because alcohol or other drug use can actually temporarily cover-up symptoms by increasing your blood level of medication. Even small amounts of alcohol or other drugs can have a negative effect on medications. In some instances, mixing medication with alcohol or drugs can cause serious complications.

Substance use can lower your motivation to comply with medications.

I've heard many people complain that their medication wasn't working, yet they were continuing to use alcohol and drugs. If you continue to drink or use drugs, don't expect to get the maximum benefit from medications. Also, be aware that some doctors may not prescribe psychiatric medications unless you agree to abstain from substances.

Medication Seeking

Some people look for a "magic bullet" medication that will cure their psychiatric illness and make everything better for them. They think that anytime their symptoms worsen or new ones develop, some pill will magically take these symptoms away. Or, they hope that a medication can make them feel better when they have serious problems at work or in their relationships. Regardless of your symptoms or how you respond to medication, you have to

Questions to Ask Your Doctor About Medications

1. What is the purpose of this medication?
2. When should I take this medicine? Should it be taken with food, or should I avoid eating right before or after taking it?
3. How long will it take for medications to have an effect on my mood symptoms, and which symptoms are most likely to be relieved?
4. How will I know if this medication isn't working for me?
5. What are the side effects? Will they go away? If they don't go away, what can I do about them, and which should I report immediately to my doctor?
6. What are the risks of not taking this medication?
7. How long will I need to take medication?
8. What happens if I drink alcohol or use other drugs while I'm taking this medication?
9. Are there other medicines that interact with this?
10. What are the dangers of missing dosages of medications or taking more than prescribed?
11. If I feel like quitting my medications, what should I do before stopping?
12. What are some of the lifestyle changes I can work on, in addition to diet and exercise, to lessen some side effects from medications?
13. How can I deal with the stigma of taking medications?
14. If I feel fine now, why do I need to stay on my medication?
15. What can I do to remember to take my medications?

learn coping skills to change your life and manage your disorders. Although medications are very helpful for many types of mood disorders and a major form of treatment for some, other strategies are also needed.

Coping With People Who Tell You to Stop Taking Medication

Because other people, sometimes even family members and friends, may suggest that you stop taking your psychiatric medications, it helps to think ahead and plan how to handle this situation if it arises. You should think about this the same way that you think about heart medication. If another person told you to get off of your heart medication would you stop it? Of course not! The same holds true for medication used for depression or bipolar illness. Tell people straight out that you need the medication, question why they would want you to stop a medication used to treat a mood disorder, or tell them that you don't appreciate their poor advice.

Some people believe they have to "white knuckle" it, that no matter how severe their symptoms are, they should cope with them without medication. I've seen people suffer needlessly because they felt that they shouldn't take medication. The reality is that many people cannot recover from a mood disorder unless they are on medications. Remind yourself what can happen if you stop taking medication and the benefits you have experienced. Ask your sponsor or treatment team for other ideas or ways to cope with pressures to get off medications. Ask other men and women in the program how they dealt with this pressure.

If your mood disorder is treated properly you have a greater chance of recovering from your addiction. There is no shame in needing medications. On the previous page is a list of questions you can consider asking your doctor about the medicines used to treat mood disorders.

Chapter 7 *Managing Feelings*

Emotional Issues in Recovery

Managing emotions or feelings is a very important part of recovery from an addiction, a mood disorder, or dual disorders.[1] Three major issues are related to managing feelings in recovery: (1) identifying or being aware of your various moods or feeling states; (2) managing and expressing your feelings appropriately; and (3) coping with feelings so that you don't use alcohol or drugs or engage in behaviors that are harmful. There are times when feeling bad is a sign of progress. For example, feeling sadness related to problems in your family relationships caused by your dual disorders is often a necessary part of recovery. The critical issue is how you manage your feelings. In this chapter, I discuss feelings that you may need to address in your recovery.

Anger

Many people deny, avoid, or internalize angry feelings. One common behavior I see is holding all angry feelings inside and letting them build up. This can lead to using substances, getting into arguments or altercations, or harming yourself with self-destructive behavior. On the other extreme is lashing out and expressing anger whenever you feel it, whether or not it is appropriate to do so. In many cases anger is exaggerated and based on a distortion of reality.

Either extreme is unhealthy. If you hold anger inside, then you have to learn if, when, and how to let it out in a reasonable manner. If you lash out when you feel angry, you need to learn to control and contain these feelings and impulses so that they are not outwardly expressed.

A number of strategies are available for managing anger.[2] Learn as much as you can about anger and how and when it is appropriate to express it. Become aware of how angry feelings show in your body, thoughts, and behaviors. Examine and change your beliefs about anger. For example, if you believe that you should keep all of your anger inside, or if you think you should let it out as soon as you feel it, then you are going to act on these beliefs. To change how you cope with your feelings, you have to reexamine and change these beliefs. If you believe that "it's not good to let my angry feelings show," you can change it to "letting anger show can be healthy as long as it is done in a constructive way."

Another strategy is to change your angry thoughts or "inner dialogue" and talk yourself out of being angry. Rather than say "I'm mad at my spouse for criticizing me," you may say instead "it was difficult to hear the criticism but it was done with good intentions, and just because my spouse criticized me doesn't mean I'm a bad person." Use the slogans of recovery programs and positive self-talk. You can say things like "this anger will pass, I'm going to keep control of my anger, let go and let God." Remind yourself or write a list of the negative effects of dealing with anger in inappropriate ways or the benefits of handling anger constructively.

Talk about your feelings and thoughts or the situations that contribute to your anger. You can talk to the person toward whom you feel angry or talk to another person as a safe way of expressing your feelings. Share your anger in a therapy session, with your sponsor, or at a support group meeting. Talking can help you better understand why you are angry and sort through your options. The best option may be to do nothing but just let go of your anger.

If people have been hurt by things you said or did while angry, it is helpful to make amends to them. You start by identifying people who were seriously hurt by your expression of anger. Then you initiate a discussion with them and apologize. Keep in mind, however, that you can apologize until you are blue in the face, but if you don't back it up with positive behavior change, it won't mean anything to other people. If your angry actions toward other people are part of a more serious problem, such as inability to control aggressive impulses or a tendency to be violent, then you are going to have to change in order to get control of your anger.

Leave situations in which you feel that your anger is building up and you seriously worry about losing control. I don't recommend that you walk away from situations that trigger anger unless you need time to calm down or are worried about saying or doing something you will later regret.

Redirect angry feelings toward an activity such as working around the house or doing something enjoyable. Creative media—such as painting, drawing, clay, or other arts and crafts—exercise, and physical exertion are excellent ways to release angry feelings and clear your head.

Write about your angry feelings and thoughts in a journal. You can track your feelings over time to see how you're improving and what strategies work for you. Make an anger log by getting a notebook and making four columns across the top of the paper. In the first column, list the situation(s) or event(s) that trigger your anger. In the second column, rate the degree to which you felt angry on a scale of 1–10 (1 = little; 5 = moderate; 10 = extreme). In the third column, write your thoughts about the situation, and in the fourth column, write two or more coping strategies that you can use.

Some people find it helpful to practice ahead of time what they are going to say to another person when they want to directly express their angry feelings. You can practice by yourself by saying out loud what you want to say in the situation at hand. Or you can practice in a role play with your counselor. This may make you feel more comfortable about what you are going to say once you are in a situation in which you talk to someone about your feelings.

If you carry around a lot of anger from the past, you have to work on letting it go, or it can cause physical symptoms and emotional discomfort. Old baggage from the past can also have a negative effect on your current relationships and your mood.

Dealing With Other People Who Are Angry With You

Dealing effectively with other people's anger toward you requires understanding and tolerating others who feel upset with you and listening to what they have to say. The anger of another person that is directed toward you may not have anything to do with you. Or, if it does, it may not be justified. In other instances, you may have done or said something to anger another. It is impos-

Strategies for Managing Anger

1. Recognize your anger and know how it shows in your body, thoughts, and behaviors.
2. Identify factors that cause you to feel angry.
3. Identify the effects of angry feelings and how you cope with anger.
4. Don't let little, insignificant things get you angry.
5. Learn to challenge yourself when feeling angry to figure out whether it is justified.
6. Change your angry thoughts in order to change angry feelings.
7. Use anger as a motivator to solve problems or conflicts or to achieve things in your life.
8. Express your angry feelings to the person you are mad at when appropriate, but do so in a controlled manner.
9. Talk about your anger with a sponsor, friend, family member, or counselor or at a support group meeting.
10. Don't let anger control you and make you say or do things that will hurt others or that you will later regret.
11. Leave situations in which you worry you will lose control and do something harmful to another person.
12. If you have hurt others by lashing out angrily at them, make amends to them.
13. Use physical or creative activities as a means of releasing angry energy.
14. Write about your feelings in a journal or anger log.
15. Pray or ask for strength from your Higher Power.
16. If severe anger and aggressive behaviors don't stop with abstinence or with therapy alone, seek an evaluation for mood-stabilizing medications.

sible to have close relationships without people getting upset or angry with each other. The chart above lists anger management strategies.[3]

Anxiety and Worry

Alcohol and drug use can increase your anxiety over the long run, even if it helps you feel better in the short run. Often, it is the use of substances to cope with anxiety that has led to the original addiction. Anxiety is sometimes caused by withdrawal from alcohol and other drugs, from which your body is adjusting to being free. Other times, anxiety is a normal part of living related to situations that you have to cope with in your daily life. Anxiety and worry are common among people with mood disorders, phobias, panic disorder, generalized anxiety disorder, or obsessive–compulsive disorder.

Anxiety may involve physical symptoms, such as shortness of breath, rapid heartbeat, chest discomfort, feeling weak, feeling on edge, sweating, blushing, dizziness, dry mouth, desire to urinate, or having a tingling sensation. People who have panic attacks sometimes feel as if they are having a heart attack and end up in a hospital emergency room.

Anxiety may be partially caused by faulty beliefs about yourself, your abilities, the world, and safety. For example, when you experience *anticipatory anxiety*, you worry about what may happen in the future. The idea of something often becomes more anxiety provoking than the reality of it. You worry excessively and unrealistically that you'll make a mistake, mess up a job interview, flunk a test, botch a speech, have a lousy time at a social event, or be criticized or that something terrible might happen. Or you may believe that it isn't safe to leave your house or to travel by plane or train. You may believe that you are an incompetent person or an imposter and that others will find out the truth about you. You may even believe that you have to be perfect and can't make any mistakes lest others judge you as incompetent. Such thoughts often lead to unnecessary suffering and discomfort. They also lead to avoiding people or situations you fear or worry about.

There are many strategies for coping with anxiety or worry.[4-6] The first is to figure out what causes these feelings. Then you can address the problems or situations that trigger them. If they are real problems, then you can work on solving them. If they are potential problems that you anticipate, you can question whether or not they are likely to occur. Change how you think, because the problem you are anxious about may never occur and may be based on distorted thinking.

Evaluate your diet, as using too much caffeine and sugar can contribute to anxiety. If you smoke a lot, nicotine can play a factor in increasing your anxiety. It also helps to evaluate your lifestyle to make sure that you get enough rest, relaxation, and exercise. Exercise can help reduce anxiety, too.

Change your anxious and worrisome thoughts, such as always expecting the worst to happen. Challenge yourself by examining the "facts." If you feel anxious about a job interview and tell yourself, "I'm not going to get this job," question how you know ahead of time that you won't get the job. Then say to yourself, "by preparing for the job interview I give myself a better chance. I won't let my anxiety control me and pull me down." Give yourself positive messages such as "I can control my anxiety, I'm not going to let it get the best of me," "it's okay to make mistakes, no one has to be perfect," "the worst is not going to happen like I predict." This helps fight off negative messages, and it can raise your confidence.

If you practice proper breathing, you can control the physical symptoms caused by your anxiety, such as a rapid heartbeat. Meditation and relaxation help calm you down and may even help prevent anxiety from building up.

Talking about your anxious feelings and thoughts with other people helps, too. You can share anxious feelings with others in 12-step or other self-help meetings or in counseling sessions. Some people find it helpful to set aside worry time each day so that they can spend 10 or 20 minutes worrying during this designated time, rather than worrying continuously the whole day long.

You can keep a journal and write down your thoughts and feelings related to anxiety-provoking situations. You can use the same four-column format as the anger log described earlier (see page 113).

One of the most effective strategies is to directly face the situations that cause you to feel anxious. Usually you will find out that the reality of the situation is seldom as bad as your worrisome thoughts about it. Start by facing the least threatening anxiety- or worry-provoking situations and then slowly build

Strategies for Coping With Anxiety and Worry

1. Know the signs and symptoms of excessive anxiety or worry so that you can "catch" yourself when you feel anxious or worry too much.
2. Find out what is causing your anxiety.
3. Get a physical exam to determine whether medical problems are contributing to anxiety.
4. Evaluate your diet to figure out whether you use excessive amounts of caffeine or sugar.
5. Make sure you get enough rest, relaxation, and exercise.
6. Meditate to help you feel calmer and reduce your anxiety.
7. Use relaxation techniques.
8. Practice proper breathing techniques.
9. Change your beliefs or thoughts that contribute to your anxiety and worry.
10. Discuss your anxious feelings and thoughts with others.
11. Set aside "worry" time each day so that you have a place and regular time to let your worries out.
12. Write your thoughts and feelings in a journal.
13. Face the situations that cause you to feel anxious and to worry.
14. If your anxiety causes you significant distress despite abstinence and involvement in therapy, seek a medication evaluation.

Source: Daley, D. C. (2000). *Dual diagnosis workbook: Recovery strategies for substance use and mental health problems* (2nd ed., pp. 81–85). Independence, MO: Independence Press.

up to the more difficult ones. As you face these situations, your confidence level will grow, and anxiety will decrease.

If you have chronic anxiety and worry, don't expect it to go away totally. A more realistic goal is to reduce your level of anxiety and worry and to live more comfortably with it. Medications are sometimes used to treat symptoms of anxiety disorders that cause considerable distress or interfere with your life (see Chapter 6). The chart on page 115 lists strategies to cope with anxiety and worry.[3]

Boredom

Boredom is often used as an excuse to use alcohol or drugs. It may result from "missing the action" of using substances. Many people with chronic mood disorders who are unemployed have a lot of time on their hands and feel bored if they don't keep busy or feel productive.

You may also feel bored with your job or with a personal relationship. This kind of boredom should be discussed with your therapist before you make any major decisions, because it is different from the type in which you don't have things to do with your time. Avoid impulsively quitting a job or ending a relationship with which you are bored.

One strategy for coping with boredom is to regain some of the activities that you gave up as your addiction or mood disorder progressed. These should be activities that bring you a sense of fun and pleasure and don't involve alcohol or other drug use. You can also develop new interests. Start by choosing one new activity and making plans to do it. Make a conscious effort to build fun into your day-to-day life. You may find it helpful to plan a daily or weekly list of pleasant activities.

Figure out your high-risk times for feeling bored. Because weekends and evenings are the times when you are most likely to desire alcohol or other drugs, structure activities that are fun and enjoyable. Involve other people so you are not alone. Attending support groups can also help you keep busy and lower your relapse risk.

If you are a "hyper" person, like to live on the edge, need a lot of action, or tend to be someone with high energy, you have to learn to appreciate some of the simple pleasures in life. It won't always be possible to engage in activities that are exciting and action oriented.

Strategies for Managing Boredom

1. Build structure in your daily life to minimize free time.
2. Set goals to work toward.
3. Know your high-risk times for boredom and develop plans to keep busy.
4. Regain enjoyable activities that you gave up due to your addiction or mood disorder.
5. Develop new leisure interests and hobbies.
6. Try something different from your usual interests.
7. Take initiative and don't expect others to keep you from being bored.
8. Plan a vacation or a trip.
9. Challenge your thinking when you become bored or feel lonely or depressed.
10. Expect some boredom and accept it as normal.
11. Participate in social activities sponsored by recovery clubs or self-help groups.
12. Go slowly in making major changes based on boredom with a relationship or job.
13. Get involved in meaningful activities, organizations, and relationships.
14. Start a club based on an interest you share with other people.

Source: Daley, D. C. (2000). *Dual diagnosis workbook: Recovery strategies for substance use and mental health problems* (2nd ed., pp. 86–90). Independence, MO: Independence Press.

Change your thoughts and beliefs about boredom, such as the belief that you need constant action in order to feel good or alive. Don't expect never to be bored and for other people to take responsibility for making your boredom go away. Keep busy or find things that make you feel good. Challenge thoughts such as "I need alcohol or drugs in order to have fun or cope with my boredom" and replace them with thoughts such as "just because I'm feeling bored doesn't mean I need to get high." Above are strategies to help manage your boredom.[3]

Depression

Alcohol or drugs or the long-term effects of addiction on your life can cause or worsen depression. Addiction or manic behaviors can lead to loss of relationships, jobs, money, and self-esteem. Dreams are often shattered and potential is wasted, causing depression. A relapse to substance use or a recurrence of mania can also cause you to feel depressed.

Some people get more depressed the longer they are sober as a result of an underlying depressive illness that is independent of addiction. Clinical depression differs from normal feelings of depression in the persistence, intensity, duration, and effects of the mood. Clinical depression can linger for weeks or months and can be crippling.

Coping with depression puts you in a better position to stay sober and to feel better about yourself.[7-15] One strategy for managing depressed feelings is to figure out what problems contribute to your feeling depressed and resolve these problems. For example, if you feel depressed because you hate your job or because you are overweight, then you need to do something about your problem.

Feeling depressed won't always be related to specific stresses, problems, or events that occur in your life. People who have recurrent depression can experience symptoms as a result of the illness itself. Internal biological factors contribute to symptoms of depression in cases such as this.

Another strategy is to evaluate your relationships with others to see whether you are involved in unsatisfying or unhealthy relationships that lower your mood. You may have to develop new relationships or improve the ones that are causing you to feel upset and depressed. For example, if your emotional needs are not being satisfied in your current relationship and this is getting you down, talk with your partner about your needs and what you would like from him or her. If you try different ways of problem solving or communication and you still feel your relationship is very dissatisfying, then you may wish to consider ending it. Relationships only work if they are mutual and if both parties want to meet each other's needs.

Unresolved or traumatic grief related to a major loss is another possible factor in depression. Usually, this relates to loss of an important relationship through separation, divorce, or death. In some cases, a loss may have resulted from an awful experience, such as a loved one dying in military combat or in an accident or even being murdered. Whereas some people work through their grief on their own with the support of loved ones or friends in self-help support groups, others need therapy or counseling.

Loss of a job or career, of financial security, of an important hobby, or of functioning can cause a grief reaction, too. Some people suffer a grief reaction when they "lose" their active addiction. Despite the damage that substances caused, you are likely to "miss" using. You may feel angry and bitter because you feel you "can't" use substances. Some people with serious mood disorders, especially bipolar illness, experience a "loss of healthy self."

Making amends to other people who have been hurt by your behaviors is another way of reducing your depression. Your sponsor or counselor can guide you in determining with whom, how, and when you should make amends. This action can lessen feelings of guilt and shame, which often contribute to depression.

Keep active and force yourself to participate in hobbies, interests, or social activities even if you don't want to. Regular physical activity—walking, running, sports, working out—can help improve your mood. So can involvement in enjoyable activities. Try to participate in at least one pleasant activity every day. It doesn't even matter what the activity is as long as it is something that you find enjoyable or relaxing. Sometimes your feelings will change only after you participate in pleasant activities. It helps to have something in life to feel passionate about, something you really look forward to doing, which brings you a sense of positive involvement or enjoyment in life. It really doesn't matter what this passion is—reading, traveling, gardening, watching old movies, writing, painting, playing a musical instrument, restoring old cars or furniture, collecting certain things, and so forth. What matters is your feeling of investment in and enjoyment of this passion.

Share your feelings and problems with your counselor, a sponsor, and close friends or at a support group meeting. This can provide relief from bothersome feelings and help you look at your problems differently. However, I recommend against constantly talking about feeling bad to other people, as this might turn other people off and push them away. Therefore, another helpful strategy is to focus on positive things in your life and even to try to say positive things in your conversations with other people.

Figure out whether other feelings contribute to your depression. It isn't unusual to feel depressed as a result of having chronic anxiety or of pushing anger deep down inside and never letting it out. You can then figure out ways to work through these other feelings to improve your depressed mood.

Learn new ways of thinking about how you evaluate problems or situations. Challenge your negative, pessimistic, or depressed thoughts. Use self-talk strategies to give yourself new messages. Instead of saying, "I made a mistake and I'm a big failure," you can tell yourself "everyone makes mistakes. I'll try to learn something from this. It's no reason to beat myself up. In fact I do a lot of things right." Instead of jumping to the wrong conclusion about a situation and making yourself feel depressed, examine all the facts to see if your conclusion is warranted.

You can write about your depression and related feelings in a journal. Use the same kind of log that I described in the section on anger. The only difference is that this is a depression log in which you keep track of situations associated with depression or sadness, the degree to which you feel depressed, your specific thoughts, and coping strategies.

Identify and plan future activities that you can look forward to enjoying, such as saving up to buy something nice, going on a trip or vacation, or going out to a social event you think will be enjoyable. This can break up the monotony of daily life and give you something to focus your attention on. It doesn't matter whether the future event relates to fun, work, school, or a family activity.

If you have chronic and persistent depression, don't expect it to go away totally. A more realistic goal is to reduce your level of depression and learn to function the best that you can despite your depressed feelings.

The more severe forms of depressive illness benefit from antidepressant medications. Medications are usually used in combination therapy or counseling (see Chapter 6). The following chart summarizes strategies for managing depressed feelings:[3]

Strategies for Managing Depressed Feelings

1. Abstain from alcohol or drugs.
2. Address personal problems that contribute to your depression.
3. Evaluate your relationships with others to determine whether changes need to be made.
4. Make amends to others who have been hurt by your behaviors.
5. Keep active in your family and social relationships and with your hobbies.
6. Exercise regularly and do something physical each day.
7. Talk about your feelings and problems.
8. Look for other emotions or feelings that may contribute to, or be associated with, depression (such as anger, loneliness, or guilt and shame).
9. Challenge and change your depressed, cynical, or negative thoughts.
10. Increase your positive thoughts and focus on positive things in your life.
11. Write about your depressed feelings in a journal.
12. Participate in pleasant activities every day.
13. Identify and plan future activities that you can look forward to enjoying.
14. Consider medications if you have a recurrent or chronic form of depression.
15. If you first try therapy for depression but don't improve despite being abstinent from alcohol or other drugs, consider an evaluation for an antidepressant medicine.

Source: Daley, D. C. (2000). *Dual diagnosis workbook: Recovery strategies for substance use and mental health problems* (2nd ed., pp. 91–96). Independence, MO: Independence Press.

Feeling Empty

Many people with an addiction and depression say they feel "empty" and don't have much in their lives that makes them feel good. If you feel empty, it's hard to experience joy or pleasure. You may feel that your life has no sense of direction, meaning, or purpose to it. This can cause you to feel miserable and puts you at risk for relapse to alcohol or drug use or to depression. Sometimes, the emptiness results from the negative consequences of your disorders. Other times it results from not being involved in important relationships or activities that make you feel good about yourself and your contributions to society.

One way to help yourself is to focus your time and energy on nurturing your relationships with others. Sharing time with family or friends, expressing love and positive feelings toward them, and taking an interest in them are ways to nurture your relationships. The more you are connected with other people, the less likely you are to feel empty, isolated, or alone.

Involvement in the spiritual aspect of recovery reduces emptiness. This involves developing a relationship with a Higher Power or God as a way of gaining a sense of meaning in your life. You can pray, read the Bible, or communicate in any personal way that you want to with your Higher Power. Involvement in services or activities at your church, synagogue, or other place of worship can help as well.

Focus on what goes right in your life, what you have achieved, what you can achieve in the future, and important activities in which you are involved. Get involved in activities that bring you a sense of excitement about life or give you something to look forward to doing.

One of the most effective ways of reducing emptiness is to help or be of service to other people. Getting involved in a cause or doing something nice for a friend, family member, or another member of a support group can make you feel good. Helping out at 12-step meetings or serving as a sponsor to others once you have made some good progress in your own recovery are just a few ways of serving other people. Even little actions, such as giving people rides to meetings or listening to their troubles over a cup of coffee after a meeting, are ways of being of service. There are numerous things you can do to help friends or family, such as lending a hand to help with a project or job or listening to their experiences, interests, concerns, or problems. Doing volunteer work or coaching sports teams are other ways of serving others.

Strategies for Managing Feelings of Emptiness

1. Build structure into your life so that you participate in activities that are both important and enjoyable.	7. Do things to help other people.
2. Figure out what has meaning and value in your life.	8. Ask your therapist to help you understand and cope with persistent feelings of emptiness.
3. Find something that you can feel passionate about (an activity, cause, etc.).	9. Become more self-reliant and tell yourself that you can function without substances.
4. Nurture your relationships with family or friends.	10. Set goals to work toward (short and long term).
5. Minimize time spent alone, especially on weekends or at times when you are vulnerable to feeling alone and empty.	11. Reduce self-critical remarks and focus on your positive qualities and achievements.
6. Ask for help from your Higher Power and get involved in the spiritual aspect of recovery.	12. Use self-comforting strategies (see page 172).
	13. Read recovery literature to gain inspiration, hope, and guidance.

Source: Daley, D. C. (2001). *Coping with feelings workbook* (2nd ed., pp. 47–49). Holmes Beach, FL: Learning Publications.

Having structure in your life or a sense of direction and goals for the future can reduce your emptiness. If you aimlessly go from day to day and have no goals, nothing to look forward to, or no structure in your life, you are likely to continue feeling empty. This puts you at risk for relapse to substance use, depression, and involvement in unhealthy relationships or activities.

Attending support group meetings and working with 12-step programs are other ways to cope with emptiness. The 12 steps provide an excellent way to develop a reliance on a Higher Power, to seek forgiveness from other people who have been hurt by your addiction, to make amends, and to carry the message of recovery to others. The chart above summarizes strategies for managing feelings of emptiness:[1]

Guilt and Shame

Many people feel guilty about and ashamed of their disorders. Guilt is feeling bad about your behaviors or things that you have done or failed to do. Shame is feeling bad about yourself, feeling that there is something defective about you, that you are "weak" or a failure. Whereas some people feel more shame and stigma because of their mood disorders, others feel more shame because of their addictions.

There is no quick or easy way to let go of your guilty or shameful feelings. Because change usually comes in small steps, you have to accept that feeling a little less guilty or shameful is a sign of progress. Your progress will be connected to making positive changes in yourself and your lifestyle, to maintaining abstinence from alcohol, street drugs, or nonprescribed substances, and to improving your mood disorder.

Talking over your feelings of guilt and shame with others in recovery and honestly admitting things you did to hurt others is an important part of the healing process. It helps to share the details of the specific things you did or failed to do that you feel hurt another person with someone who won't judge you. Steps 1–5 (see page 163) are very helpful in working through guilt and shame. Step 5 allows you to admit the things you did to hurt others. Many people find it helpful to do the fifth step with a member of the clergy or a sponsor. Be careful, however, not to rush this step. Get some sober time under your belt first.

Working steps 8 and 9 and making amends to others who were hurt by your behaviors puts you in a position to receive forgiveness or understanding

Strategies for Coping With Feelings of Guilt and Shame

1. Accept your disorders as "no-fault" illnesses (use Step 1) and accept yourself as having dual disorders rather than being a "weak" person.

2. Don't expect instant relief from feelings of guilt and shame; give yourself time to work through these.

3. Share your feelings of guilt and shame with a sponsor, therapist, minister, priest, or rabbi so that you can learn to forgive yourself (use Step 5).

4. Show responsible behaviors in your daily life and in your relationships.

5. Make amends to people hurt by your behaviors (use Steps 8 and 9).

6. Make your current relationships count by spending time with, and taking an interest in, the lives of family and friends.

7. Don't use the past as an excuse to drink or use drugs again or as an excuse to justify immature, inappropriate, or self-centered behaviors.

Source: Daley, D. C. (2001). *Coping with feelings workbook* (2nd ed., pp. 53–54). Holmes Beach, FL: Learning Publications.

from them. Your sponsor or counselor can help guide you through this process of making amends.

Asking other people whom you hurt with your behaviors for forgiveness can help reduce guilt and shame. However, there is a risk that other people may not be willing to forgive you for things that you said or did. If you ask for forgiveness, you have to be sincere, and your behaviors have to back up your words. If you apologize and seek forgiveness but continue self-destructive or hurtful behaviors toward others, they will find it hard to forgive you.

Forgiving yourself and accepting your mistakes and limitations is another healing strategy. Rather than blame yourself for having a mood disorder and addiction, accept these as "no-fault illnesses" that happened for a variety of physiological and psychological reasons. By taking responsibility for making positive changes in yourself and staying sober, you are likely to feel good about yourself. Step 1 is especially helpful in accepting your disorders as "no fault." Strategies for managing guilt and shame are summarized on page 123.[1]

Love and Positive Emotions

Sharing positive feelings such as love, joy, happiness, affection, caring, and interest with other people can improve your relationships and raise your self-esteem. Others are then likely to share positive feelings toward you.

One way to express positive feelings is to tell people directly how you feel. For example, you can tell your parents that you love them or you miss them, or tell your children how important they are to you. Show your positive feelings in your behaviors, as well, because actions speak louder than words. You can tell someone you love him or her, but if you don't back this statement with your behavior, then it is going to be less meaningful to the other person. You show love or other positive feelings by listening to others, taking an active interest in their lives, doing nice things for them, giving them gifts, making them feel important, spending time with them, and being available to give them emotional support. My experience is that people who give to others and express their positive feelings have the most satisfying relationships. Giving to other people is important in having a mutual relationship, not just "taking" from them. Giving to others requires an ability to see things from their point of view and a desire to do good for others.

Steps for Managing Feelings

1. Recognize and label your feelings.
2. Be aware of how your different feelings show in your body language, thoughts, and behavior.
3. Figure out what causes you to experience a particular feeling.
4. Take a look at how your feelings, as well as how you cope with them, affect you and your relationships with other people.
5. Identify verbal, cognitive, and behavioral coping strategies you can use to deal with your feelings.
6. Rehearse or practice verbal strategies ahead of time, before you share them directly with another person.
7. Put your coping strategies into action and use them on a regular basis.
8. Change your coping strategies as needed, based on evaluating whether or not they help you.

Source: Daley, D. C. (2001). *Coping with feelings workbook* (2nd ed., pp. 13–15). Holmes Beach, FL: Learning Publications.

A Problem-Solving Approach for Dealing With Feelings

Managing your feelings can reduce your risk of relapse, help you feel better about yourself, and lead to better personal relationships. Above is a brief summary of steps you can take to identify and cope with your feelings.[1]

Listen to how Lester, Tunisia, and Linda are coping with some of their feelings. See if you can relate to anything that they say.

Letting Go of Anger

A lot of anger and resentment had built up inside me over the years. I started dealing with this by first making a list of the people I felt angry at and figuring out how mad I really was at them versus myself 'cause I blamed others for my troubles. I talked this list over with my therapist who helped me realize most of my anger wasn't justified. She also taught me how to let my feelings out in a safe way. She taught me to overcome my fear of losing control of my anger and getting violent so I could "get even" with the people I thought done me wrong in the past. I'm learning to share my feelings with my sponsor and NA friends so that anger doesn't build up. 'Cause if I let it build, I know what will happen—I'll use again. You know, I used to think a lot of people who talked about praying and using a Higher Power were practicing religious mumbo-jumbo. But I'm getting it. Sometimes it blows me away to think that I'm praying, and asking God for help and strength. 'Cause I used to only depend on myself. —Lester

Life Is No Longer Empty

For years, I couldn't stand being alone. I felt like nothing and a nobody unless I was in a relationship with a man. The problem was that I kept picking losers, men who treated me poorly. Some even abused me but I kept putting up with them. I just hated the idea of being alone. But, as I got sober and worked hard at recovery, I accepted that I don't need to find my identity in somebody else. I have many good friends, some of whom are in AA. I stay away from relationships with men who can't give anything back. I'm more comfortable with myself now. My work is important, too. My life is no longer empty and I don't have to fill it with bad relationships or alcohol. —Linda

I'm Getting More Love in My Life

I've been a hard-core addict for a long time. Been depressed and suicidal and at the end of my rope. For a long time, I never felt nobody loved or cared for me. I had to start by loving myself and believing I was somebody. Only then was I able to show some love to others. Before, all I did was look out for me. Didn't care about nobody and only thought about how I could rip people off. I've been slowly learning to care for other people. I'm living in a halfway house. I've been learning to care about the other sisters here. I'm calling my mother every week and visiting whenever I get a chance. Since I've learned to care about others more, I'm also getting more love in my life. Last year, I didn't care if I lived or died. Now, I want to live. I want to be somebody. —Tunisia

Recognizing the Feelings of Others

According to Daniel Goleman, one of the most important "emotional intelligence" skills is the ability to show empathy toward others.[16,17] To do this requires an awareness of the feelings and experiences of others, as well as taking an interest in the things that concern them. This requires learning how to read body language, gestures, and tone of voice and being able to figure out what another is saying. Sometimes you have to hear things from others that you would prefer not hearing, such as anger or disappointment. Listening to another who expresses a feeling that causes you discomfort, without being defensive or hostile and lashing out at them, takes patience and skill. The same holds true for listening to positive feelings expressed by others. The more adept you are at listening and hearing what others are feeling, the better chance you have for genuine communication.

Chapter 8   *Building a Support System*

How a Support System Can Help You

Recovery is a "we" program in which you are encouraged to seek support from other people for help with cravings to use, ups and downs of recovery, unpleasant feelings, relapse warning signs, and other problems.[1-5] You can ask the people in your network for emotional support when you feel upset. Or you can ask for help with practical matters, such as a ride to a meeting or moving furniture. However, if you ask someone for help with a problem, then reject the ideas given to you, they may be reluctant to help you in the future.

Stay connected with other people with whom you can get your needs for love, intimacy, companionship, or even fun satisfied. Satisfying your needs should decrease any desire to use alcohol or drugs. This strategy has the added benefit of improving your mood and self-esteem. You will feel better about yourself when you are close to other people and satisfied with your relationships. Sharing time on mutual interests or hobbies with others can reduce isolation and serve as a protective factor against relapse.

Who to Include in Your Support System

Discussions with people in your support network put you in a position to identify problems early. Small problems can be caught and dealt with *before* they become large problems. This in turn helps you figure out steps that you can take to deal with problems and reduces your risk of relapse.

A sponsor in AA, NA, or DRA can guide you in "working the program" of recovery by teaching you the ropes, by sharing his or her experiences, strength, and hope, by listening to your struggles, by sharing your successes, and by introducing you to other people in recovery. A sponsor can also help you see when you are slacking off your program and at risk for a relapse. Talking regularly by phone and attending meetings together allow you to take full advantage of your sponsor's experience, wisdom, and support.

Other members of self-help groups can support you by sharing their personal experiences, discussing recovery issues, and being there for you when you need someone with whom to talk. Having a "home group" puts you in a position to regularly see people who know you. People who know you are more likely to give you help and support, as well as point out any concerns they have about you slipping back to old habits or behaviors. Also, some may reach out to you when they sense you are having a rough time or stop attending meetings.

You can attend meetings and meet others at recovery clubs. Sometimes, just being around others in recovery gives you a sense of support and security. Recovery clubs often sponsor social activities that are fun and enjoyable, such as dances, picnics, and trips to social events.

Members of your treatment team, such as your doctor, therapist or counselor, or case manager, can be consulted in times of serious psychiatric or substance use emergencies. They can also help you figure out ways to develop or expand your support network. Although professionals can help you in many ways, I recommend that you use others in your support system as much as possible, as these are the people most available to you.

Close friends or family members can be included in your support network. However, if they have been hurt by your behaviors, consider making amends to them before you ask them to be part of your network. Steps 8 and 9 of AA, NA, or DRA can help in this process (step 8 says, "made a list of all persons we had harmed and became willing to make amends to them all"; step 9 says, "made direct amends to such people wherever possible, except when to do so would injure them or others").

Friends and family whom you invite to be part of your recovery network should be those who don't harbor intense anger or hostility toward you. Ideally, they should understand your disorders and attend some treatment sessions with you and/or support groups for themselves.

How to Ask for Help and Support From Others

You may have to overcome your own reluctance to ask for help and support. Be direct in your request and let people know that you are in recovery for a mood disorder and addiction. Be as specific as you can in terms of what kind of help and support you need from them. Then be gracious in accepting help or support that is offered. Below is a summary of strategies that can help you build a recovery network.

Resisting Social Pressures to Get High

A common cause of relapse is an inability to resist social pressures to use alcohol or other drugs.[6–8] Social pressures may be direct, in which other people offer you alcohol or other drugs. Or they may be indirect and involve situations or events in which others around you are using but don't offer you alcohol or drugs. Social pressures include parties, graduation ceremonies, weddings, family gatherings, picnics, birthdays, sporting events, and socializing after work.

Strategies for Building a Recovery Network

1. Face your fears or reluctance to ask for help and support from others.
2. Identify supportive family members and friends who would be willing to be part of your recovery network.
3. Be specific when asking others to be part of your recovery network, and clarify what you want from them.
4. Get a list of phone numbers of people in mental health, addiction, or dual-recovery self-help groups.
5. Talk to someone in "the program" every day.
6. Find a "home" group.
7. Identify organizations that can be part of your recovery network.
8. Join at least one of these within the first 2 months of recovery.
9. If you have trouble asking others for help and support, see a therapist to help you figure out why, as well as how you can get support from others.
10. Don't make excuses about why you can't find a sponsor, and make a commitment to ask for a sponsor, even a temporary one.
11. Talk with your sponsor every day, and let him or her guide you in using the 12 steps.
12. Ask your sponsor for feedback regarding your progress in recovery so that you can identify changes you need to make.
13. Remember that recovery is a "we" program and is not meant to be something that you do alone.

Strategies for Resisting Social Pressures

1. Anticipate social pressures you will face, then figure out a few different ways to tell people that you don't want to use alcohol or other drugs if they offer them to you.
2. Be assertive when resisting pressures to use. Say no and mean it! Hold to your position.
3. Get out of high-pressure situations and events as quickly as you can, particularly if you are worried that you will give in to the pressure.
4. If there is a social event that is important for you to attend, such as a wedding party or graduation, and alcohol will be available, take a support person with you so that you can talk with them to help you cope with this potential social pressure.
5. Avoid situations and events in which you know deep down that there is no way you can survive without using. Don't fool yourself by pretending you can cope when you know very well that it's a setup.

It is not the situation but how it affects your thoughts or feelings and your coping skills that determines whether you will use alcohol or drugs. If you are pressured to use, a part of you that still wants to use may think, "I want to fit in," "a few won't hurt," or "how can I have fun if I'm not using and the other people are?" You may feel threatened and scared that you'll give in to pressures. Or you may feel excited about using because you miss it or you miss being with others who use.

Awareness of the social pressures and the high-risk people and situations that you may face puts you in a better position to stay sober.[6]

Relationship Traps to Avoid

Relationship problems can pose a threat to your recovery, cause major hassles in your life, and affect your mood or substance abuse. Following is a discussion of relationship traps to avoid or to ask a therapist or sponsor for help in dealing with.

Quick Romances

Establish several months or more of solid recovery before getting involved in a new romantic relationship. Quick romances can lead to focusing more on the relationship than on your recovery. A new romantic relationship with someone just starting recovery is an even higher risk situation with potential disaster written all over it.

Moving in With Someone You Don't Know Well

Avoid moving in with a lover or other person whom you don't know very well. Such arrangements often go sour because the two people who make an impulsive decision to live together don't really know enough about each other to get a feel for whether or not it will work. If one of the partners has children, they often suffer as a result, because they are not emotionally ready for another adult to move in with their mother or father. In addition, kids who become attached to the partner may feel a loss when the relationship suddenly ends, which it often does.

Relationship Hopping

Jumping from one relationship to the next in search of the "perfect" mate or partner or in search of "excitement" is another trap to avoid. This occurs as a result of immaturity, self-centeredness, an inability to make a commitment in a relationship, or a need to run away from a relationship when it has problems or scares you.

Boredom With Spouse or Partner

Most people get bored with their spouses or partners from time to time. However, avoid letting this boredom drag your relationship down. Instead, work with your partner to find new ways of making your relationship fun, enjoyable, or exciting.

Focusing Mainly on Sex

When sex is the primary focus of a relationship, you are less likely to take an interest in your partner's life. Although this may satisfy your sexual needs, seldom will it satisfy your emotional needs. Relationships with multiple partners raise the risk of diseases and infections. Too much focus on sex can detract from your recovery.

Staying in an Abusive Relationship

Despite difficulties leaving such a relationship, continuing is psychologically harmful. Physical safety can be jeopardized as well. A person who abuses another lacks respect and self-control. Do not let yourself be subject to such a relationship. And don't fool yourself into believing that you can change your abusive partner or that your partner will change simply because he apologized to you after hurting you.

Relationships With Addicts Who Still Get High

Living with, or hanging out with, addicts who still get high raises your risk of relapse. They can influence you to use substances. You can become disgusted with a mate or partner who still gets high, say "the hell with it," and start using again. If you are with friends who are using, you might "miss the action" and feel like you don't fit in if you don't use. Seeing friends with alcohol, drugs, or paraphernalia can trigger strong cravings to use.

"Me"-Centered Relationships

One-way relationships revolving around "me" are destined to fail, unless one person lacks a sense of self and constantly feeds the other person's ego. People who focus primarily on "me" burn others out, push them away, turn them off, and anger them. Balanced relationships that focus on the needs of both individuals are much healthier. This requires learning how to "give" and to focus on the needs and interests of other people, how to express your needs, and how to make demands on your partner so that you "get" something from the relationship.

"You"-Centered Relationships

Some people give too much to others and constantly focus on the other person, often at the expense of taking care of their own needs. They become doormats and get used by others. Even though they allow this to continue, they harbor resentment and feel like victims. Again, balance is needed so that you can "get" as well as "give" to others.

Ignoring Your Family

Families are affected by mood and substance use disorders. Pay attention to your family members by giving them your time, showing interest in them, doing things with and for them, and not taking them for granted. Talk with them about your problems and recovery. Invite them to some of your therapy sessions and encourage them to attend self-help programs for families. Chapter 9 focuses on working with your family.

Ignoring Your Children

Children are the innocent victims of parental addiction or mood disorders.[4,9–10] They may have been exposed to scary or confusing behaviors, such as intoxication, mania, depression, withdrawal, violence, or suicide threats. It's easy to overlook their needs as you focus on recovery and changing yourself. Your children need to understand what's been going on with you and how all of this affected them. They also need your love, time, and attention. I've heard many recovering people say they felt bad regarding the impact of their behaviors on their children, then fail to talk with or change anything in their relationship with their kids. You can't go back and change the past, but you can change the present. Be sure to focus on your children.

Improving Your Communication

A way to strengthen relationships is to improve your communication.[3] Healthy communication requires a willingness to express your thoughts, feelings, opinions, and needs. This also means sharing distress and difficulties, upsetting feelings, and positive feelings such as love or caring. It means being able to talk about things that go well for you in your life, too. If you always focus on the negative, you can push people away or turn them off.

An important part of communication involves being able to listen and understand what other people are sharing with you. Effective communication has to be mutual. You have to listen to others and hear what they say to you. Avoid turning conversations back to yourself.

Brenda is recovering from depression, an anxiety disorder, and alcoholism. She had a long history of poor communication with her family, often keeping things to herself and acting them out in passive-aggressive ways. She used to let her husband make most of the decisions, then she would secretly brood because she resented the fact that her needs weren't getting satisfied. Following is Brenda's description of how she changed her pattern of poor communication.

I used to show my feelings by giving my husband the "silent treatment" or making critical and sarcastic remarks to him. I'd act like nothing was wrong and deny I was upset when he would ask me if anything were bothering me. With my kids I was more direct, often yelling at them and criticizing them for little things. With both my husband and kids, I found myself holding onto positive feelings, too, especially if I was carrying around anger.

In recovery, I worked hard at being direct with my husband and kids. I learned to be up front with my feelings and found out that by sharing anger early, it made it easier to work out differences. I learned to calm myself down and share anger in a way that did not put others down or criticize them. Plus, I was more likely to share my positive feelings with them. I learned from my therapist to take an inventory at the end of the day to make sure I wasn't letting things build up. This helped prevent a lot of little things from becoming major problems because I caught them early.

Since I had also been passive in letting my husband know what I wanted, I worked on expressing my needs. Actually, this was very helpful because I found out if I let my needs be known he would consider them. So now, instead of letting my husband always decide where we go for vacations or where we go for a date, I express my desires. Speaking up and being assertive has helped me feel better about myself. It also has made things better at home, too.

Improving Your Relationships

There are a number of other steps you can take to improve your relationships.[3] One is to take an active interest in the lives of other people who are important to you. Don't keep all the focus on yourself. Show an interest in what others are doing and what is important to them. Ask questions to find out more about them and encourage them to talk about things they are doing or interested in. Find out their opinions about things going on in the world. Make yourself available to support other people emotionally. Simply being available to talk with or do things with others can be a great source of comfort to them.

Do helpful or positive things for others, such as helping your children with homework, helping a friend move furniture, or acknowledging important events or dates in the lives of other people, such as birthdays and holidays. Doing nice things for others will make you feel better about yourself. Although you want to keep recovery your number one priority, it helps to get outside of yourself and focus on other people.

Derrick is recovering from bipolar illness and cocaine and alcohol addiction. Prior to getting involved in recovery, his relationships were one-sided. Derrick "used" others, including his family, and seldom showed interest in anyone but himself. He ignored his son, who lives with his ex-wife. Here is his description of steps he has taken to improve his relationships.

> I was definitely self-centered, always focusing on me and what I needed. It was hard for me to care about other people because I was always looking out for number one. About the only time I would call or visit my parents was when I needed money from them. And I always forgot their birthdays and anniversary.
>
> With my girlfriend, we always did what I wanted to do. Although we had been together a good while, I didn't know too much about her because I never asked her much about herself or what she was interested in.
>
> I'm ashamed to admit that my 8-year-old son had been ignored. I seldom saw or called him. And I never knew much about what was happening in his life because I simply never asked.
>
> In recovery, I'm focusing on ways to make my relationships more mutual. I call my parents every week and visit them every few weeks, just to see how they are doing and if they need me to do anything for them. I ask my girlfriend questions about how her day went, what she thinks about things, and what she's interested in. I don't tune her out and focus only on myself like I used to.
>
> The change I feel most proud of is becoming a father to my son. I talk with him a couple times every week by phone. I ask him about school and other things going on in his life. Plus, every week I see him at least once or twice and he spends one weekend a month at my apartment. I

know I can never change the past and give him what I cheated him out of, but I'm trying hard to make things better now.

Being a responsible father has helped motivate me to work harder in my recovery because there have been a few times when I wanted to get high very bad. Remembering what my addiction and mood disorder did to my relationship with my son helps me stay on track.

Family and Interpersonal Conflict

Some people are passive and avoid conflict at all costs, often stuffing their feelings inside. They don't want "to upset the apple cart." They express their dislike or upset feelings in passive-aggressive ways, such as dragging their feet, criticizing others behind their backs, "forgetting" important occasions such as

Strategies for Coping With Relationship Conflict

1. Be aware of the specific family and interpersonal conflicts you have as a result of your mood and addiction.
2. Face these conflicts head on instead of avoiding them or wishing them away.
3. When appropriate, make amends to others who have been hurt by your behaviors.
4. Be patient with others who may still be hurt by things you said or did.
5. Stay calm and maintain control during times in which you are discussing problems or conflicts with other people.
6. If you criticize others, avoid criticizing the person or attacking their character. Instead, focus your criticisms on specific behaviors that upset you.
7. Express your feelings and differences as directly as possible.
8. Compromise during arguments or disagreements when necessary.
9. Learn to apologize when you are wrong or when you say or do hurtful things.
10. Accept that it's normal to feel angry or have conflicts with other people, and keep in mind that the important issue is to work these conflicts out in a mutually satisfying manner.
11. If your style of conflict resolution is either too passive or too aggressive, use therapy to help you change how you resolve conflicts with others.
12. Spend time with family and close friends in order to nurture your relationships.
13. If you have children, take an active role in their lives. Be an involved parent, and be there to support, teach, and love them. Show them they can depend on you.

a loved one's birthday or anniversary, giving the "silent" treatment, or making life miserable for others. Or they let others "walk on them" and take advantage of them. They don't stand up for their rights, letting others tell them what to do, even when they are in disagreement.

Others get too aggressive and push their opinions, feelings, and thoughts on others. They show little regard for other peoples' points of view and say and do whatever they believe is right. They control others and may even intimidate them because the only way to resolve conflict is to do things "their way." If either of these two styles describes you, use therapy to help you understand and change how you deal with these conflicts.

Conflict and negative interactions can be a major source of stress and a factor in relapse to your mood or substance use disorder. Therefore, it helps to face and resolve your conflicts and differences so that upsetting feelings and negative thoughts don't build up inside you. Conflict resolution requires an ability to be assertive in expressing your thoughts and feelings, as well as an ability to listen to others so that their positions and feelings can be understood. Even if you argue with a loved one, if you avoid showing contempt and instead show empathy, compassion, and humor, the chances of bad feelings building up lessen. And the chances of understanding and accepting each other increase. Sometimes it's not so much the problem or issues you argue about but the way you go about arguing that determines the impact on your relationship.

Be willing to compromise so that things don't have to go your way. When you make mistakes and do something wrong, admit this and apologize. In 12-step programs, steps 8 and 9 are helpful in repairing damaged relationships. Ask a sponsor to guide you in using these steps. The chart on the previous page provides a summary of strategies to help you cope with relationship conflicts.

Chapter 9   *Working With Your Family*

Addiction and Mood Disorders Run in Families

Rates of addiction, depression, or bipolar disorder are higher among first-degree relatives (siblings or children) than among the general population.[1,2] For example, up to 1% of the general population will have bipolar illness, whereas up to 10% of first-degree relatives will have this illness. Major depression is about three times higher among first-degree relatives than among the general population. Rates of addiction are also higher among relatives of individuals with an addiction than among the general population. For example, a study of alcoholics and their siblings found that almost 50% of brothers and 25% of sisters of the alcoholic also met criteria for alcoholism at some point in their lives; these rates are about 2–4 times higher than the rates of alcoholism found in the general population. Studies of sons adopted soon after birth whose fathers had alcoholism show that these sons have much higher rates of alcoholism than do adopted sons whose biological fathers were not alcoholic.[3]

Why All Families Aren't Affected the Same Way

In chapter 1, I listed some of the effects of dual disorders on the family that have been reported by outpatients in treatment in my clinic. These included: creating an emotional burden on their families (anger, worry, fear, distrust);

neglecting their families; being irresponsible; verbally or physically abusing family members; creating financial problems; and family breakups. Although it is clear that families are often deeply hurt, not every family is affected in the same way by exposure to a mood disorder and addiction. The following brief family case histories illustrate this point—one family was hurt very deeply, whereas the negative effects on the other family were less devastating.

> Belinda's family suffered a tremendous emotional and financial burden as a result of her verbal and physical violence toward family members, her frequent suicide threats and one actual attempt, her skirmishes with the legal system, and her inability to support herself financially. Her parents are heartbroken that she hasn't been able to finish college, because she is such a bright person. Her parents squabble over how to handle her, and their relationship has suffered because of differences of opinion on what they should do. Belinda's mother feels guilty and wonders what she possibly could have done wrong to cause Belinda to act the way she does. Her parents sometimes feel hopeless when Belinda relapses to drug use, becomes depressed, or stops outpatient treatment. They know that her depression always worsens when she stops treatment, yet she won't listen to them.

> Ray's family, on the other hand, has not experienced the same burden as Belinda's family. Although concerned about Ray's drinking and bouts of depression, they never felt the hopelessness that Belinda's parents felt. Despite his dual disorders, Ray always managed to take pretty good care of his family. He was a loving father toward his daughter and son and at times pushed himself to interact with them during episodes of depression. Although his disorders had some negative impact on his family, Ray really tried hard to make sure his family was taken care of.

The effects of your disorders on your family will depend on several factors:[4] (1) the severity and length of your depression or bipolar illness and your substance use disorder; (2) their exposure to your drunkenness, drug intoxication, or out-of-control behavior such as suicidality, violence, or aggressiveness; (3) your ability to fulfill your roles (e.g., as parent, provider, partner, etc.); (4) your ability to meet your family responsibilities (e.g., economic, emotional, etc.); (5) how each family member views you and the nature of their relationship with you; and (6) the coping skills of family members. Some family members are hurt more than others. Part of how they respond is based on their personalities and coping mechanisms. Some children, for example, are much more resilient than others are. These kids can handle tough circumstances or "bounce back" from trauma or difficult family situations or life problems.[5–7] Exposure to other life experiences and positive relationships can help offset some of the problems caused by dual disorders. A recent report by the National Institute on Alcohol Abuse and Alcoholism identifies parent-child connectedness and school connectedness as factors that "protect" children from taking risks in health areas, such as substance use (specifically, use of cigarettes, alcohol, or marijuana).[8] A parent, grandparent, sibling, or other person may provide love, support, emotional nurturance, or guidance or motivation that helps a family member cope with their feelings. The following illustrates this.

> Matt is a 14-year-old whose father has bipolar disorder, alcoholism, and cocaine addiction. Over the years, he's been exposed to several episodes of his father's mania and depression and one relapse to alcohol and drug use. Matt's parents have spent considerable time with him discussing the father's disorders and his treatment. This has helped Matt better understand and cope with his father's episodes, especially when his father says bizarre things or makes promises that he breaks. Matt knows he can stay with his grandparents if his dad's condition gets too bad. Although Matt worries about his father, he's doing well in school and has many interests and many friends. The information and support provided by his mother and grandparents have helped him through rough times.

Chances are that your family has been exposed to negative aspects of your disorders. It is not always easy to separate out the effects that are caused by your behaviors and those that are caused by other factors. Therefore, don't assume that all of the difficulties and problems in your family are related to your dual disorders.

Effects on the Family Unit

The U.S. Department of Health and Human Services issued a report stating that parental substance abuse underlies many symptoms of family dysfunction, such as divorce, spousal abuse, child abuse and neglect, welfare dependence, and criminal behavior.[9] This single statement reflects the many serious problems associated with substance abuse in the family. This report goes on to say that kids exposed to these parental problems are at risk for addictive disorders themselves.

Howard, a very successful and well-respected physician, captures the personal anguish experienced in his family over his son Jason's heroin addiction and depression:

> My wife and I have been through hell with our son. Even though he's only 25 years old, Jason has been in more than 15 detox and rehab programs. He's also been in the psychiatric hospital twice. The guilt we felt was incredible. We asked ourselves over and over what could we possibly have done that may have made contributed to these serious problems. I took him to the best programs, doctors, and counselors in the city, and he still couldn't stay off drugs. Twice, he overdosed and almost died. He's threatened suicide many times. His mother is heartbroken, and we both have prepared for the possible reality that he may die from his addiction. Our other children have washed their hands of him and told us we are enablers; they get mad at us sometimes because they feel we spend too much time and emotional energy trying to help Jason. I can tell you this, there's nothing worse than watching your child ruined by drug addiction and depression. It's awful, just awful.

Bipolar illness or depressive disorders also affect families in many ways. Kay Jamison, an expert on mood disorders, captures the impact of bipolar disorders on family when she says:[10]

> Moods are by nature compelling, contagious, and profoundly interpersonal, and disorders of mood alter the perceptions and behaviors not only of those who have them but also of those who are related or closely associated. Manic-depressive illness—marked as it is by extraordinary and confusing fluctuations in mood, personality, thinking, and behavior— inevitably has powerful and often painful effects on relationships. (25–26)

Jamison goes on to talk specifically about the impact of bipolar disorder on marriages:

> The divorce rate among marriages in which a spouse is manic-depressive is very high. It is very demoralizing for a husband or wife to endure a day-to-day relationship with someone from whom they can't get a positive response, and who they can't help. (27)

Many other articles and books about mood, addiction, or dual disorders also document powerful and painful effects on families, as well as the need for support groups for families.[4,11–21] For example, the "Big Book" of Alcoholics Anonymous, written originally in the 1930s, includes two chapters that deal with the impact of alcoholism on wives and the family.[22] Self-help programs such as Al-Anon and Nar-Anon and those sponsored by the National Alliance for the Mentally Ill (NAMI) were developed precisely because of the pain experienced by families.[23] These support programs provide families with hope, support, and ideas on how to live with an ill member, as well as how to change.

Dual disorders can have a negative effect on communication in your family. Family members may be reluctant to share their feelings and concerns directly with you. The mood or atmosphere in the family can be tense or depressing. Some members live in fear, especially when exposed to suicidal threats and manic, unpredictable, or bizarre behaviors. Others are angry and bitter. The emotional burden felt by your family can be overwhelming for them. Sherri, a mother of a 21-year-old college student with bipolar illness and alcoholism, shared the following, which clearly captures how she felt and was affected by her daughter's disorders:

> My daughter has been hospitalized three times, once for being manic and way out of control, and twice when she was depressed and suicidal. After she got sick, I worried constantly about her, even when she was out of the hospital. I often stayed home because I was afraid if I left her alone, she might overdose on pills again. We even cancelled one of our summer vacations because I just couldn't leave her at home. I became very anxious and depressed. I gained more than 35 pounds, which made me feel worse about myself. There's no doubt in my mind that her problems had a big impact on our family.

Family members may minimize, deny, or cover up your disorders, often with good intentions. Some members are more accepting of your addiction, and others may more easily accept your mood disorder. Some families also experience a financial burden. Neil, whose wife had a problem with depression and cocaine addiction, describes both the financial and emotional burden he felt:

> I'm so damn tired. For years I was a nervous wreck because I always worried about my wife. When she was depressed I tried to lift her up. When she was getting high, I tried to make her want to stop using. Guess you

could say I really burned myself out. I got real angry because she wasted so much money on drugs. We were always behind on bills and deep in debt. Plus, it took away from our kids.

In some cases, families actually break up as a result of divorce or separation or because their children were removed by social service agencies. Jackie speaks about losing her kids.

I've had depression for years but always managed to take care of my kids. But when I started using crack cocaine, I went downhill real fast. Things got so bad that I was always running the streets and hardly ever home to take care of my kids. I got reported to Children and Youth Services after getting arrested and ended up losing my kids to a foster home. I know this was the best thing for them 'cause I wasn't a good mother at the time, but I miss them. I'm working hard at staying off drugs and hope to get my kids back.

In other cases family members bond closely together. They support each other and work together in dealing with the dual-disordered member. Although they may feel upset or distressed, they do whatever they can to make sure the family stays cohesive and works together.

Effects on Individual Family Members

Numerous studies show that family members are affected in many ways by alcohol or drug dependency, mood and other psychiatric disorders, or dual disorders. Studies of children of alcoholics find increased rates of alcohol abuse, drug abuse, conduct problems, antisocial personality disorder, anxiety disorders, and combined mood and anxiety disorders.[4,24] Shirley Hill and colleagues at the University of Pittsburgh Medical Center have conducted long-term studies of high-risk children of parents with alcoholism.[25-27] They found that these children are at greater risk for depression, phobias, and anxiety, attention-deficit, conduct, oppositional, and substance use disorders. Deficits in academic performance predicted later problems in these areas, and behavioral inhibition in unfamiliar situations to the child was seen as a possible risk factor for alcoholism. Hill's group also found these high-risk children different from normal children in terms of their neuroanatomy and neurophysiology (e.g., they showed reduced right amygdala volume in the brain).

Robert Ackerman has also documented the effects of alcoholism on children in his book *Children of Alcoholics.*[5] Several of his other publications document the impact of alcoholism on adult children.[28,29] In *The Forgotten Children,* one of the first books to document the effects of alcoholism on 116 children ages 10–16, Margaret Cork reported that 43% experienced "very serious," 49% experienced "fairly serious," and 8% experienced "slight" damage. The chart below of her findings shows the negative effects of parental alcoholism on the children's' relationships, school performance, and psychological and physical health.[30]

Howard Moss, Ralph Tartar, and colleagues from the NIDA-funded Center for Education and Drug Abuse Research at the University of Pittsburgh Medical Center have been studying sons of drug-dependent fathers for well over 15 years. Findings from their scientific studies show that the following problems are overrepresented in these children: conduct disturbances, heightened aggression, impulsivity, inattention, irritability, heightened motor activity, and temperamental deviations.[31–35] These high-risk children also have significantly lower IQ scores, poorer school performance, and impairments of the executive functions of the brain. Furthermore, they found that many high-risk children have a blunted neuroendocrine response to stress that may be the result of habituation to a stressful home environment.[36,37] Importantly, these sci-

Effects of Alcoholism on Children

98%	Relationships in family hurt	61%	Anxious and afraid of the future
97%	Feels unwanted	47%	Constantly defiant
96%	Relationships outside family hurt	47%	Schoolwork affected
94%	Parents inconsistent or unpredictable	43%	Thinks constantly about escaping
94%	Unsure of self, lacks confidence	42%	Burdened by too much responsibility
77%	Ashamed, hurt, gets upset and cries easily	40%	Worries about being liked by peers
70%	Feels loss of respect or ashamed	27%	Overly self-reliant, distrustful
65%	Constantly angry or hostile	22%	Feels hopeless and depressed
63%	Worried about being different	7%	Physical health affected

Source: Cork, M. (1969). *The forgotten children.* Toronto, Ontario: Alcoholism and Drug Addiction Research Foundation.

entists also found that when a substance-dependent father stops using drugs, it can have a significant positive effect on the problem behavior profile of his children.[38]

A recent report of the Center for Substance Abuse Treatment stated that parental substance abuse underlies many family problems, including divorce, welfare dependence, spousal abuse, child abuse and neglect, and other criminal behaviors.[9] A study of children of opiate addicts conducted by Edward Nunes and colleagues found that these children had higher rates of school problems, behavior problems, anxiety disorders, and mood disorders compared with those found in community surveys.[39] A study of relatives of opiate addicts conducted by Bruce Rounsaville and colleagues showed that relatives have elevated rates of major depression and anxiety disorders.[40]

Thus, overall, the evidence shows that all types of substance abuse problems have negative effects on children and their families. Although statistics provide a glimpse into some of these problems, listening to the experiences of real people brings these feelings and thoughts to life. The following quotes from children and adults capture the essence of how they were affected by their loved ones' disorders.

Walking on Eggshells

My mom, sisters and I worry a lot about Dad. What will his mood be today? How will he treat us? It's like walking on eggshells all the time. We never know what to expect from him. His mood changes real fast, and he seems to be depressed a lot, no matter what we try to do to help him.—Matt, age 16

I Worry So Much About Him

My son Scott has bipolar illness and also abuses drugs and alcohol. When he's sober and in treatment, he does pretty good and can even live on his own. But when he uses drugs again, he always stops his medication and treatment sessions. Then it's only a matter of time before he gets manic or depressed and gets in trouble. I worry so much about him. I'm afraid something terrible is going to happen to him someday.—Scott's mother, age 54

I Don't Have a Mom Sometimes

I feel like I don't have a mom sometimes 'cause she's always so depressed. She never feels like doing anything with me and gets real mad at me, even for dumb little things. When she drinks, it gets worse because I never know how she's going to act.—Lauren, age 11

It's Wearing Me Out

My wife has depression and panic disorder. She gets these bad panic attacks and hardly ever leaves the house. Every time we make plans to go somewhere, we either cancel or I go by myself. It's wearing me out. I have to do all the shopping. And I'm tired of lying to our friends and family all the time about why she doesn't visit. She takes nerve pills like candy and sneaks alcohol during the day. Our kids are worried too.—Stan, age 42

She's Trying To Kill Herself

Our daughter is always getting into trouble for fighting or breaking the law. I know a lot of it has to do with using those damn drugs. I can't tell you how many times we bailed her out of trouble. But she continues the same behavior, over and over. Sometimes she calls when she's drunk and blames us for all her problems and threatens to kill herself. A couple of times, she cut her arms with a knife and ended up in the ER at the hospital. It worries us to death because we don't know if she's trying to kill herself or does it to get attention.—Lois, age 45

My Sons Are Scared of Him

My boyfriend goes into these rages and smashes things and calls me horrible names. He's even hit and pushed me a couple of times and threatened to hurt me real bad. He gets like a maniac. It's worse when he drinks, but he can be stone sober and still act this way. My sons are scared of him. It's so confusing to me 'cause sometimes he treats me so good and takes care of me.—Colleen, age 29

I Can't Rely on My Husband

I can't rely on my husband for anything. He's always out partying with his friends. He can't hold a job very long, and if it weren't for my income, we'd be broke all the time. I take care of the house and the kids by myself. I keep wondering what keeps us together. Sometimes, I get very depressed myself. But, I keep telling myself that things will get better. Maybe someday he'll realize what he's putting his family through. —Tamara, age 27

Dad Isn't Dependable

Mom and dad got divorced because of his drug problem. Half the time he's supposed to take my younger brother and me he doesn't show up.

It makes me mad 'cause Dad isn't dependable. He even forgot my last birthday.—BJ, age 18

As these quotations show, exposure to dual disorders can have a variety of effects on your family. A family member may refuse to accept your problem, deny it, or cover it up. A member may "overfunction" and assume your responsibilities because you "underfunction." Some family members may even develop mental health or substance abuse problems themselves.

Dual disorders produce a great deal of stress. People respond in different ways to stress. Therefore, don't be surprised if members of your family are affected differently. For couples with children, a major factor in how children are affected relates to the behavior of the partner or spouse who doesn't have addiction and a mood disorder. If your partner or spouse is emotionally upset, he or she may not be able to provide the nurturing, time, and attention your children need. In these cases, a child may feel that both parents are lost.

Some members of a family, including children, are resilient and survive difficult situations with very few negative effects. Therefore, some children will do well despite a parent's illness.

Concerns of Families

Families who have a member with both mood and substance use disorders identify many personal concerns and questions about the disorders. These are summarized in the chart opposite.[41]

When families participate in treatment and attend support group meetings, they learn information and coping strategies that aid them in dealing with their concerns. Ask your family to attend some of your treatment sessions and encourage them to attend self-help meetings. If your family refuses, ask your therapist for help in persuading them to come in for sessions or attend self-help meetings.

Making Amends

Making amends can help repair the damage caused in your family as a result of your behaviors. This requires you to understand how your behaviors have

Concerns and Questions of Family Members Regarding Mood Disorders and Addiction

1. What are the causes of depression, bipolar illness, and addiction?
2. How does one illness affect the other?
3. What's involved in treatment and recovery?
4. What is the family's role in treatment and recovery?
5. How much responsibility should the family take to get the ill member into treatment or ensure that he or she complies with the treatment plan?
6. How effective are medications and how long do they need to be taken?
7. What are the chances and causes of relapse, and what steps can be taken to prevent or reduce relapse to either disorder?
8. How do you know when psychiatric hospitalization is needed, and what are the possible repercussions if a member is involuntarily hospitalized?
9. Why do I feel guilty or responsible for the mood disorder or the addiction?
10. What steps can our family take to deal with our own feelings or reactions to the problems associated with the dual disorders (for example, anger, anxiety, depression, or disappointment)?
11. How do we ensure safety for the dual-disordered family member, as well as for other members of the family, particularly when suicidal or violent behaviors are involved?
12. What are the risks that others in the family may develop an addiction or mental health problem?
13. How do we cope with the financial burdens caused by the dual disorders?
14. What should we tell our children regarding the dual disorders and treatment?
15. How do we handle suicide or violence threats or behaviors, persistent symptoms of the mood disorder, unusual or bizarre behavior, or episodes of alcohol or drug intoxication?
16. How can we set limits on the dual-disordered family member?

Source: Daley, D. C., & Thase, M. E. (2000). *Dual disorders recovery counseling* (2nd ed., p. 64). Independence, MO: Independence Press.

affected your family. Try to "put yourself in their shoes" and know what it was like for them. Ask yourself the following questions: How have they experienced your disorders? What do they feel? What do they think? What are they concerned about in relation to you and your disorders? Talk with them directly and listen to what they say about their experiences and feelings. The timing of such a discussion depends on a variety of factors, so you should discuss this with your therapist and/or sponsor so you don't rush into it prematurely. They can help guide you in this process.

Steps 8 and 9 of the 12-step program focus on making amends. Although many family members are kind and forgiving, some may harbor pain and resentment. Therefore, be prepared to hear unpleasant things when you talk with your loved ones about your impact on them. Don't get defensive. Give your family time to get over upset feelings. It won't happen simply because you talk with them and apologize for your behaviors. Words will be hollow if you don't back them up with actions and by staying sober. Spending time with your family, giving them attention and support, and participating in activities together can help you undo damage from the past. If you borrowed or stole money from them, make arrangements to pay it back. Take responsibility for your behaviors, be willing to face the truth, and work hard at making things better today.

Family members who learn about dual disorders and recovery and who participate in support groups are more likely to accept your gestures at making amends. This is another reason why family members should be encouraged to attend meetings of support groups such as Al-Anon or Nar-Anon or those sponsored by NAMI.

The Family's Role in Treatment and Recovery

Attending assessment, treatment, education, and self-help support group meetings can help you and your family in many ways.[4,9,14,16,19–21,42–49] These groups can help your family support you and figure out what they can do to help you, as well as what they can't do. Part of what they may learn is that behaviors on their part can "enable" you or actually interfere with your recovery. For example, your family enables you when they bail you out of trouble, shield you from the consequences of your behaviors, or take on your responsibilities. They enable you by paying your bills or giving you money because you spent yours on alcohol or drugs. However, sometimes your family is in a bind and does something for you because they know your kids won't be taken care unless they help.

Treatment can help your family reduce stress, understand and accept your disorders, manage crises, learn to take better care of themselves, work through some of their own emotional pain, and improve relationships in the family. They may also learn how to focus more on other family members instead of giving most of their time, attention, and energy to you.

Family members benefit from sharing their own experiences, feelings, and concerns with other families who are dealing with dual disorders. This is the reason family support groups or treatment groups are helpful. As they gain information about illness and recovery, your family can become realistic about what treatment can and cannot do. They will learn to live with certain symptoms and limitations imposed by your illnesses, especially chronic mood disorders. Information will also help them spot early warning signs of relapse. By observing and pointing out these relapse warning signs, they can help you take action early, which can prevent a full-blown relapse to your depression or bipolar illness or your addiction. They also learn how to access treatment if you refuse or if you become unable to take care of yourself.

Children

As I said earlier in this chapter, children in families in which a parent or other close relative has dual disorders are at increased risk for emotional, behavioral, academic, and alcohol or drug abuse problems. If you think that any of your children have been seriously affected, arrange a psychiatric evaluation for them. If you are in therapy, ask your therapist or psychiatrist for help in getting your child an evaluation. For example, Gail reported to her therapist that her 9-year-old son had difficulty paying attention in school, often defied her at home, and talked about wanting to die. Gail's therapist helped her arrange an evaluation for her son, who is now in treatment. In addition, Gail participates in a program designed to help parents become more effective in managing children with emotional problems.

A child with a serious problem will probably not ask for help or even know something is wrong that requires treatment. Therefore, if you observe any of the symptoms or problems listed in the table on page 152 in your child, you should seek an evaluation by a mental health professional (or addictions specialist if the problem is with alcohol or other drug use).[41]

Even if your child does not have a serious problem that needs to be assessed by a mental health professional, you should be aware of how your disorders have affected him or her. Have a discussion with your children about your disorders. Ask them to share their thoughts and feelings about what it has been like for them. If you are uncomfortable doing this on your own, ask your therapist to conduct family sessions in which your children are guided in shar-

Symptoms and Problems of Children Requiring an Evaluation

1. Severe depression, mania, irritability, or mood swings.
2. Expression of suicidal thoughts or plans or an actual attempt.
3. Severe anxiety and worry.
4. Violent behavior toward animals or other people.
5. Hearing voices or expressing bizarre ideas, such as that people are trying to put thoughts in his or her head or take them out.
6. Severe agitation or inability to sit still for very long, or having trouble completing projects started because of a short attention span.
7. Trouble concentrating or completing schoolwork, which causes poor grades or other problems in school.
8. Running away from home.
9. Constantly defying you or other adults.
10. Serious problems getting along with others at home, school, or in the community.
11. Using alcohol or other drugs.
12. Stealing, involvement in illegal activities, or trouble with the law.
13. Inability to form relationships or maintain friendships.

Source: Daley, D. C. (2000). *Dual diagnosis workbook: Recovery strategies for substance use and mental health problems* (2nd ed., p. 102). Independence, MO: Independence Press.

ing their experiences and feelings. Children need a chance to be heard and share their experiences.

Family Rituals

Family rituals refer to activities and interactions among family members that are a regular, routine yet important part of life. These can be daily rituals, such as eating meals together, discussing the events and sharing personal experiences of the day, or enjoying a social or recreational activity, such as watching a movie or playing cards. Rituals can also revolve around social events such as shopping, eating out, going to the movies, or other activities; family events such as visiting relatives, picnics, trips or vacations, or regular telephone conversations with other family members (grandparents, siblings, etc.); celebrations of religious events, birthdays, anniversaries, graduations, or end of the school year; or other "special" occasions and achievements among family members. The list of potential rituals is endless.

Rituals can also be established with specific family members. A couple, for example, may establish the ritual of having breakfast together before work or taking a few minutes before dinner each evening to relax together and discuss how the day went. Other rituals might include watching movies every Friday evening while enjoying a favorite snack or surprising each other with unusual gifts on birthdays. A parent can establish many rituals with a child, such as discussing the child's day at school during dinner conversation, helping out with homework each evening, talking with the child before bedtime, watching TV programs or movies, cooking or playing a game together, and doing something "special" together away from home.

Rituals help families and individual members feel anchored and provide predictability to their lives. They are important, and they often occur without much thought given to them. Unfortunately, mental health and substance disorders frequently disrupt family rituals. Therefore, it helps to reestablish old rituals or develop new ones during your recovery. For example, Jay and Sandy attend a support group for individuals with bipolar illness and their families. After each meeting, they go out for coffee with several other people to discuss the meeting and to share mutual support. When they go home, they talk with their kids about the topic of discussion during the meeting. This ritual keeps this family focused on the positive aspects of recovery. Jay and Sandy also reestablished the ritual of planning family vacations together, which they had stopped for several years due to Sandy's unpredictable behaviors caused by her drinking and mania.

Family Therapy

You can seek family therapy if you and your family cannot work out problems on your own or if things at home don't improve even though you and your family go to self-help meetings. Family therapy is recommended if:

- You are worried that your family is on the verge of breaking up.
- The level of anger and hostility in your family is high.
- Violent behavior occurs in your family.
- Family members have serious trouble supporting each other or getting along.

- Family tension and problems trigger thoughts of getting drunk or high.
- Family members carry around a lot of emotional pain.

A family therapist can help you and your family focus on specific problems that you can work on together in order to make things better in your family. If your therapist or counselor does not offer family therapy, ask for a referral to a qualified family therapist.

Chapter 10 *Changing Your Lifestyle*

Using Recovery Tools on a Daily Basis

Tools of recovery are the steps you take on a regular basis to manage your disorders. The more these become part of your daily life, the greater likelihood there is that your recovery will lead to positive changes. One such tool is attending support group meetings such as Alcoholics Anonymous (AA), Narcotics Anonymous (NA), Dual Recovery Anonymous (DRA), or mental health support groups for depression or bipolar illness. Meetings provide education, support, and a sense of hopefulness about change.

Working the 12 steps can help you accept your disorders, reduce feelings of guilt and shame, rely on a Higher Power for strength, identify your strengths and weaknesses, and make amends to others hurt by your addiction and mood disorder. Take your time and seek guidance from a sponsor in working the 12-step program of recovery.

Face-to-face and telephone discussions with a sponsor or other member of support programs can help you feel connected, keep your program in perspective, and learn what others do to help themselves. Getting together for coffee after a self-help meeting is an excellent way to discuss recovery issues and share mutual concerns or support. Spiritual recovery tools include praying, reading the Bible, or using your Higher Power for strength and hope. These activities can provide you with strength or inspiration and can be very helpful during times of difficulty.

Writing your thoughts or feelings in a journal or recovery workbook can help you sort through them and track changes over time. Recovery literature such as *Alcoholics Anonymous* ("Big Book"), *Narcotics Anonymous* ("Basic Text"), the *Dual Disorders Recovery Book,* and books on depression or bipolar disorder provide information and stories of other people who have learned to manage their disorders and made positive changes.[1–6]

Talking yourself through cravings or desires to get high, calming yourself down when you are upset, practicing positive thinking, and challenging your negative thoughts can help you to feel better and manage your problems. These require practice until you get comfortable doing them. Get a list of slogans of AA, NA, and DRA and use the ones you feel can help you. Make up your own slogans, as well. For example, Steve, who had severe problems controlling anger, created these slogans: "keep the lid on," "if you feel angry, don't act on these feelings," and "I control my anger—it doesn't control me."

Keep a list of support group meetings and professional treatment activities that you regularly attend. Using slogans, positive self-talk, and talking with your Higher Power should be done on a regular basis so that they become second nature. This requires both discipline and commitment. Remember that recovery has no shortcuts. At the end of this chapter is a list of the 12 steps of Dual Recovery Anonymous, adapted from the 12 steps of AA. These steps address both mental health and addiction recovery issues.

The chart opposite summarizes the tools you can use in ongoing recovery.[7] Use these regularly, as they can help you manage your disorders, prevent small problems from becoming large problems, and stay connected with others who can help and support you.

Developing a Weekly Schedule

A way of adding structure and discipline to your recovery is to make a schedule of activities with which to get involved during the week. Although you can't fill every hour of every day, schedule enough activities so that you don't have a lot of free time on your hands, especially on weekends and in the early months of recovery. Too much free time can lead to an increase in cravings to use alcohol or drugs, restlessness, boredom, or depression. This schedule can include recovery activities such as 12-step groups, mental health support groups, and therapy sessions, as well as social, recreational, family, and work activities.

Tools for Use in Daily Recovery

Behavioral and Lifestyle Tools
- Keep busy and active.
- Participate in pleasant activities.
- Establish regular eating and sleeping habits.
- Exercise regularly.
- Avoid high-risk people, places, and events when possible.
- Set goals.

Self-Help Program Tools
- Attend and participate in self-help meetings.
- Read recovery literature.
- Talk with a sponsor or other program members.
- Practice or use the 12 steps (of AA, NA, DRA).
- Attend social events sponsored by recovery programs or clubs.

Emotional and Relationship Tools
- Be aware of your feelings and know how to express them appropriately.
- Share problems, feelings, or concerns with someone trustworthy.
- Ask others for help or support.
- Share substance-free activities with sober people.

- Develop and maintain meaningful relationships.
- Focus more on others and less on yourself.
- Do something nice for a loved one or friend.
- Spend time with family members or friends.

Cognitive (Thinking or Planning) Tools
- Challenge thoughts of using substances.
- Challenge negative thinking.
- Practice positive thinking.
- Think through your problems.
- Repeat slogans of the 12-step program.
- Remind yourself of benefits of treatment and recovery.
- Plan each day of recovery.
- Review each day of recovery to catch early warning signs of relapse.

Spiritual Tools
- Pray or relate to a Higher Power.
- Meditate.
- Read spiritual literature.
- Reflect on your blessings.
- Attend services regularly and attend prayer or Bible study groups.
- Forgive yourself or others.

Source: Daley, D. C. (2003). *Coping with dual disorders*. Center City, MN: Hazelden.

Be sure to include activities that are fun and relaxing. I find that people who schedule their time feel a greater sense of control over what they are going to be doing during the week and weekend. As a result, they feel less bored or lost. One of the worst things you can do is to have too much free time on your hands with nothing planned. If you plan activities, you are more likely to follow through and keep busy than if you wait for things to happen on the spur of the moment. You will be less likely to use drugs or alcohol to fill your time. Sam talks about how he uses a schedule to keep himself busy on weekends.

Between work, taking care of my apartment, and going to meetings, I keep busy during the week. Until I planned my weekends, it was easy to get bored, feel lonely or depressed. Now, every weekend, I plan my days so I keep active. On Saturday, I do my shopping and laundry, visit my parents or talk on the phone, and go to an evening NA meeting. We go out after the meeting for coffee and sometimes we even go to a late movie. On Sundays, I go to church, play sports, watch a game on TV, and write my kids a letter. During the evening, I usually go to a meeting, stay home and watch a movie, or visit a friend in recovery. I also read a lot on weekends, too. I like to read my NA basic text, but I also like to read novels. The important thing I learned is to keep busy doing things to help my recovery, stay connected to family and friends, and have some fun and relaxation.

Setting Goals

Goals give you a sense of purpose and direction in life. A goal is a process or end point that you wish to achieve. Goals can involve learning information, developing or improving a skill, or making a change in yourself, in a relationship, or in your lifestyle.

The more specific you set your goals, the better. However, you can also set general goals, such as "becoming a better parent, becoming a better husband/ wife, becoming a better worker, or becoming a better person." Specific goals take these general ideas and break them down into more concrete terms. For example, you could define a goal of becoming a better spouse as "to get closer to my spouse by regularly going out together to do something enjoyable." If your general goal is to become a better parent, a specific example might be "getting closer to my daughter by spending time teaching her how to play basketball or a musical instrument." If you set the general goal of becoming a better worker on your job, you might define it in terms of "to improve my ability to deal with difficult people." "Getting in shape" is a general goal that could be further defined as "losing 15 pounds over the next 3 months." A goal of "becoming a better person" could mean "showing more love and compassion to friends or family members." One other example of a general goal is "developing a new leisure interest," whereas the specific goal could be "learn woodworking so I can build things in my spare time." Goals provide you with a yardstick against which you can measure your progress. If you reach your goals, you will feel better about yourself.

Short-term goals are those that you want to achieve within the next 3 months, medium-term goals are those that you want to achieve within the next 3 to 6 months, and long-term goals are the ones you want to achieve within the next 6 to 12 months or longer. You can develop goals in any area of your life: family or social relationships, physical health or condition, weight, emotional health, how you cope with feelings, how you deal with negative thinking, your style of relating to other people, spirituality, leisure interests and hobbies, your job, school or education, and money or debt.

When you are in early recovery, avoid setting too many goals or ones that are too ambitious or unrealistic, as this can overwhelm and frustrate you. Discuss goals with your therapist or sponsor to get feedback about whether your goals and the steps you take to reach them are reasonable. Reward yourself for the effort you put forth.

Once you set a specific goal, the next step is to figure out a plan of action that you can take to reach this goal. Goals are nothing more than ideas if they are not backed up with a plan of action that you follow. Change your plan if it doesn't work. The following cases show how Linda and Derek set goals and developed plans to meet these goals.

Linda's Goals

(1) Increasing my social interaction with others

I'll do this by going out with other AA members after meetings instead of going right home, inviting a friend to my house for dinner and a movie or going out for dinner and a movie every week, and calling an AA member at least once a week to talk.

(2) Increasing my positive thinking

I'll do this by catching myself when I think negatively about myself or my future, focusing on the good things in my life and not just the problems, and writing at least two positive statements in my recovery journal every single day.

Derek's Goals

(1) Coping with boredom and my need for action

I'll keep busy by going to meetings every day. I'll hang out a lot at the local recovery club on weekends and go to dances and social events. I'll give myself pep talks about staying away from the action on the street.

(2) Becoming a more responsible father

I'll visit my son every week and call him a couple of times each week, too. When we're together, I'll talk with him about school and things he's interested in. I'll teach him how to play ball. Even though I don't have much money, I'll give him a little allowance so he has a few bucks to spend when we're together.

Handling Money and Debt

Dual disorders often cause financial problems. You may have spent a lot of money on alcohol or drugs, lost jobs or income, and become unable to pay your bills and take care of your financial responsibilities. Some people lose almost everything as a result of their addiction or manic behavior. A major cause of financial problems is poor use of money, credit cards, and loans. Many people get into financial difficulty because they don't follow a budget. A wrong attitude about money coupled with irresponsible money management can lead to financial disaster.

There are a number of strategies to help you handle financial problems, even if you are on a tight budget.[8-9] One is to keep track of your spending so you can figure out where your money is going. It is not unusual to spend more money on expenses than you thought you were spending. An easy way to track your spending is to write down everything you spend over a period of 2 months in a budget book or a notebook. Write down how much money you spent, the date you spent it, and what you spent it for. If you use a notebook, keep track of money spent according to categories such as rent, food, clothing, utilities, entertainment, child care, transportation, loans, and savings. Add other categories of expenses as needed. This can help you track spending, as well as identify patterns in your spending behaviors. For example, Carlton discovered that he spent over $60 a month buying sodas and coffee at fast-food restaurants or convenience stores, an amount he hardly could afford given that he was living on a limited fixed income. Simply by changing this pattern, he reduced this amount to less than $25 a month, saving $35 each month. Donna, who had more than enough to live on, was always falling behind on her utilities and phone bill. After tracking her spending, Donna discovered that she spent too much money on cosmetics, clothes, and gifts to her daughters. A budget helped her reduce spending, giving her more money for bills and savings. Roger, a well-paid executive, found that far too much money was spent on unplanned trips to restaurants to eat out with his wife and on unplanned shopping trips. By cutting down on unplanned dinners and shopping trips, he saved several hundreds of dollars per month.

Budgeting is important if you are on a limited income such as public assistance or disability or if you work part time or have a low-paying job. A budget works only if you follow it and guard against spending impulsively by buying things that you don't need or can't afford. Live within your financial means, or you will fall deeper into debt. One woman, for example, complained that she could barely make ends meet. Yet one of the first things she did when she got her paycheck was buy new clothes and jewelry. Although she had a nice wardrobe and selection of jewelry, she couldn't meet her financial obligations and wasted a lot of money on credit card interest because she charged her clothes and jewelry.

If you are married or involved in a close live-in relationship and share the bills, work on the budget together with your spouse or partner. This helps minimize angry arguments over money matters, which reduces the chances of blaming each other for financial problems.

Keeping a limit on, or getting rid of, loans and charge cards is another way to get better control of your finances. If you have a large charge card balance, you are likely to pay a lot of your money in interest charges. Credit cards often carry interest fees up to 20% or higher. Some loans also carry a high interest rate. This means that most of your monthly payment goes to paying the interest, which is money wasted. If possible, pay off your loans and credit cards to get control of your financial situation. For example, Lollie paid off all her credit cards over a period of about a year and a half. This reduced her monthly debts by $165, and she saved over $1,000 per year just on the interest charges she had been paying.

If you need a loan, check different banks to find out what the interest rates are. Even a 1 or 2% difference in the interest rate can mean saving between $10 and $25 dollars a month, particularly on a large loan for expensive items such as a car. Avoid loan sharks, as they charge high interest rates and your money will be eaten up very fast, causing more financial problems.

Evaluate your shopping and buying habits to identify patterns of impulsive buying. This refers to buying things at stores, malls, through TV shows, or on the Internet without considering whether you really need or can afford them. Many sale items are bought on impulse because you think you're getting a good deal. It doesn't do you any good to buy items on sale if it puts you deeper in debt.

Even if you are on a tight budget, if you regularly save money, you can prepare for emergencies. A common mistake is to save money only if there is some left over after all bills and expenses are paid. Budgeting a regular amount of money to savings is an excellent way to ensure that money is set aside for future use.

Figure out ways to cut down on your weekly expenses, such as buying food or household items in bulk quantity. This often saves 30–50% or more compared with buying things in smaller sizes at a grocery or department store. You can pick up many things very cheaply at yard or garage sales or through advertisements in papers. Buying generic food items or medicine products can save you 30–50% or more on items from medicine to cereal. Other ways to reduce spending include packing a lunch for work, sharing rides, going grocery shopping after you have eaten, shopping from a grocery list, renting items such as videotapes and DVDs rather than buying them, and not spending money on something that hasn't been budgeted. For example, Allan eliminated several unplanned stops to eat after work, saving over $90 each month. Tracy, a mother of four, saved over $80 a month by buying generic medicines and foods. Holly saved over $100 a month by buying food and household items in bulk quantities.

Money problems contribute to stress, frustration, relationship squabbles, and unhappiness. Even if you are on a limited income, there are things you can do to stretch your money and manage it more wisely. If you have a decent income, it helps to save money and think about ways of investing for your children, your family, or your future. You can go to your local library and look at financial planning books or a number of the popular magazines to get more information about money management or investment strategies. Or you can use the services of a financial consultant. If you are in debt far over your head, go to a financial counselor for help in reducing your debt. A counselor can help you learn how to budget so that you can live within your means and how to deal with your creditors.

If you are self-employed and have your own business, you can benefit from the services of an accountant or tax planner. Professionals can help you find legitimate ways to reduce your taxes and shelter your income and provide you with other suggestions on ways to save or invest money.

The 12 Steps of Dual Recovery Anonymous (DRA)

These steps were adapted from the 12 steps of AA specifically for individuals who have both a psychiatric disorder and an addiction.[3]

The 12 Steps of Dual Recovery Anonymous

1. We admitted we were powerless over our dual illness of chemical dependency and emotional or psychiatric illness—that our lives had become unmanageable.

2. Came to believe that a Higher Power of our understanding could restore us to sanity.

3. Made a decision to turn our will and our lives over to the care of our Higher Power, to help us to rebuild our lives in a positive and caring way.

4. Made a searching and fearless personal inventory of ourselves.

5. Admitted to our Higher Power, to ourselves, and to another human being the exact nature of our liabilities and our assets.

6. Were entirely ready to have our Higher Power remove all our liabilities.

7. Humbly asked our Higher Power to remove these liabilities and to help us to strengthen our assets for recovery.

8. Made a list of all people we had harmed and became willing to make amends to them all.

9. Made direct amends to such people wherever possible, except when to do so would injure them or others.

10. Continued to take personal inventory and when wrong promptly admitted it, while continuing to recognize our progress in dual recovery.

11. Sought through prayer and meditation to improve our conscious contact with our Higher Power, praying only for knowledge of our Higher Power's will for us and the power to carry that out.

12. Having had a spiritual awakening as a result of these Steps, we tried to carry this message to others who experience dual disorders and to practice these principles in all our affairs.

Source: *The dual disorders recovery book.* (1993). Center City, MN: Hazelden.

Chapter 11 *Strategies for Self-Improvement*

Changing Your Thinking

The way in which you think about yourself and the world affects your feelings and behaviors. You can talk yourself into feeling miserable, anxious, depressed, and bored. These feelings can lead to using alcohol and drugs, getting involved in unhealthy relationships, withdrawing from other people due to depression, or avoiding people or situations because of anxiety or fear.

Patterns of negative thinking are referred to as "stinking thinking," "cognitive distortions," "thinking errors," or "faulty thinking." If you learn to identify and change your negative thinking or to think through problems and options, you will feel better about yourself and are more likely to stay sober.

Aaron Beck, Albert Ellis, and David Burns are three well-known experts who have identified common examples of negative thinking that contribute to depression, anxiety, substance abuse, and other problems.[1-4] One example is making things out to be much worse than they really are, referred to as "making mountains out of molehills." Small worries or problems become insurmountable or unsolvable. For example, April's daughter brought home a sloppy school assignment on which she received the grade of D. Normally an A or B student, her daughter had rushed to finish this assignment at the last minute because she forgot it was due. When April first saw her daughter's poor grade, she became upset and angry. She berated her daughter and began making a case that her daughter would not make the honor roll because of one poor assignment. April made a big deal out of something that wasn't a big deal because her daughter had a proven track record of good grades. As a result, April upset herself and her daughter.

Other examples of negative thinking include expecting the worst thing to happen, believing that things are not going to work out, thinking you are going to fail, or focusing only on the negative side of a situation by looking at what may go wrong instead of what can go right. Some people are much more negative and cynical in their thinking and tend to have trouble seeing any good in themselves, other people, or the world. If you have this tendency, you compare yourself unfavorably to others and focus on flaws or deficits rather than strengths and achievements. For example, no matter what Richard does to help himself, he gets stuck on his shortcomings, failures, and problems. Although he has made very good progress in several areas of his life, he has trouble accepting his growth and achievements because he focuses only on his short-comings. He shrugs off compliments from others and sees himself much less favorably than others do. Richard is stuck in a vicious cycle of negative thinking about himself and his future. To get better, he has to learn to reverse this pattern of negative thinking and to focus on what he does well.

Another example is believing that you can't make any changes in your life or that you are not capable of staying off alcohol or other drugs. Thinking that you can't cope without using alcohol or drugs or that a few drinks, joints, or hits off a crack pipe can't really hurt you are common thoughts expressed by people in recovery.

Dwelling too much on your shortcomings, your symptoms, your problems, and what may go wrong in the future are common negative thought patterns. Another is having hopeless thoughts about yourself and the future or even thoughts that life isn't worth living.

If you keep your bothersome thoughts to yourself and don't share them with others, it is harder to change them. This is especially true in the first couple of months in recovery. Half of the battle in changing negative thoughts is being aware of and admitting them. You can then figure out whether there is evidence to support these thoughts. For example, if you tell yourself that you are a failure at everything and then look closely at your life, you will find that, even if you have made a lot of mistakes, you have not failed at everything. You will discover some successes in your life. Always examine the evidence for negative thinking, which contributes to feeling depressed.

Challenge yourself when you think negatively. If any of the examples I gave earlier pop into your mind, think of ways that you can fight them off. For example, if you have a flat tire and think, "this is going to be a rotten day and my life is falling apart," you can challenge this by saying "it's an inconvenience that I had this flat tire; I'm going to have to fix it," and then let the day go on without letting this drag you down. If you have a job interview and tell yourself "I'll never get this job because I'm not good enough," you can challenge this and say "I'm going to prepare the best way I can and this will give me a decent chance of getting this job. If I don't get this job I'll keep trying and look for other jobs." Or, if you tell yourself "staying clean is a drag; I'm not having fun," you can challenge this and say "I can get through my boredom without using. I refuse to let this be an excuse to use drugs. The truth is, I am much better off since I quit drugs."

Practicing positive thinking each day, such as "I'm going to be able to cope with my problem today," "I'm not going to drink or use drugs today," "I'm going to make this a decent day," or "I'm going to do something to make myself feel good today." If you increase positive thinking by 10%, you are making a step in the right direction.

Take a look at things you have achieved and the progress you are making in recovery. This can help you think more positively about how things are really going. Sometimes it is easy to focus on one thing that goes wrong rather than on the big picture, in which many things go all right or very well. Give yourself credit, even for small steps in your recovery.

Use the slogans you learned in AA or NA or the Serenity Prayer. Remind yourself of the benefits of recovery, especially the benefits of staying alcohol and drug free during periods of time in which you feel like using.

Keep a written journal in which you write down the situations that trigger negative thinking. Then write three to five counter statements for each negative thought that you list in your journal. There are many books about how to change your thinking. I recommend books written by Aaron Beck, David Burns, Albert Ellis, and others.[1–5] They have developed cognitive therapies based on the fact that if you change your beliefs and how you think, you can change your feelings and behaviors. This leads to positive changes in your life and a greater ability to solve your problems, stay sober, and cope with depression, bipolar illness, anxiety, and other mental health problems.

Changing Self-Defeating Behaviors

Self-defeating behaviors hurt you emotionally, harm your relationships, cause you significant losses, or get in the way of reaching your goals. These behaviors may be deliberate or a by-product of other actions. Self-defeating behaviors show in your interpersonal behaviors, in how you approach responsibilities, in your health care habits, and in how you spend your time. They also show in your involvement in illegal behaviors or in other types of addiction, such as compulsive gambling, sex, or overeating. Self-defeating behaviors can contribute to substance abuse or depression, cause you to feel dissatisfied and unhappy, interfere with your recovery, or cause problems with the law.

Ignoring your family or children is a common self-defeating behavior that can lead to unhappiness and bad feelings. For example, Stan spent little time with his two kids during the past 4 years. As he got more heavily into using crack cocaine, nobody mattered much to him. Consequently, his wife divorced him. Although Stan has been in recovery for well over a year, it has only been recently that he has taken actions to get involved in the lives of his two kids. Early in recovery he complained about missing his children, yet he continued to ignore them. Stan didn't start feeling better about himself until he began taking more responsibility as a father. This meant taking time and showing a genuine interest in his kids on a consistent basis, not only when he wanted to.

Relationships require commitment to make them work. This means spending time with important people and being concerned with their needs and interests. If your depression is related to your inability to stick with an intimate relationship, then you have to take a look at this pattern in order to understand it. Only then will you be able to figure out how you can change this pattern of behavior. Changing this behavior pattern, in turn, can have a positive effect on your mood and self-esteem.

A physically or emotionally abusive relationship can cause you suffering and pose a risk of relapse to substances, of feeling depressed, or of becoming violent or suicidal. Lisa, for example, had a history of feeling suicidal after fights with her boyfriend. During arguments, he pushed and slapped her around and called her rotten names, telling her she was no good and worthless. Staying in this relationship played a major role in Lisa's thoughts of hurting herself, in her feelings of depression, and in her alcohol use. Lisa did not get well until she ended this relationship and accepted that it was better to be alone than in an abusive relationship.

Another self-defeating behavior is using violence, intimidation, or anger to keep other people on their guard or from getting close to you. This behavior is a way of controlling other people. It interferes with being able keep satisfying relationships that involve give and take. J. J. describes himself as a "miserable SOB." He says, "I use hostility as a weapon. People are afraid of me, and some think I'm crazy. But I know exactly what I'm doing and how to control others." Seeking revenge on others who hurt you is a variation of this behavior.

Conning, manipulating, or taking advantage of other people in order to get your needs met can destroy a relationship. These behaviors may occur in relation to getting money or something else you need or even in trying to make others feel guilty and blame them for your problems.

Self-defeating behaviors show up in other areas of your life, such as work and school, in money mismanagement, or in your daily life structure. Quitting a job impulsively without having another one, jumping from job to job, being irresponsible and not showing up on time or missing work, or performing your job poorly are other examples of self-defeating behaviors. The same holds true with school. Not completing your assignments or courses, not working hard while you are in school, or quitting are also behaviors that hurt you and block your personal growth.

Poor money management, getting yourself deep in debt, spending money that you or your family needs for basic necessities on things that you don't need, and not planning ahead for future financial obligations are other self-defeating behavior patterns. So are buying excessively on credit cards and borrowing money from loan sharks or institutions that charge an excessively high rate of interest. These behaviors put you further in financial debt. They also raise your levels of anxiety, depression, frustration, and anger.

Other areas in which your self-defeating behaviors show are how you live your life on a day-to-day basis and how you plan for the future. Failure to finish projects you start, not setting any goals or action plans to achieve goals, chronic procrastination, acting helpless, and not building structure into your day put you at risk for relapse to your mood disorder, your addiction, or both. Failure to plan for the future puts you in a position in which you have nothing to strive for. It can take away your motivation and lead to an "I don't care" attitude.

Failure to accept responsibility for your behaviors and blaming others for your misfortune is self-defeating. It is easy to blame family, friends, bad luck, or other factors for your difficulties. Another self-defeating behavior is not following through with your treatment sessions or not taking the advice of people who are trying to help you. Refusing help from others is often a sure way to set yourself up to do poorly. In early recovery you need to trust others and take their advice without questioning them too much. The professionals who care for you or other people in recovery often know what works. Even if you don't agree with what they advise you to do, you give yourself a better chance of recovery if you follow through on their recommendations. I hear people say time and time again that being stubborn and insisting that they don't need anyone to guide them in recovery usually leads to disaster and relapse to alcohol or other drug use.

Any excessive, addictive, or compulsive behavior can be self-defeating.[6–8] These include compulsive gambling, overeating, and sexual behavior; spending too much time on a computer or on the Internet; or working too much. For example, since getting involved in recovery 7 months ago, Dave has managed to stay drug free, and his depression has improved significantly. Yet he reports that he feels unhappy and burnt out because all he does is work and go to a few NA meetings. He usually works 7 days a week, often up to 10 hours or more each day. Dave has little time for anything else. Also, he's often tired and feels resentful that he has so little free time. On the one hand, he feels he has to work in order to make money to get out of debt created by his addiction. On the other hand, excessive work takes a big toll on him. If he doesn't start cutting back and relaxing a little, he puts himself at risk for relapse to depression or to alcohol or drugs.

Self-directed violence is another example of a destructive behavior. This includes cutting or burning yourself or damaging your body in other ways, such as getting tattoos plastered all over your body. A more severe form of self-violence is making an actual suicide attempt.

Involvement in illegal activities or criminal behaviors is common among addicted people.[9–10] Such dishonesty is likely to show up in other areas of your life, including lying about whether or not you are using drugs or alcohol or lying about other symptoms of your mood disorder. You also put yourself at risk of being arrested and ending up in jail or prison. Changing antisocial behaviors will increase your chances of staying sober, feeling better about yourself, developing better relationships, and managing your mood disorder.

Once you identify your self-defeating behaviors, you can figure out which ones to change, why and how to change, and the benefits of change. Because some behaviors are ingrained in your personality, it may take a long time to change them. Other self-defeating behaviors may be easier to change. The key with all change is to stick with your program and do things differently. Listen to Debra's story of how she changed some of her self-defeating patterns of behavior.

I used to stay in bad relationships far too long. I always tried to rescue a failing relationship, even when it just wasn't meant to be and it was clear that I was doing all the work. When my relationship would end, I had a bad habit of hooking up with another man long before I was emotionally ready. I felt so needy that I couldn't get along without a man that I made a lot of very bad decisions. Now, I do things different. I go slow and don't jump into relationships. And I don't stay around at all if I find out a guy I'm involved with is violent or gets high. I also don't threaten suicide or try to hurt myself if a relationship doesn't work out. There isn't anybody in the damn world worth hurting myself over. Since changing some of my behaviors, I gained self-respect and feel a whole lot better about myself.

Spirituality in Recovery

Although most people think of spirituality in terms of religion, in recovery it has a broader meaning. It refers to your relationships with God or a Higher Power and the values that bring you a sense of purpose and meaning in your life. According to Bowen White and John MacDougall, spirituality encompasses principles such as honesty, hope, faith, courage, integrity, willingness, humility, compassion, justice, perseverance, spiritual awareness, and service.[11] I would add forgiveness to this list (of oneself and others).[12] Although spirituality has always been an important part of recovery from addiction, more attention is now being paid to this area among mental health professionals.[13]

Many people find it helpful to attend services or to participate in religious activities because this brings a sense of hope, connectedness, and strength. Services and prayer bring comfort to many and help people get through hard times.

Recovery is a "we" rather than an "I" program, so stay connected with other people and a Higher Power so that you won't feel alone. Connecting with other people gives you a sense of purpose and an opportunity to get support, which helps you both in times of difficulty and during times in which you are doing well. Praying and reading the Bible or other inspirational works can help you find knowledge, guidance, and motivation and give meaning and direction to your life.

You can talk about spirituality issues in treatment sessions or at support group meetings. Several of the 12 steps focus on spirituality. Working step 5 with a member of the clergy can be very helpful ("We admitted to God, to ourselves, and to another human being the exact nature of our wrongs").

Being of service to others and doing things for the greater good of society can help your spirituality. Even small contributions can have a big impact on how you feel about yourself. You can do volunteer work for a homeless shelter, a soup kitchen, a hospital, a church or synagogue, a school, or other community organizations. Helping your own children and family members by spending time with them, showing love and compassion to them, or doing things for them is another way of serving others who are close to you.

Working though feelings of guilt and shame helps you further develop your spirituality. This process involves making amends to others hurt by your

Strategies for Developing Your Spirituality

1. Rely on God or your Higher Power for strength, guidance, purpose in life, and understanding.
2. Participate in religious services and other religious activities.
3. Make praying a regular part of your day or join a prayer group.
4. Attend a religious retreat or spend time at a monastery or other spiritual place.
5. Meditate.
6. Read the Bible or other spiritual and inspirational guides in order to seek knowledge, guidance, and motivation.
7. Discuss spirituality issues in therapy sessions or with your AA/NA/DRA sponsor.
8. Focus on the 12-step program of AA, NA, or DRA, especially steps 2, 3, 4, 5, 6, 7, 11, and 12.
9. Seek spiritual advice from a priest, minister, rabbi, or other spiritual person.
10. Focus on the greater good of society and contributions that you can make to make the world a better place.
11. Be of service to others.
12. Show love and compassion in your daily life in your interactions with other people.
13. Be kind and forgiving to people whom you believe have hurt you.
14. Accept your own weaknesses and limitations and be kind to yourself and tolerant of your shortcomings and mistakes.
15. If you feel guilty for things you've done that hurt others, stop the hurtful behavior and decide whether you need to make amends to undo some of the damage.

Source: Daley, D. C. (2000). *Dual diagnosis workbook: Recovery strategies for substance use and mental health problems* (2nd ed.). Independence, MO: Independence Press.

behaviors, accepting your weaknesses and limitations, and giving yourself credit for all the steps you are taking to improve yourself.

Working on your spirituality helps you feel better about yourself, stay off alcohol or drugs, and become a better person. One of the longer term goals of recovery is growth as a person. Focusing on spiritual development is one excellent way of achieving this personal growth.

The chart on page 171 summarizes ways to develop your spirituality in recovery.[14]

Using Self-Comforting Strategies

Self-comforting strategies are physical, mental, or spiritual activities that make you feel good and help you calm yourself down, cope with unpleasant thoughts or feelings, or gain a greater sense of self-control. These can be used to cope with difficult circumstances or serve as a "prevention" function. Many of these were discussed in previous sections, and they are listed in the chart that follows:[15]

Self-Comforting Strategies

1. Breathe slowly when feeling upset.
2. Talk yourself out of feeling upset by making positive self-coping statements.
3. Think calm thoughts.
4. Slow down and don't let your life get too hectic.
5. Make sure you get sufficient sleep and rest.
6. Release your tensions with regular physical activity or exercise.
7. Jog or take a walk to clear your head.
8. Relax during every single day.
9. Listen to soothing music under candlelight.
10. Engage in creative activities (music, writing, sculpting, etc.).
11. Read inspirational writings.
12. Write about your thoughts, feelings, and experiences in a journal.
13. Give yourself body time (take a long bath, get a massage).
14. Pray or meditate.
15. Reach out to others for support.

Source: Linehan, M. M. (1993). *Skills training manual for treating borderline personality disorder.* New York: Guilford Press.

Chapter 12 *Maintaining Gains Over Time: Relapse Prevention Strategies*

Stories of Relapse

I Was Doing Well, Then Things Started Getting Bad

I had been in recovery off and on for a long time for depression, an anxiety and phobic disorder, and addiction to tranquilizers and alcohol. I had over 3 years sober, and my psychiatric problems were well under control. I was able to get off my medications because I was doing very well. Then I lost my job. Over a period of the next few months, things started getting bad. I got real depressed and kept to myself. Then I started feeling intense anxiety and fear again. I couldn't go anywhere unless my son went with me. I even stopped going to AA meetings and got to the point where I only went out of my house when I had to buy food or pay bills. In no time, I became a prisoner of my own home because of my fear.

When I started thinking about drinking alcohol to help calm my nerves and give me courage to leave my house, I knew it was time to do something. So I made an appointment at the clinic that took care of me before. They helped get my depression, anxiety, and phobia under control with the right treatment. Even though my symptoms returned, I felt good that I didn't use alcohol again because this would have made things much worse.—Roberta, age 39

So What's Wrong With a Few Beers?

Things were going good for me. I was taking lithium for my bipolar illness, seeing a therapist and psychiatrist regularly, and going to AA meetings. My home remodeling business was going well, too. Then I got a call from Pete, an old friend who wanted an estimate on finishing a game room. He asked if I could meet him down at the local bar. I didn't think this was any big deal because I had been sober for a long time and hadn't had any desires to drink for some time.

So I met Pete at the bar and had a sandwich with him as we talked about the job. As I watched him drink, I thought to myself, "so what's wrong with a few beers?" After all, I was doing well, how could a few beers hurt? I drank two beers and that was it. No big deal, really. Each day, when I was done working on Pete's basement, he'd bring some beers and we would drink and talk. Of course, I never told anybody else I was drinking again because I was controlling how much I drank and not getting drunk. Well, this was just the beginning. Within a month, I missed two outpatient appointments and stopped taking lithium because my prescription ran out. At the same time, my drinking got heavier. Soon, I was in a manic episode again, flying around like a madman from one job to the next, and spending a lot of time talking on the phone. I'd be up and dressed and ready to go at 4 in the morning and often didn't come home until late at night.

Things would have gotten much worse if my wife hadn't insisted I see my therapist and doctor because she knew something was wrong, even though I outright lied to her and denied I was drinking. Lucky for me, my therapist and doctor helped me stop drinking and get back on the lithium. I'm doing OK now, but I was really flirting with disaster. I always have to keep in mind that drinking any alcohol will put me at greater risk for a relapse to mania because I end up stopping my lithium. There's no way of getting around this fact.—Jackson, age 53

Relapse is a reality in mood disorders and/or addiction.[1–6] In the preceding story, Roberta ignored her early warning signs of relapse to her depression and anxiety disorders. Fortunately, she reached out for help *before* she used alcohol. Had she started drinking again, her condition would have gotten worse. Jackson, on the other hand, relapsed to alcohol use. He started with a few beers, then increased the amount and frequency of his drinking over the next several weeks. Jackson then stopped taking his lithium, which put him at risk for a manic relapse. Soon, both of his disorders were out of control, and he went downhill fast. Who knows how much more damage may have resulted from his relapse if his wife hadn't insisted he get help? These cases show that people can do well and then relapse to either or both disorders, even after a period of sobriety or mood stability.

Definitions of Relapse

With depression, bipolar illness, or another psychiatric disorder, relapse refers to a return of the symptoms of your disorder after a period of recovery from your current episode. Relapse also refers to a significant worsening of some of the persistent symptoms of your illness. This means that symptoms that more or less remain with you continuously over time get much worse and interfere with your well-being. *Recurrence* is a term used to describe a new episode of depression, mania, or other psychiatric illness following months or years of being virtually symptom free.

With addiction, relapse refers to the process of going back to using alcohol or drugs. The relapse process can start before you use alcohol or drugs. This is sometimes referred to as "building up to drink or use drugs, the dry drunk syndrome, the dry drug syndrome, or a mental relapse."[2] You may not be using, but your behaviors and attitudes indicate that you are likely to use if you don't do something to stop the relapse process.

You are at higher risk for relapse to either of your disorders than those who have only a single disorder. This is the reason that it is important to work hard at your recovery and to put together a solid relapse prevention plan. Although doing this won't guarantee that your symptoms won't return or that you won't use substances again, it will decrease your chances of relapse.

Causes of Relapse to Depression or Mania

A number of factors can contribute to your depression or mania returning or worsening.[7-12] One of the most common is failure to comply with your treatment plan.[13,14] This involves missing or stopping therapy sessions, cutting down or stopping your medications, not taking them as prescribed, or mixing alcohol or other street drugs with them. This is often a private decision made for the wrong reasons and one that is not discussed first with your therapist or doctor. The case of Jackson shows that he started drinking alcohol and soon quit taking his lithium. He never discussed any of these decisions with his therapist, doctor, or sponsor.

If you miss your appointments, stop therapy, or stop taking medications, you place yourself at risk for relapse. And you are more likely to need inpatient hospitalization if your mood symptoms significantly worsen. People who stabilize in a psychiatric hospital often end up back again because they don't attend outpatient sessions or drop out early.

One of the most common causes of relapse is failure to catch early warning signs. Usually, mild symptoms precede more severe ones. Ignoring, wishing them away, or not discussing symptoms with your treatment team can contribute to an increase in their severity. If you ignore early signs, symptoms of your mood disorder can break through, and you can have a full-blown episode of illness. Contrary to what some people believe, you don't need to experience any specific event or upsetting situation to suffer a mood disorder relapse. The chronic and recurrent nature of many types of mood disorders is such that symptoms can return as a result of the illness itself.

Occasionally, medications used to treat one type of illness may trigger symptoms of another illness. Keep in close contact with your treatment team and let them know if your symptoms return or worsen, particularly after medication changes have been made by your doctor.

Some people are more vulnerable to stress and have a harder time coping with ordinary life experiences than others due to their biological and psychological makeup. Therefore, your personal vulnerability may make you more apt to have a relapse of your illness. This is why it is so important to spot symptom changes early. In addition, it helps to learn ways to cope with stressful and upsetting situations.

Another major factor in mood disorder relapse is using alcohol, street drugs, or other, nonprescribed drugs. Even small amounts of substances can make your psychiatric medications less effective, negatively affect your motivation, or make your illness worse. For this reason I advise working a program of *total abstinence* from alcohol or other drugs. This gives you a better chance of recovering from your mood disorder. Jackson's case is an example of a common pattern seen among individuals with dual diagnosis—alcohol or drugs are used, psychiatric treatment is stopped, and then the symptoms return. When symptoms return, life problems often result.

If you lack structure, routine, or goals, you are more vulnerable to relapse. Being engaged in productive work, leisure, or volunteer or community activities keeps you busy, provides you opportunities to feel good about yourself, and gives you a sense of purpose and direction. It also gives you less time to turn your thoughts inward and focus on your problems.

Major medical problems, changes in your health status, and major life stresses such as a serious illness of a partner or family member or losing your job can affect a relapse, as well. It is usually not the event or stress in and of itself that causes a relapse but lacking the coping skills to deal with it. Roberta's relapse started with feeling depressed and isolating herself from others following the loss of her job. She was unable to cope with her depression after ignoring the early signs of her mood relapse.

Relationship stress, losing an important relationship, being disconnected from others and feeling alone, lacking support from others, getting rejected, experiencing severe criticism, or having serious conflicts with others in your life can influence relapse, too. This is the reason you should focus on improving relationships and developing a strong support system as part of your recovery.

You can also set yourself up to relapse if you take on major roles before you are stable from your depression or bipolar disorder. For example, if you have a major episode of illness that requires you to be in a psychiatric hospital and you go back to work too soon, you may put yourself in a stressful situation with which you are not ready to deal. This is not to say that you can't go to work after being discharged from a psychiatric hospital. Everyone is different, and what is best for you depends on your specific situation. For example, Mike lost his job following relapse to cocaine addiction and to his mood disorder. He insisted he needed another job right away and chose to work rather than attend a day hospital treatment program. Within 2 weeks, he lost his new job. Although it is understandable that Mike wanted to work, he was in no shape psychologically. Putting treatment low on his priority list worked against him. Fortunately, he finally followed the recommendations of his treatment team, finished the day program, got some drug-free time under his belt, and stabilized on medications. He then was able to find and keep a job.

Sometimes receiving inadequate treatment can cause your relapse. If you have major life problems or stresses that contribute to your depressive illness and your only treatment is medications, you may be more vulnerable to relapse. This is the reason that therapy is important, unless you have been stable on medications for several years or longer. Therapy gives you the chance to work out problems that contribute to or result from your disorders. Or, if your mood symptoms are severe and disabling but you refuse to take medications, your chances of improvement are much smaller than if you take medications. Finally, if going to treatment sessions once a week doesn't help you manage your mood symptoms or stop substance abuse, you probably need a higher level of care, such as a partial-hospital or intensive outpatient program.

I conducted a survey of 140 outpatients with dual diagnoses and asked them to tell me the different factors they think contributed to a relapse to their mood disorders. They identified the most common factors that contribute to relapse as follows: (1) stress and upsetting emotional states; (2) relationship and family conflicts; (3) poor compliance with treatment; (4) lifestyle factors; (5) using alcohol or other drugs to medicate themselves; and (6) negative thinking.

Causes of Addiction Relapse

Many of the same factors mentioned previously can contribute to addiction relapse.[2,15,16] These include failure to comply with your treatment plan, missing treatment sessions, stopping treatment or self-help meetings, ignoring early signs of relapse, lacking structure or direction in your life, inability to manage major life changes or stresses, lacking coping skills to deal with your problems, or involvement in unhealthy or violent relationships.

Upsetting moods or feelings—such as anxiety, anger, boredom, depression, emptiness, guilt, loneliness, and joylessness—can affect relapse, too. Sometimes these feelings are part of a mood disorder. It is not just the upsetting emotion but the lack of coping skills to manage it that contributes to relapse.

Another cause of addiction relapse is being around people or in places in which alcohol or drugs are offered or readily available. If you are unable to refuse offers to drink alcohol or use other drugs or to resolve problems and conflicts with other people, or if you lack a support system, you increase your risk for relapse. Therefore, it helps to cut ties with others who are getting high and become involved with people who are sober and can support your recovery.

You still may feel anxious or depressed or have sleep difficulties, making you feel vulnerable to relapse even weeks or months after you stop alcohol or drugs. Your addiction also triggers cravings and urges to use. This may be a conditioned response to seeing people, places, and things in your environment that remind you of using. Other times it results from complex interactions of neurotransmitters in your brain.

Physical illness or pain, premenstrual syndrome (PMS), failure to get proper rest or relaxation, eating a poor diet, and using medications for dental, medical, or psychiatric problems can trigger your addictive urge. For example, your body does not know the difference between an addictive drug used get high and one used to treat a medical problem. Tell your doctor or dentist about your addiction so that, if medicines are prescribed, they are used under close supervision. Phil, for example, who had been doing quite well for several years, relapsed to heroin use after taking pain medication following dental work. After just a few days of using pain medications, Phil's desire for drugs resurfaced quickly and overwhelmed him. Rather than tell his dentist or people in his support system, he let his addictive urge lead him to using drugs again. His relapse lasted months and caused much damage in his life and with his family.

If you self-medicate your mood symptoms with alcohol, street drugs, or someone else's medication, you are more vulnerable to addiction relapse. For example, mania can impair your judgment, or depression can lower your motivation to work your recovery plan. Either way, you could end up using alcohol or drugs again.

Spiritual factors—such as intense shame and guilt, not having any meaning or purpose in life, feeling a chronic sense of emptiness or lacking joy in your life, and feeling no connection with other people—can contribute to relapse. Using may "fill the void" and temporarily let you escape from spiritual pain or emptiness. This is the reason that your life has to change and that you need positive replacements for drugs and alcohol.

It is usually several factors that cause a relapse rather than just one. You need to figure out your relapse risk factors and devise prevention strategies. The more you work on your life problems and remain aware of factors that cause relapse, the more you reduce your risk.

In the survey I mentioned earlier, I also asked the 140 patients to tell me what contributed to addiction relapse. They identified these factors as follows: (1) stress or upsetting emotional states; (2) relationship and family conflicts; (3) poor compliance with treatment; (4) negative thinking; (5) low motivation to change; and (6) lifestyle factors. All of these overlap with the causes of mood disorder relapse. I spoke with Dr. Roger Weiss, director of substance abuse treatment at McLean Hospital of Harvard Medical School, about his research with patients who have both bipolar disorders and addiction. Dr. Weiss told me that the dynamics of relapse are similar in both disorders and that poor compliance with medications is a major factor in relapse to the bipolar disorder.[17]

Identifying and Managing Relapse Warning Signs

Before a recurrent episode of depression or mania occurs or you relapse to substance use, you are likely to experience warning signs.[2,18–20] Learning to spot warning signs early can help you take action to reduce the likelihood of relapse to either of your disorders.

Relapse warning signs can be obvious to you or others. However, because of denial and other psychological defenses or poor judgment, you may not be aware of warning signs when they show. The more you increase your awareness of common general warning signs and warning signs specific to your mood and substance use disorders, and the more you involve significant others in your recovery, the better able you will be to take action to protect your recovery and reduce relapse risk.

General indicators of relapse to mood disorders or addiction show in changes in your thoughts, moods, behaviors, and health habits. For example, cutting down or stopping treatment or self-help sessions frequently precedes relapse. Specific indicators of relapse include symptoms of your mood disorder, which can return after a period of partial or full remission. With bipolar disorder, first signs of relapse may be sleep disturbance, racing thoughts, or thoughts that medications make you less productive, creative, or interesting to others. Learn as much as you can about your disorder so that you can spot early signs of relapse. Chronic and persistent symptoms that had been fairly well controlled can suddenly worsen, causing you personal distress or difficulties in your life. For example, Patrick, who was recovering from major depression, dysthymia, and alcoholism, was able to cope successfully with his mood symptoms for a long time. Then, after he resumed drinking alcohol, to his surprise he felt increasingly depressed, isolated, and hopeless about his life.

Relapse warning signs can show in your thinking or attitudes. You may stop caring about your recovery or think that you no longer need help. You may have more negative and pessimistic thoughts about your ability to recover or critical thoughts about your treatment team, sponsor, or self-help programs.

Increased difficulty concentrating or paying attention or racing thoughts may indicate a relapse to your mood disorder. The return of persistent thoughts about hurting yourself or other people is also a relapse sign.

Significant changes in your feelings or mood states often precede a relapse. Examples include becoming increasingly moody, depressed, anxious, agitated, fearful, or angry. You may start feeling euphoric, as though you are on top of the world, or your moods may shift rapidly from feeling depressed to feeling euphoric. Feelings of depression are very common in mood disorder relapse and addiction relapse. Feeling bored and losing interest can also be a warning sign of relapse with depression, mania, and addiction.

Changes in your health habits or daily routine may tip you off that you are headed toward a relapse. These show in changes in your personal hygiene, sleep difficulties, significant changes in your appetite or energy level, or changes in your daily routine.

Other warning signs may be an increase or decrease in your interactions with other people, becoming more or less talkative than usual, acting without thinking about the consequences of your action, or hurting yourself or others. With all types of mood and substance use disorders, stopping treatment, self-help meetings, or other important social, recreational, or church activities can indicate movement toward relapse.

Keep in mind that you may have nonillness symptoms of relapse, as well as illness-specific symptoms. Discuss the possibility of relapse with your therapist so that you are clear about the signs of relapse that are associated with your disorders.

Once you identify warning signs of relapse, the next step is to develop an action plan. This plan involves the steps you can take to deal with your warning signs so that you don't use alcohol or drugs and so that you have a chance of heading off a full-blown episode of mood relapse. Your plan should include actions you can take on your own, such as talking yourself out of using alcohol or drugs, talking yourself out of acting on thoughts to hurt yourself or another person, fighting off negative thoughts that make you feel bad, or distracting yourself with an activity. Your plan should also include steps you can take to reach out for help and support from people such as your treatment team, your sponsor and other members of support groups, and your family and friends. By paying attention to warning signs, you can spot changes early. For example, if you notice mild symptoms of depression and take action to cope with them, you put yourself in a better position to avoid a full episode of major depressive illness. Or, if you notice signs of an impending manic episode early, it is possible that you could head it off by getting an adjustment in your medications or extra support from your treatment team. The same holds true with addiction. If you can catch your early warning signs, you have a greater chance of not picking up the first drink or drug.

Identifying and Managing High-Risk Relapse Factors

High-risk factors are situations that increase your vulnerability to drinking or using drugs, feeling depressed or becoming hypomanic, stopping your medications, or dropping out of treatment. One of the best ways to manage high-risk factors is to attend support group meetings. It helps to have structure and a sense of direction in your life in which you set and work toward specific goals. You should have a list of problems that you are working on in order to get well and improve your life. By facing and resolving your problems and conflicts and complying with medication and therapy, you decrease the chances of relapse to alcohol or drug use. You also decrease the chances that stress will trigger your mood symptoms. This is precisely the reason that recovery requires commitment, as well as a willingness to deal head-on with your problems and high-risk factors.

Developing a Written Relapse Prevention Plan

Make a written list of your warning signs of relapse for both disorders and of your high-risk factors. Then list some specific steps you can take to manage them. If you have been in recovery before, review the times in which you did well. Identify the specific things you did before that helped you. For example, if participation in support groups, talking openly with others about your problems or struggles, praying or asking for help from your Higher Power, or positive self-talk helped you before, continue to use these recovery tools.

Discussing Your Relapse Prevention Plan With Others

Discuss your relapse prevention plan with your therapist, your sponsor, or others who know you well so you can get their input. Talk with your family about steps they can take to help you if they see early warning signs of relapse. It is better to have this discussion during a period in which you are doing well, because in the midst of an actual relapse, you may not listen to feedback from your family. Make an agreement that includes the steps they can take to point out warning signs or to provide you with help and support if you ignore their pleas. Give your family permission to let your doctor or therapist know if your symptoms get much worse and you refuse to listen to them. For example, Luisa's husband Shawn was able to help avert a more serious relapse for his wife when he alerted her therapist and doctor that some of her mood symptoms were worsening. When her treatment team ordered lab tests, they discovered low levels of antidepressant medication in her blood. The laboratory reports also showed that she was smoking pot again. Although she was in a relapse, quick action on the part of her husband helped keep things from getting worse, particularly as she initially denied using marijuana when asked by her treatment team.

In more severe cases of mood disorder relapse, it may be necessary for an involuntary commitment to be initiated by your loved ones. This usually occurs only when you can't take care of your basic needs or are at serious risk to hurt yourself or someone else. Always remember that family members do this out of love and concern and a desire to help you get back on track.

Preparing for Setbacks and Emergencies

Preparing for emergencies puts you in a position to get help before a lot of damage is done. Should you have a setback, keep in mind that the longer you ignore your depression or manic symptoms, and the longer your use of substances goes on, the greater the degree of damage that can occur.

Emergencies include a return of more serious mood or other psychiatric symptoms, a significant worsening of persistent symptoms, or a return to alcohol or other drug abuse. Feeling severely depressed, agitated, suicidal, homicidal, psychotic, and manic or being unable to take care of yourself are specific examples of emergencies. Because your illness may cause you to deny or minimize the severity of an emergency, you should involve others in your emergency plan. This is self-protection for you, because your judgment may be so impaired that your life is in jeopardy.

Your emergency plan can include:

- The specific steps you can take if you actually use alcohol or drugs again
- Steps you can take if you have a serious psychiatric emergency
- Figuring out under what conditions you should go to a psychiatric hospital
- Figuring out under what circumstances you would need to go back to the hospital for detoxification from addictive substance use
- Determining under what conditions you would need to be committed to psychiatric care involuntarily
- Determining the specific steps that your family or members of your support network can take to help you in any of these emergency situations, including when you refuse their efforts to help you

Prepare ahead of time so that you are not taken by surprise by an emergency. Put together your plan when you are doing well. I have seen many emergen-

---

Strategies for Managing Relapse Warning Signs and High-Risk Situations

1. Know the causes and warning signs of mood disorder and addiction relapse, as well as signs unique to you.
2. Develop a plan to manage the early relapse warning signs of both your disorders.
3. Identify your high-risk situations (people, places, events, feelings, and problems).
4. Develop a plan to deal directly with these high-risk factors.
5. Work a daily recovery plan.
6. Complete a daily inventory to monitor relapse warning signs, high-risk factors, and close calls.
7. Ask people in your recovery network to point out relapse warning signs if they spot them early.
8. Discuss strong cravings and desires to use, close calls, and persistent thoughts of using with your sponsor, therapist, or someone whom you trust.
9. If you use, stop immediately and get back on the sober track. Seek help if you feel unable to stop on your own.
10. Review your relapse prevention plan with a sponsor, therapist, or someone who understands recovery.
11. If you have had multiple relapses, try to figure out whether any patterns exist.
12. Use your relapses as a learning experience and figure out what you need to do differently in the future.
13. Learn to cope with persistent symptoms of recurrent or chronic mood disorders.

---

cies dealt with quickly because people took action early in the relapse process rather than waiting until things were out of control. If you need to go back to the hospital, then remember that the hospital is for helping people who have severe psychiatric problems. Any time that you have a severe emergency, once things have settled down, you can take a look at what led up to it and caused it. This in turn can help you with your future recovery plans.

The chart opposite lists strategies to manage relapse warning signs and high-risk situations.

Appendix   *Helpful Resources*

Many resources are available on mood disorders, addiction, or dual disorders. These include informational resources (books, guides, workbooks, audiotapes, and videotapes), as well as self-help programs. Check the telephone book or call information for local phone numbers of treatment agencies. In addition to the Internet list that follows, resources can be accessed on the Internet through names of bookstores (e.g., Amazon, Barnes and Noble, Borders) or of publishers of recovery literature or by conducting a search of key terms or words, such as addiction; alcohol abuse, alcohol addiction, alcohol dependence, or alcoholism; bipolar disorder; depression, major depression, or dysthymia; drug abuse, drug addiction, or drug dependency; families and addiction, alcoholism, drug addiction, bipolar disorder or depression; mood disorders; recovery, recovery from addiction, bipolar illness, depression, or dual disorders; or the name of a specific person or organization associated with addiction, mood disorders, or dual disorders.

Alcoholics Anonymous, www.alcoholics-anonymous.org

Al-Anon Family Groups, www.alanon.org

American Foundation for the Prevention of Suicide, www.afsp.org

American Psychiatric Association, www.psych.org

American Psychological Association, www.apa.org

Anxiety Disorders Association of America, www.adaa.org

Bipolar Focus, www.moodswing.org

Daley Publications, www.drdenniscdaley.com

Depression and Related Affective Disorders Association, www.drada.org

Dual Recovery Anonymous (DRA), www.dualrecovery.org

Hazelden: Educational Materials, www.hazelden.org

International Foundation for Research and Education on Depression, www.ifred.org

Mental Health Infosource, www.mhsource.com

Narcotics Anonymous, www.na.org

Nar-Anon Family Groups, www.naranon.com

National Alliance for the Mentally Ill, www.nami.org

National Clearinghouse for Alcohol & Drug Information, www.health.org

National Depressive and Manic-Depressive Association, www.ndmda.org

National Institute on Alcohol Abuse and Alcoholism, www.niaaa.nih.gov

National Institute on Drug Abuse, www.nida.nih.gov

National Institute of Mental Health, www.nimh.nih.gov

National Mental Health Association, www.nmha.org

Pendulum Resources: Bipolar and Affective Disorders, www.pendulum.org

Substance Abuse and Mental Health Services, www.samhsa.gov

Suicide Prevention Action Network, www.spanusa.org

Support Group.Com Home Page, www.support-group.com

References

* Denotes readings for clients and/or families

Chapter 1. Dual Disorders

1. McGovern, G. (1997). *Terry.* New York: Plume.
2. Robins, L. N., & Regier, D. A. (1991). *Psychiatric disorders in America.* New York: Free Press.
3. Regier, D. (1990). Comorbidity of mental disorders with alcohol and other drug abuse: Results from the Epidemiologic Catchment Area Study. *Journal of the American Medical Association, 264,* 2511–2518.
4. Daley, D. C., & Moss, H. M. (2002). *Dual disorders: Counseling clients with chemical dependency and mental illness* (3rd ed.). Center City, MN: Hazelden.
5. O'Connell, D.F. (Ed.). (2002). *Managing the dually diagnosed patient: Current issues and clinical approaches* (2nd ed.). New York: Haworth.
6. Salloum, I. M., Daley, D. C., & Thase, M. E. (2000). *Male depression, alcoholism, and violence.* London: Dunitz.
7. Ross, H., Germanson, T., & Glaser, F. (1988). The prevalence of psychiatric disorders in clients with alcohol and other drug problems. *Archives of General Psychiatry, 45,* 1023–1031.
8. Drake, R. E., & Mueser, K. T. (Eds.). (1996). *Dual diagnosis of major mental illness and substance abuse* (Vol. 2). San Francisco: Jossey-Bass.
9. Rosenthal, R. N., & Weinrich, L. (1999). Treatment of persons with dual diagnoses of substance use disorder and other psychological problems. In B. S. McCrady & E. E. Epstein (Eds.) *Addictions: A comprehensive guidebook* (pp. 439–476). New York: Oxford University Press.

10. Bernadt, M., & Murray, R. (1986). Psychiatric disorder, drinking, and alcoholism: What are the links? *British Journal of Psychiatry, 148,* 393–400.

11. Daley, D. C., & Thase, M. E. (2000). *Dual disorders recovery counseling: Integrated treatment for substance use and mental health disorders* (2nd ed.). Independence, MO: Independence Press.

12. Meyer, R. (Ed.) (1986). *Addictive disorders and psychopathology.* New York: Guilford Press.

13. Salloum, I. M., & Thase, M. E. (2000). Impact of substance abuse on the course and treatment of bipolar disorder. *Bipolar Disorders, 2,* 269–280.

14. Styron, W. (1990). *Darkness visible: A memoir of madness.* New York: Random House.

15. Drake, R. E., Mercer-McFadden, C., Mueser, K. T., McHugho, G., & Bond, G. (1998). A review of integrated mental health and substance abuse treatment for patients with dual disorders. *Schizophrenia Bulletin, 24,* 589–608.

16. Galanter, M., & Kleber, H. D. (Eds.). (1999). *Textbook of substance abuse treatment* (2nd ed.). Washington, DC: American Psychiatric Press.

17. Clark, H. W., Masson, C. L., Delucchi, K. L., Hall, S. M., & Sees, K. L. (2000). Violent traumatic events and drug abuse severity. *Journal of Substance Abuse Treatment, 20,* 121–127.

18. Daley, D. C., & Salloum, I. M. (Eds.). (2001). *A clinician's guide to mental illness.* New York: McGraw-Hill.

19. Frank, E., Swartz, H. A., & Kupfer, D. J. (2000). Interpersonal and social rhythm therapy: Managing the chaos of bipolar disorder. *Biological Psychiatry, 48,* 593–604.

20. Goodwin, F. K., & Jamison, K. R. (1990). *Manic-depressive illness.* New York: Oxford University Press.

21. Hirschfeld, R. M., & Shea, M. T. (2000). Mood disorders: Psychotherapy. In B. J. Sadock & V. A. Sadock (Eds.) *Comprehensive textbook of psychiatry* (7th ed., pp. 1431–1440). Baltimore: Lippincott Williams & Wilkins.

22. Jaffe, J. H. (2000). Substance-related disorders: Introduction and overview. In B. J. Sadock & V. A. Sadock (Eds.) *Comprehensive textbook of psychiatry* (7th ed., pp. 924–952). Baltimore: Lippincott Williams & Wilkins.

23. Kocsis, J. H., & Klein, D. N. (Eds.). (1995). *Diagnosis and treatment of chronic depression.* New York: Guilford Press.

24. McCrady, B., & Epstein, E. (Eds.). (1999). *Addictions: A comprehensive guidebook.* New York: Oxford University Press.

25. Montimore, F. M. (1999). *Bipolar disorder: A guide for patients and families.* Baltimore: Johns Hopkins Press.*

26. Ott, P. J., Tarter, R. E., & Ammerman, R. T. (Eds.). (1999). *Sourcebook on substance abuse: Etiology, epidemiology, assessment, and treatment.* Needham Heights, MA: Allyn & Bacon.

27. Papolos, D., & Papolos J. (1997). *Overcoming depression: The definitive resource for patients and families who live with depression and manic-depression* (3rd ed.). New York: HarperCollins.*

28. Pirzada, S. R., Ries, R., & LoGerfo, J. P. (1997). Cost of comorbid alcohol and drug problems. *American Journal on Addictions, 6,* 193–204.

29. Post, R. M. (2000). Mood disorders: Treatment of bipolar disorder. In B. J. Sadock & V. A. Sadock (Eds.) *Comprehensive textbook of psychiatry* (7th ed., pp. 1385–1430). Baltimore: Lippincott Williams & Wilkins.

30. Schuckit, M. A. (2000). *Drug and alcohol abuse: A clinical guide to diagnosis and treatment* (5th ed.). New York: Plenum.

31. Blazer, D. G., II. (2000). Mood disorders: Epidemiology. In B. J. Sadock & V. A. Sadock (Eds.), *Comprehensive textbook of psychiatry* (7th ed., pp. 1298–1307). Baltimore: Lippincott Williams & Wilkins.

32. Fink, M. (1999). *Electroshock therapy: Restoring the mind.* New York: Oxford University Press.

33. Center for Substance Abuse Treatment. (1999). *Treatment succeeds in fighting crime.* Rockville, MD: Author.

34. Daley, D. (1992). Substance abuse and offending: Clinical and social perspectives. *Current Opinion in Psychiatry, 5,* 792–798.

35. Daley, D. C. (2003). *Understanding suicide and addiction.* Center City, MN: Hazelden.

36. Cornelius, J. R., Salloum, I. M., Day, N. L., Thase, M. E., & Mann, J. J. (1996). Patterns of suicidality and alcohol use in alcoholics with major depression. *Alcoholism: Clinical and Experimental Research, 20,* 1451–1455.

37. Shea, S. C. (1999). *The practical art of suicide assessment: A guide for mental health professionals and substance abuse counselors.* New York: Wiley.

38. Jamison, K. R. (1999). *Night falls fast: Understanding suicide.* New York: Knopf.*

39. Akiskal, H. S. (2000). Mood disorders: Introduction and overview. In B. J. Sadock & V. A. Sadock (Eds.), *Comprehensive textbook of psychiatry* (7th ed., pp. 1284–1297). Baltimore: Lippincott Williams & Wilkins..

40. Daley, D. C., & Miller, J. (2001). *Addiction in your family: Helping yourself and your loved ones.* Holmes Beach, FL: Learning Publications.*

41. Fawcett, J., Golden, B., & Rosenfeld, N. (2000). *New hope for people with bipolar disorder.* Roseville, CA: Prima Health.*

42. Hatfield, A. B., & Lefley, H. P. (Eds.). (1987). *Families of the mentally ill: Coping and adaptation.* New York: Guilford Press.

43. Johnson, V. (1989). *Intervention: How to help someone who doesn't want help.* Minneapolis, MN: Johnson Institute.*

44. Keitner, G. I. (1990). *Depression and families: Impact and treatment.* Washington, DC: American Psychiatric Association.

45. Mueser, K. T., & Glynn, S. M. (1999). *Behavioral family therapy for psychiatric disorders* (2nd ed.). Oakland, CA: New Harbinger.

46. Rosen, L. E., & Amador, X. F. (1996). *When someone you love is depressed.* New York: Free Press.*

47. Yapko, M. D. (2000). *Hand me down blues: How to stop depression from spreading in families.* New York: St. Martin's Griffin.*

48. National Institute on Alcohol Abuse and Alcoholism.(2001). Alcohol and health. *Alcohol Research and Health, 25*(1), 1–79.

49. Liepman, M. R. (1998). The family in addiction. In A. W. Graham & T. K. Schultz (Eds.), *Principles of addiction medicine* (2nd ed., pp. 1093–1098). Chevy Chase, MD: American Society of Addiction Medicine.

50. Daley, D. C. (2001). *Money and recovery workbook.* Holmes Beach, FL: Learning Publications.

51. Mueser, K. T., Drake, R. E., Noordsy, D. L., & Fox, L. (2003). *Integrated treatment for dual disorders: A guide to effective practice.* New York: Guilford Press.

Chapter 2. Understanding Addiction

1. *Alcoholics Anonymous.* (1976). New York: AA World Services.

2. Robins, L. N., & Regier D. A. (1991). *Psychiatric disorders in America.* New York: Free Press.

3. Galanter, M., & Kleber, H. D. (Eds.). (1999). *Textbook of substance abuse treatment* (2nd ed). Washington, DC: American Psychiatric Press.

4. Jaffe, J. H. (2000). Substance-related disorders: Introduction and overview. In B. J. Sadock & V. A. Sadock (Eds.), *Comprehensive textbook of psychiatry* (7th ed., pp. 924–952). Baltimore: Lippincott Williams & Wilkins.

5. Jaffe, J. H. (2000). Cocaine-related disorders. In B. J. Sadock & V. A. Sadock (Eds.), *Comprehensive textbook of psychiatry* (7th ed., pp. 999–1014). Baltimore: Lippincott Williams & Wilkins.

6. Lowinson, J. H., Ruiz, P., Millman, R. B., & Langrod, J. G. (Eds.). (2005). *Substance abuse: A comprehensive textbook* (4th ed.). Baltimore: Williams & Wilkins.

7. McCrady, B., & Epstein, E. (Eds.). (1999). *Addictions: A comprehensive guidebook.* London: Oxford University Press.

8. National Institute on Alcohol Abuse and Alcoholism. (2000). *Alcohol and health: Tenth special report to the U.S. Congress.* Rockville, MD: U.S. Department of Health and Human Services.

9. Leshner, A. I. (1998). What we know: Drug addiction is a brain disease. In A. W. Graham & T. K. Schultz (Eds.), *Principles of addiction medicine* (2nd ed., pp. xxix–xxxvi). Chevy Chase, MD: American Society of Addiction Medicine.

10. Schuckit, M. A. (2000). *Drug and alcohol abuse: A clinical guide to diagnosis and treatment* (5th ed.). New York: Plenum Press.

11. Graham, A. W., & Schultz, T. K. (Eds.). (2003). *Principles of addiction medicine* (3rd ed.). Chevy Chase, MD: American Society of Addiction Medicine.

12. American Psychiatric Association. (2000). *Diagnostic and statistical manual of mental disorders* (4th ed., text rev.). Washington, DC: Author.

13. Andreasen, N. C. (2001). *Brave new brain: Conquering mental illness in the era of the genome.* New York: Oxford University Press.*

14. Anthenelli, R. M., & Schuckit, M. A. (1997). Genetics. In J. H. Lowinson, P. Ruiz, R. B. Millman, & J. G. Langrod (Eds.), *Substance abuse: A comprehensive textbook* (3rd ed., pp. 41–50). Baltimore: Williams & Wilkins.

15. Cloninger, C. R. (1987) Neurogenetic adaptive mechanisms in alcoholism. *Science, 236,* 410–416.

16. Daley, D. C., & Moss, H. M. (2002). Dual disorders: Counseling clients with chemical dependency and mental illness (3rd ed.). Center City, MN: Hazelden.

17. O'Brien, C. P., Childress, A. R., Ehrman, R., & Robbins, S. J. (1998). Conditioning factors in drug abuse: Can they explain compulsion? *Psychopharmacology, 12,* 15–22.

18. Tarter, R., Moss, H., & Vanyukov, M. (1995). Behavior genetic perspective of alcoholism etiology. In H. Begleiter & B. Kissin (Eds.), *Alcohol and alcoholism: Genetic factors and alcoholism* (Vol. 1, pp. 294–327). New York: Oxford University Press.

19. Volkow, N. D., & Fowler, J. S. (2000). Addiction, a disease of compulsion and drive: Involvement of the orbitofrontal cortex. *Cerebral Cortex, 10,* 318–325.

20. Wise, R. A. (1998). Drug activation of brain reward pathways. *Drug and Alcohol Dependence, 51,* 13–22.

21. National Institute on Drug Abuse. (1997). Study sheds new light on the state of drug abuse treatment nationwide. *NIDA Notes, 12*(5), 1–8.

22. McLellan, A. T., Lewis, D. C., O'Brien, C. P., & Kleber, H. D. (2000). Drug dependence, a chronic medical illness: Implications for treatment, insurance, and outcomes evaluation. *Journal of the American Medical Association, 284*(13), 1689–1695.

23. Anderson, D. (1985). *The psychopathology of denial.* Center City, MN: Hazelden.*

24. Gorske, T. T., & Grinstead, S. F. (2000). *Denial management counseling.* Independence, MO: Independence Press.

25. Goodwin, F. K., & Jamison, K. R. (1990). *Manic-depressive illness.* New York: Oxford University Press.

26. Salloum, I. M., & Thase, M. E. (2000). Impact of substance abuse on the course and treatment of bipolar disorder. *Bipolar Disorders, 2,* 269–280.

27. Carroll, K. M. (1996). Relapse prevention as a psychosocial treatment: A review of controlled clinical trials. *Experimental and Clinical Psychopharmacology, 4,* 46–54.

28. Center for Substance Abuse Treatment. (2000). *Substance abuse treatment reduces family dysfunction, improves productivity.* Rockville, MD: Author.

29. Center for Substance Abuse Treatment. (2000). *Treatment cuts medical costs.* Rockville, MD: Author.

30. Center for Substance Abuse Treatment. (1999). *Treatment succeeds in fighting crime.* Rockville, MD: Author.

31. Daley, D. C., & Zuckoff, A. (1999). *Improving treatment compliance: Counseling and system strategies for substance use and dual disorders.* Center City, MN: Hazelden.

32. Galanter, M., & Brook, D. (2000). Network therapy for addiction: Bringing fam-

ily and peer support into office practice. *International Journal of Group Psychotherapy, 51*(1), 101–123.

33. Hester, R. K., & Miller, W. R. (Eds.). (1995). *Handbook of alcoholism treatment approaches: Effective alternatives* (2nd ed.). Boston: Allyn & Bacon.

34. Maisto, S. A., McKay, J. R., & O'Farrell, T. J. (1995). Relapse precipitants and behavioral marital therapy. *Addictive Behaviors, 20*(3), 383–393.

35. Moos, R. H., Moos, B. S., & Andrassy, J. M. (1999). Outcomes of four treatment approaches in community residential programs for patients with substance use disorders. *Psychiatric Services, 50*(12), 1577–1583.

36. Nathan, P. E., & Gorman, J. M. (Eds.). (1998). *A guide to treatments that work.* New York: Oxford University Press.

37. National Institute on Alcohol Abuse and Alcoholism. (1995). *Project Match Series: Vol. 1. Twelve-step facilitation therapy manual.* Rockville, MD: U.S. Department of Health and Human Services..

38. National Institute on Alcohol Abuse and Alcoholism. (1995). *Project Match Series: Vol. 2. Motivational enhancement therapy manual.* Rockville, MD: U.S. Department of Health and Human Services.

39. National Institute on Alcohol Abuse and Alcoholism. (1995). *Project Match Series: Vol. 3. Cognitive-behavioral coping skills therapy manual.* Rockville, MD: U.S. Department of Health and Human Services.

40. National Institute on Alcohol Abuse and Alcoholism. (1999). Update on approaches to alcoholism treatment. *Alcohol Research and Health, 23*(2), 1999.

41. National Institute on Drug Abuse. (1993). *Cue extinction.* Rockville, MD: U.S. Department of Health and Human Services.

42. National Institute on Drug Abuse. (1994). *Addict aftercare: Recovery training and self-help* (2nd ed.). Rockville, MD: Author.

43. Obert, J. L., McCann, M. J., Marinelli-Casey, P., Weiner, A., Minsky, S., Brethen, P., et al. (2000). The matrix model of outpatient stimulant abuse treatment: History and description. *Journal of Psychoactive Drugs, 32*(2), 157–164.

44. O'Connell, D. F., & Alexander, C. N. (1994). *Self-recovery treating addictions using transcendental meditation and Maharishi Ayur-Veda.* New York: Haworth Press.

45. O'Farrell, T. J., & Fals-Stewart, W. (1999). Treatment models and methods: Family models. In B. S. McCrady & E. E. Epstein (Eds.), *Addictions: A comprehensive guidebook* (pp. 287–305). London: Oxford University Press.

46. Project MATCH. (1998). Matching alcoholism treatments to client heterogeneity: Project MATCH three-year drinking outcomes. *Alcoholism: Clinical and Experimental Research, 22*(6), 1300–1311.

47. Rawson, R. A., Shoptaw, S. J., Obert, J. L., McCann, M. J., Hasson, A. L., Marinelli-Casey, P. J., et al. (1995). An intensive outpatient approach for cocaine abuse treatment. *Journal of Substance Abuse Treatment, 12*(2), 117–127.

48. Stanton, M. D., & Shadish, W. R. (1997). Outcome, attrition, and family-couples

treatments for drug abuse: A meta-analysis and review of the controlled, comparative studies. *Psychological Bulletin, 122*(2), 170–191.

49. Vannicelli, M. (1995). Group psychotherapy with substance abusers and family members. In A. M. Washton (Ed.), *Psychotherapy and substance abuse: A practitioner's handbook* (pp. 337–356). New York: Guilford Press.

50. Daley, D. C., & Thase, M. E. (2004). *Dual-disorders recovery counseling: Integrated treatment for substance use and mental health disorders* (3rd ed.). Independence, MO: Independence Press.

51. Drake, R. E., & Mueser, K. T. (Eds.). (1996). *Dual diagnosis of major mental illness and substance abuse* (Vol. 2). San Francisco: Jossey-Bass.

52. Drake, R. E., Mercer-McFadden, C., Mueser, K. T., McHugho, G., & Bond, G. (1998). A review of integrated mental health and substance abuse treatment for patients with dual disorders. *Schizophrenia Bulletin, 24,* 589–608.

53. Mueser, K. T., Drake, R. E., & Noordsy, D. L. (1998). Integrated mental health and substance abuse treatment for severe psychiatric disorders. *Journal of Practical Psychiatry and Behavioral Health, 4*(3), 129–139.

Chapter 3. Understanding Mood Disorders

1. Akiskal, H. S. (2000). Mood disorders: Introduction and overview. In B. J. Sadock & V. A. Sadock (Eds.), *Comprehensive textbook of psychiatry* (7th ed., pp. 1284–1297). Baltimore: Lippincott Williams & Wilkins.

2. American Psychiatric Association. (2000). *Diagnostic and statistical manual of mental disorders* (4th ed., text rev.). Washington, DC: Author.

3. Akiskal, H. S., & Cassano, G. B. (Eds.). (1997). *Dysthymia and the spectrum of chronic depressions.* New York: Guilford Press.

4. Howland, R. H., & Thase, M. E. (1993). A comprehensive review of cyclothymic disorder. *Journal of Nervous and Mental Disease, 181,* 485–493.

5. Thase, M. E., & Lang, S. S. (2004). *Beating the blues: New approaches to overcoming dysthymia and chronic mild depression.* New York: Oxford University Press.

6. Jamison, K. R. (1993). *Touched by fire: Manic-depressive illness and the artistic temperament.* New York: Free Press.*

7. Cronkite, K. (1995). *On the edge of darkness.* New York: Delta.*

8. Fawcett, J., Golden, B., & Rosenfeld, N. (2000). *New hope for people with bipolar disorder.* Roseville, CA: Prima Health.*

9. Montimore, F. M. (1999). *Bipolar disorder: A guide for patients and families.* Baltimore: Johns Hopkins Press.*

10. Post, R. M. (2000). Mood disorders: Treatment of bipolar disorder. In B. J. Sadock & V. A. Sadock (Eds.), *Comprehensive textbook of psychiatry* (7th ed., pp. 1385–1430). Baltimore: Lippincott Williams & Wilkins.

11. Frank, E., Swartz, H. A., & Kupfer, D. J. (2000). Interpersonal and social rhythm therapy: Managing the chaos of bipolar disorder. *Biological Psychiatry, 48,* 593–604.

12. Jamison, K. R. (1995). *An unquiet mind: A memoir of moods and madness.* New York: Knopf.*

13. Regier, D. (1990). Comorbidity of mental disorders with alcohol and other drug abuse: Results from the Epidemiologic Catchment Area Study. *Journal of the American Medical Association, 264,* 2511–2518.

14. Blazer, D. G., II. (2000). Mood disorders: Epidemiology. In B. J. Sadock & V. A. Sadock (Eds.), *Comprehensive textbook of psychiatry* (7th ed., pp. 1298–1307). Baltimore: Lippincott Williams & Wilkins.

15. Basco, M. R., & Rush, A. J. (1996). *Cognitive-behavioral therapy for bipolar disorder.* New York: Guilford Press.

16. Goodwin, F. K., & Jamison, K. R. (1990). *Manic-depressive illness.* New York: Oxford University Press.

17. Medina, J. (1998). *Depression: How it happens, how it's healed.* Oakland, CA: New Harbinger Publications.*

18. Paykel, E. S. (Ed.). (1992). *Handbook of affective disorders.* New York: Guilford Press.

19. Rush, A. J. (2000). Mood disorders: Treatment of depression. In B. J. Sadock & V. A. Sadock (Eds.), *Comprehensive textbook of psychiatry* (7th ed., pp. 1377–1384). Baltimore: Lippincott Williams & Wilkins.

20. Thase, M. E., &, Daley, D. C. (1995). *Understanding depression and addiction.* Center City, MN: Hazelden.*

21. Weissman, M. M. (1995). *Mastering depression through interpersonal psychotherapy: Client workbook.* San Antonio, TX: Psychological Corporation.*

22. Frank, E., & Kupfer, D. J. (2000). Peeking through the door to the 21st century. *Archives of General Psychiatry, 57,* 83–85.

23. Kendler, J. S., Karkowski, L. M., & Prescott, C. A. (1999). Causal relationship between stressful life events and the onset of major depression. *American Journal of Psychiatry, 156,* 837–841.

24. Sheehy, G. (1995). *New passages: Mapping your life across time.* New York: Ballantine Books.

25. Thase, M. E., & Rush, A. J. (1997). *Depression: A guide for patients.* San Ramon, CA: HIN.*

26. Styron, W. (1990). *Darkness visible: A memoir of madness.* New York: Random House.

27. Seligman, M. E. P. (1990). *Learned optimism: How to change your mind and your life.* New York: Pocket Books.

28. Daley, D. C., & Moss, H. M. (2002). *Dual disorders: Counseling clients with chemical dependency and mental illness* (3rd ed.). Center City, MN: Hazelden.

29. Craske, M. G., Barlow, D. H., & Meadows, E. (2000). *Mastery of your anxiety and panic: Therapist guide* (3rd ed.). San Antonio, TX: Psychological Corporation.

30. Craske, M. G., & Barlow, D. H. (2001). *Mastery of your anxiety and panic: Client workbook for agoraphobia* (3rd ed.). San Antonio, TX: Psychological Corporation.

31. Antony, M. M., Barlow, D. H., & Craske, M. G. (1997). *Mastery of your specific phobia: Therapist guide.* San Antonio, TX: Psychological Corporation.

32. Antony, M. M., & Swinson, R. P. (2000). *The shyness and social anxiety workbook.* Oakland, CA: New Harbinger.

33. Bourne, E. (2004). *The anxiety and phobia workbook* (4th ed.). Oakland, CA: New Harbinger.

34. Clark, D. B., Feske, U., Masia, C. L., Spaulding, S. A., Brown, C., Mammen, O., et al. (1997). Systemic assessment of social phobia in clinical practice. *Depression and Anxiety, 6,* 47–61.

35. Myrick, H., & Brady, K. T. (1997). Social phobia in cocaine-dependent individuals. *American Journal on Addictions, 6*(2): 99–104.

36. Steketee, G. S. (1996). *Treatment of obsessive–compulsive disorder.* New York: Guilford Press.

37. Hyman, B. M., & Pedrick, C. (1999). *The OCD workbook: Your guide to breaking free from obsessive-compulsive disorder.* Oakland, CA: New Harbinger.

38. Foa, E. B., Keane, T. M., & Friedman, M. J. (Eds.). (2000). *Effective treatments of PTSD.* New York: Guilford Press.

39. Ouimette, P. C., Wolfe, J., & Chrestman, K. R. (1996). Characteristics of post-traumatic stress disorder–alcohol abuse comorbidity in women. *Journal of Substance Abuse, 8*(3), 335–346.

40. Najavits, L. M., Weiss, R. D., & Shaw, S. R. (1997). The link between substance abuse and posttraumatic stress disorder in women. *American Journal on Addictions, 6*(4), 273–283.

41. Craske, M. G., Barlow, D. H., & O'Leary, T. (1992). *Mastery of your anxiety and worry.* Albany, NY: Graywind.

42. Daley, D. C., & Salloum, I. M. (2003). *Understanding major anxiety disorders and addiction.* (2nd ed.). Center City, MN: Hazelden.

43. National Institute on Drug Abuse. (2001). NIDA scientific panel reports on prescription drug misuse and abuse. *NIDA Notes, 16*(1), 1–15.

44. Linehan, M. M. (1993). *Cognitive-behavioral treatment of borderline personality disorder.* New York: Guilford Press.

45. Soloff, P. (1998). Algorithms for pharmacological treatment of personality dimensions: Symptom-specific treatments for cognitive-perceptual, affective, and impulsive-behavioral dysregulation. *Bulletin of the Menninger Clinic, 62*(2), 195–214.

46. Weiss, R. D., & Daley, D. C. (2003). *Understanding personality problems and addiction* (2nd ed.). Center City, MN: Hazelden.

47. Beck, A. T., & Freeman, A. (1990). *Cognitive therapy of personality disorders.* New York: Guilford Press.

48. American Psychiatric Association. (1999). The practice of electroconvulsive ther-

apy: Recommendations for treatment, training, and privileging. In *A task force report of the American Psychiatric Association.* Washington, DC: Author.

49. Fink, M. (1999). Electroshock therapy: Restoring the mind. New York: Oxford University Press.

50. Isenberg, K. E., & Zorumski, C. F. (2000). Electroconvulsive therapy. In B. J. Sadock & V. A. Sadock (Eds.), *Comprehensive textbook of psychiatry* (7th ed., pp. 2503–2515). New York: Lippincott Williams & Wilkins.

51. Kupfer, D. J. (1993). Management of recurrent depression. *Journal of Clinical Psychiatry, 54,* 34–35.

52. Kupfer, D. J., Frank, E., Perel, J. M., Cornes, C., Mallinger, A. G., Thase, M. E., et al. (1992). Five-year outcome for maintenance therapies in recurrent depression. *Archives of General Psychiatry, 49,* 769–773.

53. Frank, E. (2005). *Treating bipolar disorder: A clinician's guide to interpersonal and social rhythm therapy,* New York: Guilford Press.

54. Thase, M. E. (1999). Long-term nature of depression. *Journal of Clinical Psychiatry, 60*(Suppl. 14), 3–9.

55. Rush, A. J., & Kupfer, D. J. (2001). Strategies and tactics in the treatment of depression. In G. O. Gabbard (Ed.), *Treatments of psychiatric disorders* (3rd ed., 1417–1437). Washington, DC: American Psychiatric Press.

56. Spanier, C. A., Frank, E., McEachran, A. B., Grochocinski, V. J., & Kupfer, D. J. (1999). Maintenance interpersonal psychotherapy for recurrent depression. In D. S. Janowsky (Eds.), *Psychotherapy indications and outcomes* (pp. 249–273). Washington, DC: American Psychiatric Press.

57. Kupfer, D. J., & Frank, E. (2001). The interaction of drug- and psychotherapy in the long-term treatment of depression. *Journal of Affective Disorders, 62,* 131–137.

58. Hirschfeld, R. M., & Shea, M. T. (2000). Mood disorders: Psychotherapy. In B. J. Sadock & V. A. Sadock (Eds.), *Comprehensive textbook of psychiatry* (7th ed., pp. 1431–1440). Baltimore: Lippincott Williams & Wilkins.

59. Frank, E., Swartz, H. A., Mallinger, A. G., Thase, M. E., Weaver, E. V., & Kupfer, D. J. (1999). Adjunctive psychotherapy for bipolar disorder: Effects of changing treatment modality. *Journal of Abnormal Psychology, 108*(4), 579–587.

60. Sammons, M. T., & Schmidt, N. B. (2001). *Combined treatments for mental disorders: A guide to psychological and pharmacological interventions.* Washington, DC: American Psychological Association.

61. Craighead, W. E., Miklowitz, D. J., Vajk, F. C., & Frank, E. (1998). Psychosocial treatments for bipolar disorder. In P. E. Nathan & J. M. Gorman (Eds.), *A guide to treatments that work* (pp. 240–248). New York: Oxford University Press.

62. Beck, A. T. (1976). *Cognitive therapy and the emotional disorders.* New York: New American Library.

63. Rush, A. J., & Beck, A. T. (2000). Cognitive therapy. In B. J. Sadock & V. A. Sadock (Eds.), *Comprehensive textbook of psychiatry* (7th ed., pp. 2167–2177). Baltimore: Lippincott Williams & Wilkins.

64. Weissman, M. M., Markowitz, J. C., & Klerman, G. L. (2000). *Comprehensive guide to interpersonal psychotherapy.* New York: Basic Books.

65. Miklowitz, D. J., & Goldstein, M. J. (1997). *Bipolar disorder: A family-focused treatment approach.* New York: Guilford Press.*

66. Mueser, K. T., & Glynn, S. M. (1999). *Behavioral family therapy for psychiatric disorders* (2nd ed.). Oakland, CA: New Harbinger.

Chapter 4. The Recovery Process for Addiction and Mood Disorders

1. Daley, D. C., & Thase, M. E. (2003). *Understanding depression and addiction.* Center City, MN: Hazelden.*

2. Daley, D. C. (2000). *Dual diagnosis workbook: Recovery strategies for substance use and mental health problems* (2nd ed.). Independence, MO: Independence Press.*

3. Daley, D. C., & Marlatt, G. A. (1997). *Managing your drug or alcohol problem: Client workbook.* San Antonio, TX: Psychological Corporation.*

4. Daley, D. C., & Moss, H. M. (2002). *Dual disorders: Counseling clients with chemical dependency and mental illness.* (3rd ed.). Center City, MN: Hazelden.

5. White, B. F., & MacDougall, J. A. (2001). *A clinician's guide to spirituality.* New York: McGraw-Hill.

6. Daley, D. C., & Roth, L. (2001). *When symptoms return: A guide to relapse in psychiatric illness* (2nd ed.). Holmes Beach: FL: Learning Publications.*

7. Daley, D. C., & Haskett, R. (2003). *Understanding bipolar illness and addiction.* Center City, MN: Hazelden.*

8. Daley, D. C. (2004). *Relapse prevention workbook for recovering alcoholics and drug dependent persons* (4th ed.). Apollo, PA: Daley Publications.

9. Thase, M. E. (1999). Long-term nature of depression. *Journal of Clinical Psychiatry, 60*(Suppl. 14), 3–9.

10. Frank, E., Kupfer, D. J., Perel, J. M., Cornes, C., Jarrett, D. B., Mallinger, A. G., et al. (1990). Three-year outcomes for maintenance therapies in recurrent depression. *Archives of General Psychiatry, 47,* 1093–1099.

11. Kupfer, D. J., Frank, E., Perel, J. M., Cornes, C., Mallinger, A. G., Thase, M. E., et al. (1992). Five-year outcome for maintenance therapies in recurrent depression. *Archives of General Psychiatry, 49,* 769–773.

12. Daley, D. C., & Thase, M. E. (2000). *Dual-disorders recovery counseling: Integrated treatment for substance use and mental health disorders* (2nd ed.). Independence, MO: Independence Press.

13. Drake, R. E., Mercer-McFadden, C., Mueser, K. T., McHugo, G., & Bond, G. (1998). A review of integrated mental health and substance abuse treatment for patients with dual disorders. *Schizophrenia Bulletin, 24,* 589–608.

14. Drake, R. E., & Mueser, K. T. (Eds.). (1996). *Dual diagnosis of major mental illness and substance abuse* (Vol. 2). San Francisco, CA: Jossey-Bass.

15. Minkoff, K. (2001). Developing standards of care for individuals with co-occurring psychiatric and substance use disorders. *Psychiatric Services, 52*(4), 597–599.

16. Mueser, K. T., Drake, R. E., & Noordsy, D. L. (1998). Integrated mental health and substance abuse treatment for severe psychiatric disorders. *Journal of Practical Psychiatry and Behavioral Health, 4*(3), 129–139.

17. O'Connell, D. F. (Ed.). (2001). *Managing the dually diagnosed patient: Current issues and clinical approaches* (2nd ed.). New York: Haworth.

18. Cornelius, J. R., Salloum, I. M., Ehler, J. G., Jarrett, P. J., Cornelius, M. D., and Perel, J. M. (1997). Fluoxetine in depressed alcoholics: A double blind, placebo-controlled trial. *Archives of General Psychiatry, 54*(8), 700–705.

19. Salloum, I. M., Cornelius, J. R., Thase, M. E., Daley, D. C., Kirisci, L. & Spotts, C. E. (1998). Naltrexone utility in depressed alcoholics. *Psychopharmacology Bulletin, 34*(1), 111–115.

Chapter 5. Setting the Foundation for Dual Recovery

1. Daley, D. C., & Thase, M. E. (2000). *Dual disorders recovery counseling: Integrated treatment for substance use and mental health disorders* (2nd ed.). Independence, MO: Independence Press.

2. Daley, D. C. (2000). *Dual diagnosis workbook: Recovery strategies for substance use and mental health problems* (2nd ed.). Independence, MO: Independence Press.*

3. Weiss, R. D., & Daley, D. C. (2003). *Understanding personality problems and addiction* (2nd ed.). Center City, MN: Hazelden.*

4. Anderson, D. (1985). *The psychopathology of denial.* Center City, MN: Hazelden.*

5. Gorske, T. T., & Grinstead, S. F. (2000). *Denial management counseling.* Independence, MO: Independence Press.

6. American Society of Addiction Medicine. (2003). *Principles of addiction medicine* (3rd ed.). Chevy Chase, MD: Author.

7. Galanter, M., & Kleber, H. D. (Eds.). (2005). *Textbook of substance abuse treatment* (3rd ed.). Washington, DC: American Psychiatric Press.

8. McCrady, B., & Epstein, E. (Eds.). (1999). *Addictions: A comprehensive guidebook.* New York: Oxford University Press.

9. National Institute on Alcohol Abuse and Alcoholism. (2000). *Alcohol and health: Tenth special report to the U.S. Congress.* Rockville, MD: U.S. Department of Health and Human Services.

10. National Institute on Drug Abuse. (2000). *Drug abuse and drug abuse research: The third triennial report to Congress from the Secretary, Department of Health and Human Services.* Rockville, MD: Author.

11. Jaffe, J. H. (2000). Substance-related disorders: Introduction and overview. In

B. J. Sadock & V. A. Sadock (Eds.), *Comprehensive textbook of psychiatry* (7th ed., pp. 924–952). Baltimore: Lippincott Williams & Wilkins.

12. Schuckit, M. A. (2000). *Drug and alcohol abuse: A clinical guide to diagnosis and treatment* (5th ed.). New York: Plenum Press.

13. Schuckit, M. A. (2000). Alcohol-related disorders. In B. J. Sadock & V. A. Sadock (Eds.), *Comprehensive textbook of psychiatry* (7th ed., pp. 953–970). Baltimore: Lippincott Williams & Wilkins.

14. Smith, D. E., & Seymour, R. B. (2001). *A clinician's guide to substance abuse.* New York: McGraw-Hill.

15. Volkow, N. D., & Fowler, J. S. (2000). Addiction, a disease of compulsion and drive: Involvement of the orbitofrontal cortex. *Cerebral Cortex, 10,* 318–325.

16. Cornelius, J. R., Salloum, I. M., Day, N. L., Thase, M. E., & Mann, J. J. (1996). Patterns of suicidality and alcohol use in alcoholics with major depression. *Alcoholism: Clinical and Experimental Research, 20,* 1451–1455.

17. Jamison, K. R. (1999). *Night falls fast: Understanding suicide.* New York: Knopf.*

18. Shea, S. C. (1999). *The practical art of suicide assessment: A guide for mental health professionals and substance abuse counselors.* New York: Wiley.

Chapter 6. Medications in Dual Recovery

1. Frank, E., Kupfer, D. J., Perel, J. M., Cornes, C., Jarrett, D. B., Mallinger, A. G., et al. (1990). Three-year outcomes for maintenance therapies in recurrent depression. *Archives of General Psychiatry, 47,* 1093–1099.

2. Goodwin, F. K., & Jamison, K. R. (1990). *Manic-depressive illness.* New York: Oxford University Press.

3. Jefferson, J. W., & Greist, J. H. (2000). Lithium. In B. J. Sadock & V. A. Sadock (Eds.), *Comprehensive textbook of psychiatry* (7th ed., pp. 2377–2390). Baltimore: Lippincott Williams & Wilkins.

4. Kupfer, D. J. (1993). Management of recurrent depression. *Journal of Clinical Psychiatry, 54,* 34–35.

5. Kupfer, D. J., Frank, E., Perel, J. M., Cornes, C., Mallinger, A. G., Thase, M. E., et al. (1992). Five-year outcome for maintenance therapies in recurrent depression. *Archives of General Psychiatry, 49,* 769–773.

6. Medina, J. (1998). *Depression: How it happens, how it's healed.* Oakland, CA: New Harbinger Publications.*

7. Post, R. M. (2000). Mood disorders: Treatment of bipolar disorder. In B. J. Sadock & V. A. Sadock (Eds.), *Comprehensive textbook of psychiatry* (7th ed., pp. 1385–1430). Baltimore: Lippincott Williams & Wilkins.

8. Rush, A. J. (2000). Mood disorders: Treatment of depression. In B. J. Sadock & V. A. Sadock (Eds.), *Comprehensive textbook of psychiatry* (7th ed., pp. 1377–1384). Baltimore: Lippincott Williams & Wilkins.

9. Salloum, I. M., Daley, D. C., & Thase, M. E. (2000). *Male depression, alcoholism, and violence.* London: Dunitz.

10. Thase, M. E. (1999). Long-term nature of depression. *Journal of Clinical Psychiatry, 60*(Suppl. 14), 3–9.

11. Akiskal, H. S., & Cassano, G. B. (Eds.). (1997). *Dysthymia and the spectrum of chronic depressions.* New York: Guilford Press.

12. Kocsis, J. H., & Klein, D. N. (Eds.) (1995). *Diagnosis and treatment of chronic depression.* New York: Guilford Press.

13. Howland, R. H. (1991). Pharmacotherapy of dysthymia: A review. *Journal of Clinical Psychopharmacology, 11,* 83–92.

14. Greenfield, S. F, Weiss, R. D., Muenz, L. R., et al. (1998). The effect of depression on return to drinking: A prospective study. *Archives of General Psychiatry, 55,* 259–265.

15. Daley, D. C., & Moss, H. M. (2002). *Dual disorders: Counseling clients with chemical dependency and mental illness* (3rd ed.). Center City, MN: Hazelden.

16. Gordis, E. (1998). What we know: Conceptual advances in alcoholism research. In A. W. Graham, T. K. Schultz, & B. B. Wilford (Eds.), *Principles of addiction medicine* (2nd ed., pp. xvii-xxvii). Chevy Chase, MD: American Society of Addiction Medicine.

17. Leshner, A. I. (1998). Understanding drug addiction: Insights from research. In A. W. Graham, T. K. Schultz, & B. B. Wilford (Eds.), *Principles of addiction medicine* (2nd ed., pp.47–56). Chevy Chase, MD: American Society of Addiction Medicine.

18. National Institute on Alcohol Abuse and Alcoholism. (1999). Update on approaches to alcoholism treatment. *Alcohol Research and Health, 23*(2), 1999.

19. National Institute on Alcohol Abuse and Alcoholism. (2000). *Alcohol and health: Tenth special report to the U.S. Congress.* Rockville, MD: U.S. Department of Health and Human Services.

20. National Institute on Drug Abuse. (1997). Study sheds new light on the state of drug abuse treatment nationwide. *NIDA Notes 12*(5), 1–8.

21. Salloum, I. M., & Cornelius, J. R. (1999). Management of side effects of drugs used in treatment of alcoholism and drug abuse. In R. Balon (Ed.), *Practical management of side effects of psychotropic drugs* (pp. 169–197). New York: Dekker.

22. Schuckit, M. A. (2000). *Drug and alcohol abuse: A clinical guide to diagnosis and treatment* (5th ed.). New York: Plenum Press.

23. Schuckit, M. A. (2000). Alcohol-related disorders. In B. J. Sadock & V. A. Sadock (Eds.), *Comprehensive textbook of psychiatry* (7th ed., pp. 953–970). Baltimore: Lippincott Williams & Wilkins.

24. American Society of Addiction Medicine. (2003). Intoxication, overdose and acute withdrawal. In A. W. Graham, T. K. Schultz, & B. B. Wilford (Eds.), *Principles of addiction medicine* (3rd ed., pp. 497–592). Chevy Chase, MD: American Society of Addiction Medicine.

25. American Society of Addiction Medicine. (2003). Pharmacologic therapies for ad-

diction. In A. W. Graham, T. K. Schultz, & B. B. Wilford (Eds.), *Principles of addiction medicine* (3rd ed., pp. 421–496). Chevy Chase, MD: American Society of Addiction Medicine.

26. Rabinowitz, J., Cohen, H., & Atias, S. (2002). Outcomes of naltrexone maintenance following ultra rapid opiate detoxification versus inpatient detoxification. *American Journal of Addiction, 11,* 52–56.

27. Gorelick, D. A. (1998). Pharmacologic therapies for cocaine and other stimulant addiction. In A. W. Graham, T. K. Schultz, & B. B. Wilford (Eds.), *Principles of addiction medicine* (2nd ed., pp. 531–544). Chevy Chase, MD: American Society of Addiction Medicine.

28. Payte, J. T., & Zweben, J. E. (2003). Opioid maintenance therapies. In A. W. Graham, T. K. Schultz, & B. B. Wilford (Eds.), *Principles of addiction medicine* (3rd ed., pp. 557–570). Chevy Chase, MD: American Society of Addiction Medicine.

29. O'Malley, S., Krishnan-Saran, S., & Rounsaville, B. J. (2000). Naltrexone. In B. J. Sadock & V. A. Sadock (Eds.), *Comprehensive textbook of psychiatry* (7th ed., pp. 2407–2411). Baltimore: Lippincott Williams & Wilkins.

30. Pani, P. P., Maremmani, I., Pirastu, R., Tagliamonte, A., & Luigi-Gessa, G. (2000). Buprenorphine: A controlled clinical trial in the treatment of opioid dependence. *Drug and Alcohol Dependence, 60,* 39–50.

31. Fuller, R. K., & Gordis, E. (2004). Does disulfiram have a role in alcoholism treatment today? *Addiction, 99*(1), 21–24.

32. Thomas, J. (2001). Buprenorphine proves effective, expands options for treatment of heroin addiction. *NIDA Notes, 16*(2), 8–11.

33. Garbutt, J. C., West, S. L., Carey, T. S., Lohr, K. N., & Crews, F. T. (1999). Pharmacological treatment of alcohol dependence: A review of the evidence. *Journal of the American Medical Association, 281*(14), 1318–1325.

34. Volpicelli, J. R., Alterman, A. I., Hayashida, M., & O'Brien, C. P. (1992). Naltrexone in the treatment of alcohol dependence. *Archives of General of Psychiatry, 49*(11), 876–880.

35. Salloum, I. M., Cornelius, J. R., Thase, M. E., Daley, D. C., Kirisci, L., & Spotts, C. E. (1998). Naltrexone utility in depressed alcoholics. *Psychopharmacology Bulletin, 34*(1), 111–115.

36. Overman, G. P., Teter, C. J., Guthrie, S. K. (2003) Acamprosate for the adjunctive treatment of alcohol dependence. *Annals of Pharmacotherapy, 37,* 1090–1099.

37. Daley, D. C., & Marlatt, G. A. (2006). *Overcoming your drug or alcohol problem: Effective treatment approaches. Therapist guide.* New York: Oxford University Press.

38. Silagy, M. B., and Associates. (2004). Nicotine replacement therapy for smoking cessation. *Cochrane Database System Review, 3,* CD000146.

39. Schmitz, J. M., Henningfield, J. E., & Jarvik, M. E. (2003). Pharmacologic therapies for nicotine dependence. In A. W. Graham, T. K. Schultz, & B. B. Wilford (Eds.), *Principles of addiction medicine* (3rd ed., pp. 571–582). Chevy Chase, MD: American Society of Addiction Medicine.

40. Kranzler, H. R., Burleson, J. A., Del Boca, F. K., Babor, T. F., Korner, P., Brown, J., et al. (1994). Buspirone treatment of anxious alcoholics. A placebo-controlled trial. *Archives of General Psychiatry, 51*(9), 720–731.

41. Cornelius, J. R., Salloum, I. M., Ehler, J. G., et al. (1997). Fluoxetine in depressed alcoholics: A double-blind, placebo-controlled trial. *Archives of General Psychiatry, 54*(8), 700–705.

42. Kelsey, J. E., & Nemeroff, C. B. (2000). Selective serotonin reuptake inhibitors: Introduction and overview. Rush, A. J. (2000). In B. J. Sadock & V. A. Sadock (Eds.), *Comprehensive textbook of psychiatry* (7th ed., pp. 2432–2454). Baltimore: Lippincott Williams & Wilkins.

43. Calabrese, J. R., Rapport, D. J., et al. (1993). Rapid cycling bipolar disorder and its treatment with valproate. *Canadian Journal of Psychiatry, 38,* 57–61.

44. Bowden, C. L. (1993). Predictors of response to divalproex and lithium. *Journal of Clinical Psychiatry, 56,* 25–30.

45. Calabrese, J. R., Markovitz, P. J., Kimmel, S. E., et al. (1992). Spectrum of efficacy of valproate in 78 rapid cycling bipolar patients. *Journal of Clinical Psychopharmacology, 12,* 53–56.

46. Salloum, I. M., Cornelius, J. R., Daley, D. C., et al. (2005). Efficacy of valproate maintenance in patients with bipolar disorder and alcoholism: A double-blind placebo-controlled study. *Archives of General Psychiatry, 62,* 37–45.

47. Fink, M. (1999). *Electroshock: Restoring the mind.* New York: Oxford University Press.

48. Lake, J. (2005, November). Integrative management of depressed mood: Evidence and treatment guidelines. *Psychiatric Times,* pp. 91–97.

49. Rosenberg, S. D., Goodman, L. A., Osher, F. C., et al. (2001). Prevalence of HIV, hepatitis B, hepatitis C in people with severe mental illness. *American Journal of Public Health, 91*(1), 31–36.

50. McElroy, S. L., Frye, M.A., Suppes, T., et al. (2002). Correlates of overweight and obesity in 644 patients with bipolar disorder. *Journal of Clinical Psychiatry, 63,* 207–213.

51. Schneider, J. P. (2005). Guidelines for psychiatrists working with patients with sexual addiction. *Psychiatric Times,* pp. 66–71.

52. Danon, P. N., Lowengrub, K., Gonopolski, Y., et al. (2005). Topiramate versus fluvoxamine in the treatment of pathological gambling. *Clinical Neuropharmacology, 28*(1), 6–10.

Chapter 7. Managing Feelings

1. Daley, D. C. (2001). *Coping with feelings workbook* (2nd ed.). Holmes Beach, FL: Learning Publications.*

2. Daley, D. C. (2004). *Managing anger workbook* (3rd ed.). Apollo, PA: Daley Publications.

3. Daley, D. C. (2000). *Dual diagnosis workbook: Recovery strategies for substance use and mental health problems* (2nd ed.). Independence, MO: Independence Press.*

4. Daley, D. C., & Salloum, I. M. (2003). *Understanding major anxiety disorders and addiction.* Center City, MN: Hazelden.

5. Hallowell, E. M. (1997). *Worry: Controlling it and using it wisely.* New York: Random House.

6. Beck, A. T. (1976). *Cognitive therapy and the emotional disorders.* New York: New American Library.

7. Burns, D. (1999). *Feeling good.* New York: Morrow.*

8. Burns, D. (1999). *Feeling good workbook.* New York: Morrow.*

9. Lewinsohn, P. M., Munoz, R. F., Youngren, M. A., & Zeiss, A. M. (1986). *Control your depression.* New York: Prentice Hall.*

10. Medina, J. (1998). *Depression: How it happens, how it's healed.* Oakland, CA: New Harbinger Publications.*

11. Kocsis, J. H., & Klein, D. N. (Eds.). (1995). *Diagnosis and treatment of chronic depression.* New York: Guilford Press.

12. Rush, A. J. (2000). Mood disorders: Treatment of depression. In B. J. Sadock & V. A. Sadock (Eds.), *Comprehensive textbook of psychiatry* (7th ed., pp. 1377–1384). Baltimore: Lippincott Williams & Wilkins.

13. Salloum, I. M., Daley, D. C., & Thase, M. E. (2000). *Male depression, alcoholism, and violence.* London: Dunitz.

14. Thase, M. E. (1999). Long-term nature of depression. *Journal of Clinical Psychiatry, 60*(Suppl. 14), 3–9.

15. Daley, D. C., & Thase, M. E. (2003). *Understanding depression and addiction.* Center City, MN: Hazelden.*

16. Goleman, D. (1995). *Emotional intelligence: Why it can matter more than IQ.* New York: Bantam.

17. Goleman, D. (2000). Emotional intelligence. In B. J. Sadock & V. A. Sadock (Eds.), *Comprehensive textbook of psychiatry* (7th ed., pp. 446–462). Baltimore: Lippincott Williams & Wilkins.

Chapter 8. Building a Support System

1. *Alcoholics anonymous.* (1976). New York: World Services.

2. *Narcotics anonymous.* (1998). Van Nuys, CA: World Service Office.*

3. Daley, D. C. (1996). *Improving communication and relationships.* Holmes Beach, FL: Learning Publications.*

4. Daley, D. C. (2000). *Dual diagnosis workbook: Recovery strategies for substance use and mental health problems* (2nd ed.). Independence, MO: Independence Press.*

5. Daley, D. C., & Marlatt, G. A. (2006). *Overcoming your drug or alcohol problem: Effective recovery strategies, Workbook* (2nd ed.). New York: Oxford University Press.*

6. Daley, D. C. (2000). *Relapse prevention workbook for recovering alcoholics and drug dependent persons* (3rd ed.). Holmes Beach, FL: Learning Publications.*

7. Marlatt, G. A. (1996). Taxonomy of high-risk situations for alcohol relapse: Evolution and development of a cognitive-behavioral model. *Addiction, 91*(Suppl. 1), S37–S49.

8. Marlatt, G. A., & Gordon, J. R. (Eds.). (1985). *Relapse prevention: Maintenance strategies in the treatment of addictive behaviors.* New York: Guilford Press.

9. Daley, D. C., & Spear, J. (2003). *A family guide to coping with dual disorders* (3rd ed.). Center City, MN: Hazelden.

10. Daley, D. C., & Miller, J. (2001). *Addiction in your family: Helping yourself and your loved ones.* Holmes Beach, FL: Learning Productions.

Chapter 9. Working With Your Family

1. Akiskal, H. S. (2000). Mood disorders: Introduction and overview. In B. J. Sadock & V. A. Sadock (Eds.), *Comprehensive textbook of psychiatry* (7th ed., pp. 1284–1297). Baltimore: Lippincott Williams & Wilkins.

2. Jaffe, J. H. (2000). Substance-related disorders: Introduction and overview. In B. J. Sadock & V. A. Sadock (Eds.), *Comprehensive textbook of psychiatry* (7th ed., pp. 924–952). Baltimore: Lippincott Williams & Wilkins.

3. Schuckit, M. A. (2000). *Drug and alcohol abuse: A clinical guide to diagnosis and treatment* (5th ed.). New York: Plenum.

4. Daley, D. C., & Miller, J. (2001). *Addiction in your family: Helping yourself and your loved ones.* Holmes Beach, FL: Learning Publications.*

5. Ackerman, R. (1983). *Children of alcoholics: A guidebook for educators, therapists and parents* (2nd ed.). Holmes Beach, FL: Learning Publications.

6. Higgins, G. O. (1994). *Resilient adults: Overcoming a cruel past.* San Francisco: Jossey-Bass.*

7. Wolin, S. J., & Wolin, S. (1993). *The resilient self: How survivors of troubled families rise above adversity.* New York: Villard Books.*

8. National Institute on Alcohol Abuse and Alcoholism. (2000). *Alcohol and health: Tenth special report to the U.S. Congress.* Rockville, MD: U.S. Department of Health and Human Services.

9. Center for Substance Abuse Treatment. (2000). *Substance abuse treatment reduces family dysfunction, improves productivity.* Rockville, MD: Author.

10. Jamison, K. R. (1993). *Touched by fire: Manic-depressive illness and the artistic temperament.* New York: Free Press.*

11. Daley, D. C., & Moss, H. M. (2002). *Dual disorders: Counseling clients with chemical dependency and mental illness* (3rd ed.). Center City, MN: Hazelden.

12. Fawcett, J., Golden, B., & Rosenfeld, N. (2000). *New hope for people with bipolar disorder.* Roseville, CA: Prima Health.*

13. Frank, E., Swartz, H. A., & Kupfer, D. J. (2000). Interpersonal and social rhythm therapy: Managing the chaos of bipolar disorder. *Biological Psychiatry, 48,* 593–604.

14. Galanter, M., & Brook, D. (2000). Network therapy for addiction: Bringing family and peer support into office practice. *International Journal of Group Psychotherapy, 51*(1), 101–123.

15. Hatfield, A. B., & Lefley, H. P. (Eds.). (1987). *Families of the mentally ill: Coping and adaptation.* New York: Guilford Press.

16. Keitner, G. I. (1990). *Depression and families: Impact and treatment.* Washington, DC: American Psychiatric Association.

17. Lowinson, J. H., Ruiz, P., Millman, R. B., & Langrod, J. G. (Eds.). (1997). *Substance abuse: A comprehensive textbook* (3rd ed.). Baltimore: Williams & Wilkins.

18. McCrady, B., & Epstein, E. (Eds.). (1999). *Addictions: A comprehensive guidebook.* New York: Oxford University Press.

19. Papolos, D., & Papolos, J. (1997). *Overcoming depression: The definitive resource for patients and families who live with depression and manic-depression* (3rd ed.). New York: HarperCollins.*

20. Rosen, L. E., & Amador, X. F. (1996). *When someone you love is depressed.* New York: Free Press.*

21. Daley, D. C., & Sinberg-Spear, J. (2003). *A family guide to dual disorders* (3rd ed.). Center City, MN: Hazelden.*

22. *Alcoholics anonymous.* (1976). New York: World Services.

23. Al-Anon. (1984). *Al-anon faces alcoholism.* (2nd ed.). New York: Al-Anon Family Group Headquarters.

24. Schuckit, M. A. (2000). Alcohol-related disorders. In B. J. Sadock & V. A. Sadock (Eds.), *Comprehensive textbook of psychiatry* (7th ed., pp. 953–970). Baltimore: Lippincott Williams & Wilkins.

25. Hill, S. Y., DeBellis, M. D., Keshavan, M. S., Lowers, L., Shen, S., Hall, J., et al. (2001). Right amygdala volume in adolescent and young adult offspring from families at high risk for developing alcoholism. *Society of Biological Psychiatry, 49,* 894–905.

26. Hill, S. Y., Locke, J., Lowers, L., & Connolly, J. (1999). Psychopathology and achievement in children at high risk for developing alcoholism. *Journal of the American Academy of Child and Adolescent Psychiatry, 38*(7), 883–891.

27. Hill, S. Y., Lowers, L., Locke, J., Snidman, N., & Kagan, J. (1999). Behavioral inhibition in children from families at high risk for developing alcoholism. *Journal of the American Academy of Child and Adolescent Psychiatry, 38*(4), 410–417.

28. Ackerman, R. (1991). *Perfect daughters: Adult daughters of alcoholics.* Hollywood, FL: Health Communications.

29. Ackerman, R. (1993). *Silent sons: A book for and about men.* New York: Simon & Schuster.

30. Cork, M. (1969). *The forgotten children.* Toronto, Ontario, Canada: Alcoholism and Drug Addiction Research Foundation.*

31. Martin, C., Earleywine, M., Blackson, T., Vanyukov, M., Moss, H., & Tarter, R. (1994). Aggressivity, inattention, hyperactivity, and impulsivity in boys at high and low risk for substance abuse. *Journal of Abnormal Child Psychology, 22,* 177–203.

32. Moss, H., Blackson, T., Martin, C., & Tarter, R. (1992). Heightened motor activity in male offspring of substance abusing fathers: Association with temperament, behavior, and psychiatric diagnosis. *Biological Psychiatry, 32,* 1135–1147.

33. Moss, H., Mezzich, A., Yao, J., Gavaler, J., & Martin, C. (1995). Aggressivity among sons of substance abusing fathers: Association with psychiatric disorder in the father and son, paternal personality, pubertal development, and socioeconomic status. *American Journal of Drug and Alcohol Abuse, 21,* 195–208.

34. Tarter, R., Blackson, T., Brigham, J., Moss, H., & Caprara, G. (1995). The association between childhood irritability and liability to substance use in early adolescence: A two-year follow-up study of boys at risk for substance abuse. *Drug Alcohol Dependence, 39,* 253–261.

35. Moss, H., Vanyukov, M., Majumder, P., Kirisci, L., & Tarter, R. (1995). Prepubertal sons of substance abusers: Influences of parental and familial substance abuse on behavioral disposition, IQ, and school achievement. *Addictive Behaviors, 20,* 1–14.

36. Moss, H., Vanyukov, M., & Martin, C. (1995). Salivary cortisol responses and the risk for substance abuse in prepubertal boys. *Biological Psychiatry, 38,* 547–555.

37. Vanyukov, M., Moss, H., Plail, J., Blackson, T., Mezzich, A., & Tarter, R. (1993). Antisocial symptoms in preadolescent boys and their parents: Associations with cortisol. *Psychiatric Research, 46,* 9–17.

38. Moss, H., Clark, D., & Kirisci, L. (1997). Timing of paternal substance use disorder cessation and the effects on problem behaviors in sons. *American Journal on Addictions, 6,* 30–37.

39. Nunes, E. V., Weissman, M. M., Goldstein, R., Rise, B., McAvay, G., & Seracani, A. M., et al. (2000). Psychiatric disorders and impairment in the children of opiate addicts: Prevalences and distribution by ethnicity. *American Journal on Addictions, 9,* 232–241.

40. Rounsaville, B. J., Kosten T. R., Weissman, M. M., Prusoff, B., Pauls, D., Anton, S. F., et al. (1991). Psychiatric disorders in relatives of probands with opiate addiction. *Archives of General Psychiatry, 48,* 33–42.

41. Daley, D. C. (2000). *Dual diagnosis workbook: Recovery strategies for substance use and mental health problems* (2nd ed.). Independence, MO: Independence Press.*

42. Costantini, M., Wermuth, L., Sorensen, J., & Lyons, J. (1992). Family functioning as a predictor of progress in substance abuse treatment. *Journal of Substance Abuse Treatment, 9*(4), 331–335.

43. Jacob, M., Frank, E., Kupfer, D. J., Cornes, C., & Carpenter, L. L. (1987). A psychoeducational workshop for depressed patients, family, and friends: Description and evaluation. *Hospital and Community Psychiatry, 38,* 968–972.

44. Maisto, S. A., McKay, J. R., & O'Farrell, T. J. (1995). Relapse precipitants and behavioral marital therapy. *Addictive Behaviors, 20*(3), 383–393.

45. Miklowitz, D. J., & Goldstein, M. J. (1997). *Bipolar disorder: A family-focused treatment approach.* New York: Guilford Press.*

46. Mueser, K. T., & Glynn, S. M. (1999). *Behavioral family therapy for psychiatric disorders* (2nd ed.). Oakland, CA: New Harbinger.

47. O'Farrell, T. J., & Fals-Stewart, W. (1999). Treatment models and methods: Family models. In B. S. McCrady & E. E. Epstein (Eds.), *Addictions: A comprehensive guidebook* (pp. 287–305). London: Oxford University Press.

48. Stanton, M. D., & Shadish, W. R. (1997). Outcome, attrition, and family-couples treatments for drug abuse: A meta-analysis and review of the controlled, comparative studies. *Psychological Bulletin, 122*(2), 170–191.

49. Yapko, M. D. (2000). *Hand me down blues: How to stop depression from spreading in families.* New York: St. Martin's Griffin.*

Chapter 10. Changing Your Lifestyle

1. *Alcoholics anonymous.* (1976). New York: World Services.

2. *Narcotics anonymous.* (1998). Van Nuys, CA: World Service Office.*

3. *The dual disorders recovery book.* (1993). Center City, MN: Hazelden.

4. Lewinsohn, P. M., Munoz, R. F., Youngren, M. A., & Zeiss, A. M. (1986). *Control your depression.* New York: Prentice Hall.*

5. Medina, J. (1998). *Depression: How it happens, how it's healed.* Oakland, CA: New Harbinger.*

6. Greenberger, D., & Padesky, C. A. (1995). *Mind over mood: A cognitive therapy manual for clients.* New York: Guilford Press.*

7. Daley, D. C. (2003). *Preventing relapse* (2nd ed.). Center City, MN: Hazelden.*

8. Daley, D. C. (2001). *Money and recovery workbook.* Holmes Beach, FL: Learning Publications.

9. Daley, D. C. (2000). *Dual diagnosis workbook: Recovery strategies for substance use and mental health problems* (2nd ed.). Independence, MO: Independence Press.*

Chapter 11. Strategies for Self-Improvement

1. Beck, A. T. (1976). *Cognitive therapy and the emotional disorders.* New York: New American Library.

2. Beck, A. T., Wright, F. D., Newman, C. F., & Liese, B. S. (1993). *Cognitive therapy of substance abuse.* New York: Guilford Press.

3. Burns, D. (1999). *Feeling good.* New York: Morrow.*

4. Ellis, A., McInerney, J. F., DiGiuseppe, R., & Yeager, R. J. (1989). *Rationale-emotive therapy with alcoholics and substance abusers.* Elmsford, NY: Pergamon Press.

5. Greenberger, D., & Padesky, C. A. (1995). *Mind over mood: A cognitive therapy manual for clients.* New York: Guilford Press.*

6. Daley, D. C. (1998). *Kicking addictive habits once and for all.* Lexington, MA: Lexington Books.

7. Carnes, P. (1983). *The sexual addiction.* Minneapolis, MN: CompCare.

8. Carnes, P., Delmonico, D. L., & Griffin, E. (2001). *In the shadows of the net.* Center City, MN: Hazelden.

9. Martin, S. E. (2001). The links between alcohol, crime and the criminal justice system: Explanations, evidence and interventions. *American Journal on Addictions, 10,* 136–158.

10. Center for Substance Abuse Treatment. (1999). *Treatment succeeds in fighting crime.* Rockville, MD: Author.

11. White, B. F., & MacDougall, J. A. (2001). *A clinician's guide to spirituality.* New York: McGraw-Hill.

12. Enright, R. D., & Fitzgibbons, R. P. (2000). *Helping clients forgive: An empirical guide for resolving anger and restoring hope.* Washington, DC: American Psychological Association.

13. Miller, W. R. (1999). *Integrating spirituality into treatment: Resources for practitioners.* Washington, DC: American Psychological Association.

14. Daley, D. C. (2000). *Dual diagnosis workbook: Recovery strategies for substance use and mental health problems* (2nd ed.). Independence, MO: Independence Press.*

15. Linehan, M. M. (1993). *Skills training manual for treating borderline personality disorder.* New York: Guilford Press.

Chapter 12. Maintaining Gains Over Time

1. Berlanga, C., Heinze, G., Torres, M., Apiquian, R., & Caballero, A. (1999). Personality and clinical predictors of recurrence of depression. *Psychiatric Services, 50,* 376–380.

2. Daley, D. C. (2000). *Relapse prevention workbook for recovering alcoholics and drug dependent persons* (3rd ed.). Holmes Beach, FL: Learning Publications.*

3. Marlatt, G. A., & Gordon, J. R. (Eds.). (1985). *Relapse prevention: Maintenance strategies in the treatment of addictive behaviors.* New York: Guilford Press.

4. Haskett, R., & Daley, D. C. (1995). *Understanding bipolar illness and addiction.* Center City, MN: Hazelden.*

5. Thase, M. E. (1999). Long-term nature of depression. *Journal of Clinical Psychiatry, 60*(Suppl. 14), 3–9.

6. Thase, M. E., &, Daley, D. C. (1995). *Understanding depression and addiction.* Center City, MN: Hazelden.*

7. Frank, E., Kupfer, D. J., Perel, J. M., Cornes, C., Jarrett, D. B., Mallinger, A. G., et al. (1990). Three-year outcomes for maintenance therapies in recurrent depression. *Archives of General Psychiatry, 47,* 1093–1099.

8. Kupfer, D. J., Frank, E., Perel, J. M., Cornes, C., Mallinger, A. G., Thase, M. E., et al. (1992). Five-year outcome for maintenance therapies in recurrent depression. *Archives of General Psychiatry, 49,* 769–773.

9. Maj, M., Veltro, F., Pirozzi, R., Lobrace, S., & Magliano, L. (1992). Pattern of recurrence of illness after recovery from an episode of major depression: A prospective study. *American Journal of Psychiatry, 149,* 795–800.

10. Montimore, F. M. (1999). *Bipolar disorder: A guide for patients and families.* Baltimore: Johns Hopkins Press.*

11. Post, R. M. (2000). Mood disorders: Treatment of bipolar disorder. In B. J. Sadock & V. A. Sadock (Eds.), *Comprehensive textbook of psychiatry* (7th ed., pp. 1385–1430). Baltimore: Lippincott Williams & Wilkins.

12. Rush, A. J., & Beck, A. T. (2000). Cognitive therapy. In B. J. Sadock & V. A. Sadock (Eds.), *Comprehensive textbook of psychiatry* (7th ed., pp. 2167–2177). Baltimore: Lippincott Williams & Wilkins.

13. Daley, D. C., & Zuckoff, A. (1999). *Improving treatment compliance: Counseling and system strategies for substance use and dual disorders.* Center City, MN: Hazelden.

14. Tomasson, K., & Vaglum, P. (1998). Psychiatric co-morbidity and aftercare among alcoholics: A prospective study of a nationwide representative sample. *Addiction, 93*(3), 423–431.

15. Marlatt, G. A. (1996). Taxonomy of high-risk situations for alcohol relapse: Evolution and development of a cognitive-behavioral model. *Addiction, 91*(Suppl. 1), S37–S49.

16. Greenfield, S. F., Weiss, R. D., Muenz, L. R., Vagge, L. M., Kelly, J. F., Bello, L. R., et al. (1998). The effect of depression on return to drinking: A prospective study. *Archives of General Psychiatry, 55*(3), 259–265.

17. Personal communication, Dr. Roger Weiss, April 2000.

18. Daley, D. C., & Roth, L. (2001). *When symptoms return: A guide to relapse in psychiatric illness* (2nd ed.). Holmes Beach: FL: Learning Publications.*

19. Daley, D. C. (1994). *Preventing relapse.* Center City, MN: Hazelden.*

20. Gorske, T. T. (1992). *The staying sober workbook.* Independence Press, MO: Independence Press.

About the Author

Dennis C. Daley, PhD, is associate professor of psychiatry, chief of Addiction Medicine Services, and director of the Center for Psychiatric and Chemical Dependency Services at Western Psychiatric Institute and Clinic (WPIC) of the University of Pittsburgh Medical Center in Pittsburgh, PA. He is also former director of Family Studies and Social Work at WPIC.

Daley is a principal and coprincipal investigator on several research studies sponsored by the National Institute on Drug Abuse and the National Institute on Alcohol Abuse and Alcoholism that are related to the treatment of individuals with substance use disorders and mood disorders. He has been a consultant to two federally funded research projects: one at Harvard Medical School that involved treatment of bipolar disorder and addiction and one at Spalding University that addressed treatment of adolescent alcohol abuse. Daley has also consulted with numerous treatment programs in the United States and Europe and has presented lectures and training seminars in more than 30 states and in Canada and Europe.

He is codirector of the Education Core for the Veteran Administration's Mental Illness Research, Education, and Clinical Care project, a joint project between the Philadelphia and Pittsburgh VA Medical Centers. Daley was also a consultant to a criminal justice program for incarcerated youth who have substance use and psychiatric disorders.

Daley developed and managed several dual-disorders treatment programs and has been involved in providing clinical services to patients and families for more than 30 years. His publications number more than 250 and include books, recovery guides, journal articles, and educational films on dual disorders, recovery, relapse prevention, and family issues. He has authored many books and workbooks on dual disorders, including: *A Clinician's Guide to Mental Illness; Improving Treatment Compliance: Counseling and Systems Strategies for Substance Use and Dual Disorders; Dual Disorders: Counseling Clients with Chemical Dependency and Mental Illness; Preventing Relapse; Understanding Major Anxiety Disorders and Addiction; Understanding Bipolar Disorders and Addiction; Understanding Depression and Addiction; Understanding Personality Problems and Addiction; Understanding Schizophrenia and Addiction; Understanding Suicide and Addiction: A Family Guide to Dual Disorders;* and *When Symptoms Return: Relapse Prevention and Psychiatric Illness.* Daley has also authored recovery materials for children and adolescents. His recovery materials for clients and families are viewed as informative, user friendly, and very helpful in the recovery process.

Daley has written more than 30 educational videos for patients and families, including the *Living Sober I* (eight videos on early recovery issues), *Living Sober II* (six videos on middle recovery issues) *and Living Sober III* (five videos on motivation and compliance) interactive video programs, *Promise of Recovery* (an 11-video program on recovery from psychiatric illness), and *Double Trouble,* which addresses addiction and mood disorders. His practical recovery materials are used in many treatment programs in the United States and other countries, and several of his books have been translated into foreign languages.